ALSO BY AMERICA'S TEST KITCHEN

Boards

Gatherings

A Very Chinese Cookbook

Kitchen Gear

The Complete Modern Pantry

Everyday Bread

The Outdoor Cook

The Complete Beans and Grains Cookbook

The Healthy Back Kitchen

Desserts Illustrated

The Complete Guide to Healthy Drinks

Vegan Cooking for Two

Modern Bistro

The Complete Small Plates Cookbook

Fresh Pasta at Home

More Mediterranean

The Complete Plant-Based Cookbook

Cooking with Plant-Based Meat

The Savory Baker

The New Cooking School Cookbook: Advanced Fundamentals

The New Cooking School Cookbook: Fundamentals

The Complete Autumn and Winter Cookbook

One-Hour Comfort

The Everyday Athlete Cookbook

Cook for Your Gut Health

Foolproof Fish

Five-Ingredient Dinners

The Ultimate Meal-Prep Cookbook

The Complete Salad Cookbook

The Chicken Bible

The Side Dish Bible

Meat Illustrated

Vegetables Illustrated

Bread Illustrated

Cooking for One

The Complete One Pot

How Can It Be Gluten-Free Cookbook Collection

The Complete Summer Cookbook

Bowls

100 Techniques

Easy Everyday Keto

Everything Chocolate

The Perfect Cookie

The Perfect Pie

The Perfect Cake

How to Cocktail

Spiced

The Ultimate Burger

The New Essentials Cookbook

Dinner Illustrated

America's Test Kitchen Menu Cookbook

Cook's Illustrated Revolutionary Recipes

Tasting Italy: A Culinary Journey

Cooking at Home with Bridget and Julia

The Complete Mediterranean Cookbook

The Complete Vegetarian Cookbook

The Complete Cooking for Two Cookbook 10th Anniversary Edition

The Complete Diabetes Cookbook

The Complete Slow Cooker

The Complete Make-Ahead Cookbook

Just Add Sauce

How to Braise Everything

How to Roast Everything

Nutritious Delicious

What Good Cooks Know

Cook's Science

The Science of Good Cooking

Master of the Grill

Kitchen Smarts

Kitchen Hacks

100 Recipes

The New Family Cookbook

The Cook's Illustrated Baking Book

The Cook's Illustrated Cookbook

The America's Test Kitchen Family Baking Book

The Complete America's Test Kitchen TV Show Cookbook 2001–2024

Ultimate Air Fryer Perfection

Healthy Air Fryer

Healthy and Delicious Instant Pot

Mediterranean Instant Pot

Cook It in Your Dutch Oven

Vegan for Everybody

Sous Vide for Everybody

Air Fryer Perfection

Toaster Oven Perfection

Multicooker Perfection

Food Processor Perfection

Pressure Cooker Perfection

Instant Pot Ace Blender Cookbook

Naturally Sweet

Foolproof Preserving

Paleo Perfected

The Best Mexican Recipes

Slow Cooker Revolution Volume 2: The Easy-Prep Edition

Slow Cooker Revolution

The America's Test Kitchen D.I.Y. Cookbook

Cook's Country Titles

Big Flavors from Italian America

One-Pan Wonders

Cook It in Cast Iron

Cook's Country Eats Local

The Complete Cook's Country TV Show Cookbook

For a Full Listing of All Our Books:

CooksIllustrated.com

AmericasTestKitchen.com

PRAISE FOR AMERICA'S TEST KITCHEN

"A mood board for one's food board is served up in this excellent guide . . . This has instant classic written all over it."

Publishers Weekly (starred review) on *Boards: Stylish Spreads for Casual Gatherings*

"This comprehensive guide is packed with delicious recipes and fun menu ideas but its unique draw is the personal narrative and knowledge-sharing of each ATK chef, which will make this a hit."

Booklist on *Gatherings*

"An exhaustive but approachable primer for those looking for a 'flexible' diet. Chock-full of tips, you can dive into the science of plant-based cooking or just sit back and enjoy the 500 recipes."

Minneapolis Star Tribune on *The Complete Plant-Based Cookbook*

Best Overall Mediterranean Cookbook 2022

Runner's World on *The Complete Mediterranean Cookbook*

"Reassuringly hefty and comprehensive, *The Complete Autumn and Winter Cookbook* by America's Test Kitchen has you covered with a seemingly endless array of seasonal fare . . . This overstuffed compendium is guaranteed to warm you from the inside out."

NPR on *The Complete Autumn and Winter Cookbook*

"Here are the words just about any vegan would be happy to read: 'Why This Recipe Works.' Fans of America's Test Kitchen are used to seeing the phrase, and now it applies to the growing collection of plant-based creations in *Vegan for Everybody*."

The Washington Post on *Vegan for Everybody*

"The book's depth, breadth, and practicality makes it a must-have for seafood lovers."

Publishers Weekly (starred review) on *Foolproof Fish*

"If you're one of the 30 million Americans with diabetes, *The Complete Diabetes Cookbook* by America's Test Kitchen belongs on your kitchen shelf."

Parade.com on *The Complete Diabetes Cookbook*

A Best Cookbook of 2023

New York Times on *A Very Chinese Cookbook*

"Another flawless entry in the America's Test Kitchen canon, *Bowls* guides readers of all culinary skill levels in composing one-bowl meals from a variety of cuisines."

BuzzFeed Books on *Bowls*

"*The Perfect Cookie* . . . is, in a word, perfect. This is an important and substantial cookbook . . . If you love cookies, but have been a tad shy to bake on your own, all your fears will be dissipated. This is one book you can use for years with magnificently happy results."

Huffpost on *The Perfect Cookie*

"The book offers an impressive education for curious cake makers, new and experienced alike. A summation of 25 years of cake making at ATK, there are cakes for every taste."

The Wall Street Journal on *The Perfect Cake*

"The go-to gift book for newlyweds, small families, or empty nesters."

Orlando Sentinel on *The Complete Cooking for Two Cookbook*

Selected as the Cookbook Award Winner of 2021 in the General category

International Association of Culinary Professionals (IACP) on *Meat Illustrated*

"True to its name, this smart and endlessly enlightening cookbook is about as definitive as it's possible to get in the modern vegetarian realm."

Men's Journal on *The Complete Vegetarian Cookbook*

FOOD GIFTS

150+ Irresistible Recipes for Crafting Personalized Presents

with food stylist and best-selling author of *Boards*
Elle Simone Scott

AMERICA'S TEST KITCHEN

CONTENTS

Library of Congress Cataloging-in-Publication Data has been applied for.

ISBN 978-1-954210-82-0

AMERICA'S TEST KITCHEN
21 Drydock Avenue, Boston, MA 02210

Printed in Canada
10 9 8 7 6 5 4 3 2 1

Distributed by Penguin Random House Publisher Services
Tel: 800.733.3000

Pictured on front cover: Afternoon Tea basket (page 54)

Pictured on back cover: Sweet Zucchini Pickle Chips (page 34), Stuffed Shells with Amatriciana Sauce (page 159), Millionaire's Shortbread (page 224), Iced Lemon–Poppy Seed Bundt Cake (page 268), Ultracreamy Hummus with Spiced Walnut Topping (page 94)

- - - - - - - - - - - - - - - - - - -

FRONT COVER

Food Styling: Elle Simone Scott

Photography: Kevin White

Editorial Director, Books: Adam Kowit

Executive Food Editor: Dan Zuccarello

Deputy Food Editor: Stephanie Pixley

Executive Managing Editor: Debra Hudak

Project Editor: Valerie Cimino

Senior Editors: Camila Chaparro and Sara Mayer

Test Cooks: Olivia Counter, Carmen Dongo, Hannah Fenton, Laila Ibrahim, José Maldonado, and David Yu

Editorial Assistant: Julia Arwine

Kitchen Intern: Olivia Goldstein

Design Director: Lindsey Timko Chandler

Art Director and Designer: Katie Barranger

Photography Director: Julie Bozzo Cote

Senior Photography Producer: Meredith Mulcahy

Senior Staff Photographers: Steve Klise and Daniel J. van Ackere

Staff Photographers: Kritsada Panichgul and Kevin White

Additional Photography: Elizabeth Fuller, Joseph Keller, and Carl Tremblay

Featured Food Stylist: Elle Simone Scott

Contributing Food Stylists: Joy Howard, Sheila Jarnes, Catrine Kelty, Chantal Lambeth, Ashley Moore, Christie Morrison, Marie Piraino, Kendra Smith, and Sally Staub

Hair and Make-Up Artists: Rachel Berkowitz, Luiz Filho, Rose Fortuna, Sarai Martinez, and Jen Tawa

Project Manager, Publishing Operations: Katie Kimmerer

Senior Print Production Specialist: Lauren Robbins

Production and Imaging Coordinator: Amanda Yong

Production and Imaging Specialist: Tricia Neumyer

Copy Editor: Deri Reed

Proofreader: Ann-Marie Imbornoni

Indexer: Elizabeth Parson

Chief Creative Officer: Jack Bishop

Executive Editorial Directors: Julia Collin Davison and Bridget Lancaster

WELCOME TO AMERICA'S TEST KITCHEN

This book has been tested, written, and edited by the folks at America's Test Kitchen, where curious cooks become confident cooks. Located in Boston's Seaport District in the historic Innovation and Design Building, it features 15,000 square feet of kitchen space including multiple photography and video studios. It is the home of *Cook's Illustrated* magazine and *Cook's Country* magazine and is the workday destination for more than 60 test cooks, editors, and cookware specialists. Our mission is to empower and inspire confidence, community, and creativity in the kitchen.

So many people across the company worked together to make this book possible. These food gifts truly came to life in the photo studio, thanks to the tireless creative collaboration among food stylists, photographers, art directors, editors, and test cooks. Elle Simone Scott was joined by talented stylists Sheila Jarnes, Catrine Kelty, Chantal Lambeth, and Ashley Moore. Photographers Steve Klise, Kritsada Panichgul, Daniel van Ackere, and Kevin White all contributed to making this process so successful. None of it would have been possible without photography director Julie Bozzo Cote and the entire photoshoot kitchen team: Olivia Counter, Carmen Dongo, Hannah Fenton, Laila Ibrahim, José Maldonado, and David Yu. Olivia Counter also took a deep dive into gift-worthy packaging ideas. Thanks to Lindsey Chandler, Valerie Cimino,

Catrine Kelty, Meredith Mulcahy, Stephanie Pixley, and Elle Simone Scott for contributing props from their personal collections. A special shout-out goes to senior photography producer Meredith Mulcahy, who in addition to her regular duties cheerfully and efficiently took on the daunting role of chief prop wrangler.

Valerie Cimino was the project editor and worked closely with Elle from the studio to the page, ensuring that all the editorial and visual pieces were cohesive. Deputy food editor Stephanie Pixley oversaw the recipe side of things and provided guidance on storage times and food packaging. Stephanie, along with senior editor Camila Chaparro and the test cooks, brainstormed countless great ideas for food gift pairings. Thanks to Julia Arwine for invaluable editorial support. Special thanks to Jack Bishop and Adam Kowit for their guidance overseeing the entire editorial process.

Along with art direction, Katie Barranger designed the entire book you hold in your hands, from the cover to the endsheets, conceiving of the look and feel of the book and making the layout as fun, versatile, and approachable as the gifts themselves. Design director Lindsey Chandler provided design guidance every step of the way and assisted greatly with visual direction of the photography.

The production team, Lauren Robbins, Amanda Yong, and Tricia Neumyer, worked hard to ensure that the photos look as good in print as they do on screen. The book was copyedited by Deri Reed, proofread by Ann-Marie Imbornoni, and indexed by Elizabeth Parson, who all thankfully have keen eyes for detail. The contributions of Katie Kimmerer and Debra Hudak kept the book schedule on track thanks to their top-notch project management and organizational skills, and they helped tie up the many loose ends that present themselves at the end of a project.

To see what goes on behind the scenes at America's Test Kitchen, check out our social media channels for kitchen snapshots, exclusive content, video tips, and much more. You can watch us work (in our actual test kitchen) by tuning in to *America's Test Kitchen* or *Cook's Country* on public television or on our websites. Listen to *Proof*, *Mystery Recipe*, and *The Walk-In* (AmericasTestKitchen.com/podcasts) to hear engaging, complex stories about people and food. Want to hone your cooking skills or finally learn how to bake—with an America's Test Kitchen test cook? Enroll in one of our online cooking classes.

However you choose to visit us, we welcome you into our kitchen, where you can stand by our side as we test our way to the best recipes in America.

- facebook.com/AmericasTestKitchen
- instagram.com/TestKitchen
- youtube.com/AmericasTestKitchen
- tiktok.com/@TestKitchen
- x.com/TestKitchen
- pinterest.com/TestKitchen

AmericasTestKitchen.com
CooksIllustrated.com
CooksCountry.com
OnlineCookingSchool.com

join our community of recipe testers

Our recipe testers provide valuable feedback on recipes under development by ensuring that they are foolproof in home kitchens. Help the America's Test Kitchen book team investigate the how and why behind successful recipes from your home kitchen.

LET'S GET GIFTING

Introducing the only guide you need for cooking, baking, assembling, and crafting homemade food gifts that will look as fabulous as they taste. Along with more than 150 irresistible recipes, you'll learn hundreds of practical tips about how to store and package food gifts to keep them fresh as well as inspirational yet totally achievable ideas for presenting your gifts in showstopping ways.

With *Food Gifts*, all of us at America's Test Kitchen have broadened expectations around food gift giving. A homemade gift of food is always going to be higher quality—and more thoughtful—than store bought. Making a food gift doesn't have to be complicated or expensive; you can customize and personalize your gift in any number of ways; and you can give a food gift for literally any occasion— or for no particular reason at all. So never again will you need to resort to an impersonal, expensive store-bought gift basket of questionable quality. Here you will find all the foods your friends and family will want to enjoy, transformed into foods you'll be delighted to give to them.

HI, I'M ELLE

I grew up in a food-gifting household. My family has been potlucking for as long as I can remember. Even though I was young, I fully understood that "bringing a dish" to someone's home was vitally important and deeply traditional. So much intentionality went into the planning and preparation of the dishes, and even more so into how they would be presented. These are my first memories of giving food as a gift.

When I was approached with the idea of conceptualizing this book, I hadn't potlucked in a few years, so the thought of returning to the essence of giving food out of love excited me! What was even more outstanding was that, in addition to my professional food-styling skills, I'd have the opportunity to bring my personal creativity and crafting skills to the table, and maybe even push those skills to the next level.

What I enjoyed most about co-creating this book was discovering the ways that gifting food could be made personal, enjoyable, and—most important—approachable for everyone. So many of us who collaborated on this book are food gift givers! We all spent a lot of time reminiscing about the traditional elements that our respective families and cultures use to share food in such loving ways. I think it's safe to say that we were all constantly inspired by each other, and that certainly built the foundation of these perfect-for-gifting recipes and the unique, crafty ways to give them.

Working on this book has reminded me that the occasion for giving food as a gift is . . . *always*. The joy of giving lies in the way it makes people feel. Handmade gifts of food, with their personal touches, make people feel seen and, certainly, deeply considered. And though the gifts in these pages are all gorgeously presented, we go leaps beyond just pretty ribbons and labels; this book is an insightful journey through the many ways that food gifts can and should be given. I have learned so much more about the "whys" of gifting food and even more so about the cute, practical, and, in many cases, eco-friendly ways that I can create a gift at home using crafting items I likely already have access to.

If you are already a food gift giver, I hope this book challenges you to step your gifting game all the way up. And if you're new to food gifting, well, I hope that it inspires you to give food in ways that you never thought you would. Let your inner crafty-home-cook flag fly!

IN FOOD & LOVE,

Elle

HOW TO GIVE MEMORABLE FOOD GIFTS

There are so many fantastic recipes and ideas in this book that, if you're anything like me, you'll have a hard time choosing. To help you decide on the best gift every time, start by asking yourself a few questions.

WHAT'S THE OCCASION?

It's impossible to list every occasion when a food gift would be appropriate—because a consumable gift is *always* appropriate! Here's just a sampling of some of my favorite reasons for giving them.

Holiday

Yes, the end-of-year holiday season is prime time for giving food gifts, but don't forget that there are holidays year-round, y'all! I often find myself looking for one or two gifts that I can make in bigger batches, so that I can divide them up and make small presents for lots of people. These types of gifts can be quite simple, like BBQ Party Mix (page 83) and Granola (page 60). Or they could be a little fancier, like Blue Cheese Log with Pistachio Dukkah and Honey (page 100) or Fruits of the Forest Liqueur (page 122).

Celebration

When I'm attending an event, from a bridal shower to a Mother's Day brunch to a barbecue, I often turn to larger-format food gifts. Check out the Grapefruit Tart with Pumpernickel-Caraway Crust (page 282), the Iced Lemon–Poppy Seed Bundt Cake (page 268), or the Triple-Berry Slab Pie (page 279). Other celebration gift ideas that always seem to be well-received are cute individual servings, like a big batch of Pear-Rosemary Muffin Tin Pies (page 291) for Friendsgiving.

Helping Hands

When a friend, relative, or neighbor is in need for any reason, I instinctively want to take some mealtime burdens off their hands and make sure they feel nourished and well-fed. There's an entire chapter of meals that can be made ahead, are easy to transport, and require little effort for the recipient to get on the table. Drop off Turkey Picnic Sandwiches with Sun-Dried Tomato Spread (page 142) to new parents, or give my go-to Chicken and Ramen Soup (page 164) to someone who's under the weather.

Going All Out

If I'm contemplating one elevated gift for one special someone, I might consider an elegant box of handmade Chocolate Truffles (page 189) or a jar of Brandied Cherry and Hazelnut Conserve (page 32). Or I might craft a show-stopping gift basket of assorted homemade and store-bought items that I know will outshine any mail-order basket. You'll find loads of customizable basket ideas throughout this book.

WHAT'S YOUR BANDWIDTH?

The versatility of food gifts extends to how much you want to expend—in effort, time, and money. Any one of the recipes stands alone as a wonderful gift and I also give suggestions for expanding gifts if you want to do a little more. Here are some examples of the ideas that you'll find.

Make It a Duo

Give the Hot Chocolate Mix (page 52) on its own, or use the Make It a Duo suggestion and add a bag of Fluffy Vanilla Marshmallows (page 201). The Cinnamon-Ginger Spiced Nuts (page 77) are special on their own, or use the Make It a Duo suggestion to add a wheel of Brie cheese.

Make It a Trio

Give the Smoked Trout Pâté (page 92) on its own, or use the Make It a Trio suggestion and add bagels and cream cheese for a simple yet elevated brunch gift. The Stuffed Dates (page 210) are so special by themselves presented in a pretty box, but make them even more so by following the Make It a Trio suggestion and giving them with a Turkish coffeepot and a bag of ground Turkish coffee.

Make It a Basket

When I'm creating a basket, one of the first things I decide is whether to make everything from scratch or add store-bought items. You could make an entirely homemade dim sum basket with Chinese Pork Dumplings (page 181), Egg Tarts (page 286), and Chili Crisp (page 67). Or turn the Sweet Vermouth (page 126) into a basket by adding all store-bought items: bourbon, cocktail cherries, assorted bitters, a jigger, a bar spoon, and salted nuts. In addition to the basket ideas that come with the recipes, the Make It a Basket features found throughout the book give you plenty of additional options depending on your budget.

WHAT'S YOUR TIME FRAME?

There are two time-management aspects that I think are important to consider: First, how much time do you have to devote to creating your food gift or gifts? And second, how far ahead of the occasion do you want or need to make your gift?

Total Time

Every recipe includes a total time to let you know how long each recipe will take to prepare or assemble.

Storage Time

Every recipe also includes the storage time for the gift, so you can plan how far ahead to make it and tell your recipient when it's best enjoyed by.

---

my top 5 tips for personalizing a food gift

- **Make it yourself!** Your cookies may look imperfect, but they really do show a sign of thoughtfulness. Embrace that.

- **Upcycle and regift.** I always save containers, gift bags, and ribbons that are too nice to toss. Even something like a tea towel or lovely scarf can really give a personal touch.

- **Say something sweet.** Including a personalized note to your receiver is a great way to put your personal stamp on a gift.

- **Give their "favorite thing."** Nothing shows you care better than giving someone exactly what they love to nosh on. It shows how much you know what brightens their day and will make them feel like you "get" them.

- **Go the extra mile.** Add-ons are a great way to personalize a gift: Add a favorite topping to the Pancake Mix (page 51) or include cocktail glasses with the Coffee Liqueur (page 125).

WHEN TO GIVE FOOD GIFTS

I give gifts of food year-round: for holidays;
for commemorative occasions like birthdays,
anniversaries, and graduations; for life
markers like a new baby or a new home;
to friends simply in need of a pick-me-up;
and for countless other reasons. Sometimes
my schedule dictates what I can make, but
there are still so many adaptable options.
Here are some of my favorite recipes along
with times when I most often give them.

Home for the Holidays

Bring along a special treat for fall or year-end holidays.

- Apple-Shallot Chutney (page 33)
- Cinnamon-Ginger Spiced Nuts (page 77)
- Smoked Trout Pâté (page 92)
- Coquito (page 118)
- Pistachio-Cherry Torrone (page 197)
- Easy Holiday Sugar Cookies (page 216)
- Nutella Rugelach (page 222)
- Chocolate Matzo Toffee (page 207)
- Peppermint Bark (page 204)
- Pumpkin Cupcakes with Cream Cheese Frosting (page 266)
- Pear-Rosemary Muffin Tin Pies (page 291)

Good Neighbors

Thank a helpful neighbor or welcome someone new to the area.

- Classic Raspberry Jam (page 31)
- Herbes de Provence (page 46)
- Ultracreamy Hummus with Spiced Walnut Topping (page 94)
- Feta Cheese Log with Advieh and Olive Oil (page 100)
- Gruyère, Mustard, and Caraway Cheese Coins (page 107)
- One of the simple syrups (page 115)
- Italian Pasta Salad (page 149)
- Brigadeiros (page 192)
- Blueberry-Lemon-Cardamom Bread (page 251)
- Chocolate–Sour Cream Bundt Cake (page 270)

Showing Some Hospitality

Offer a little something for the host or hostess.

- Easy Homemade Hot Sauce (page 68)
- Marinated Green and Black Olives (page 75)
- Basil Pesto (page 41)
- Bloody Mary Mix (page 120)
- Seeded Pumpkin Crackers (page 108)
- Southern Cheese Straws (page 86)
- Chocolate-Covered Caramels (page 194)
- Walnut-Pomegranate Stuffed Dates (page 210)
- Baci di Dama (page 227)
- A mini loaf of Chocolate-Coffee-Hazelnut Bread (page 252)

Built to Last

Make your gifts well ahead of gifting time.

- Classic Strawberry Jam (page 30)
- Summer Tomato Sauce (page 38)
- Sweet Zucchini Pickle Chips (page 34)
- Any of the spice blends (pages 44–47)
- Vanilla Extract (page 49)
- Tea Blends: Citrus Burst, Immunitea, or Cozy and Calm (page 57)
- Tonic Syrup (page 110)
- Fruits of the Forest Liqueur (page 122)
- Earl Grey Baked Oatmeal in a Jar (page 139)

Sharing a Big Batch

Make one gift for a crowd of lucky recipients.

- Any of the spice blends (pages 44–47)
- Chili Crisp (page 67)
- Tea Blends: Citrus Burst, Immunitea, or Cozy and Calm (page 57)
- Sichuan Spiced Nuts (page 78)
- Summer Tomato Sauce (page 38)
- Hot Chocolate Mix (page 52)
- Pancake Mix (page 51)
- One of the granolas (pages 60–61)
- Bloody Mary Mix (page 120)
- Coffee Liqueur (page 125)

Birthdays

Celebrate someone's big day in style.

- Dark Chocolate Fudge Sauce (page 62)
- Dulce de Leche (page 63)
- Any of the marshmallows (pages 201–202)
- Millionaire's Shortbread (page 224)
- Macarons (page 229)
- Ultimate Chocolate Cupcakes with Ganache Filling (page 264)
- Peanut Butter Ganache–Filled Brownies (page 237)
- Party Cake Pops (page 274)
- Banana-Caramel Pie in a Jar (page 294)

Major Milestones
Tackle luxe project-y gifts for extra-special occasions.

- Brandied Cherry and Hazelnut Conserve (page 32)
- Sweet Vermouth (page 126)
- Chinese Pork Dumplings (page 181)
- Chocolate Truffles (page 189)
- Pistachio-Cherry Torrone (page 197)
- Macarons (page 229)
- Chocolate Babka Buns (page 260)
- Grapefruit Tart with Pumpernickel-Caraway Crust (page 282)

Friends in Need
Bring powerful comfort and support to someone who's under the weather or when there's a family emergency.

- Ginger Syrup (page 116)
- Chicken and Ramen Soup (page 164)
- Chicken Pot Pie (page 170)
- Hearty Meat Lasagna (page 172)
- Baked Macaroni and Cheese (page 175)
- Vegetarian Curried Lentil Soup (page 167)
- Thin and Crispy Chocolate Chip Cookies (page 213)
- Nutella Rugelach (page 222)
- Cinnamon Coffee Cake (page 255)
- No-Knead Rustic Loaf (page 299)

Low-Lift Gifts
Give a thoughtful kitchen gift anytime, with minimal effort.

- Marinated Green and Black Olives (page 75)
- One of the popcorn seasonings (page 81)
- Whipped Feta Dip (page 97)
- One of the simple syrups (page 115)
- Coffee Liqueur (page 125)
- Turkish Bride Soup in a Jar (page 132)
- Mushroom Risotto in a Jar (page 134)
- Earl Grey Baked Oatmeal in a Jar (page 139)
- Peppermint Bark (page 204)
- Stuffed Dates (page 210)
- Chocolate Cream Pie in a Jar (page 297)

SUPPLIES TO PACKAGE LIKE A PRO

As a food stylist, I'm always on the lookout for one-of-a-kind containers at flea markets, vintage markets, yard sales, gift shops, and kitchen shops. Wooden or wire crates, boxes, tins, baskets, deep trays, and other containers of all sizes tend to be plentiful at these types of venues, and they always catch my eye. When I see something that I know will be perfect for building a basket (no matter what size), I buy it, even if I'm not entirely sure yet when or how I'll use it.

For the food storage containers that will go into those baskets, when I'm thinking about big-batch gifting and I need, say, a dozen pint-size Mason jars for Sweet Zucchini Pickle Chips (page 34) or a couple dozen takeout box containers for a big batch of Southern Cheese Straws (page 86), it's tough to beat large retailers such as Michael's, Target, IKEA, Ace Hardware, and Amazon.

I also look to my own kitchen for individual gift-worthy storage containers. I thoroughly clean and save all my interesting-looking condiment jars, spice jars, and beverage bottles after they've been emptied. It's easy to remove the labels (see page 27) and then decorate them with your own handmade labels to give gifts like Basil Pesto (page 41), Dark Chocolate Fudge Sauce (page 62), and Easy Homemade Hot Sauce (page 68).

If you're gifting a meal, you have lots of choices about how to pack the food, from disposable aluminum pans and inexpensive plastic food storage containers found in any supermarket, to kitchen-workhorse baking pans and casserole dishes, all the way up to wedding-gift-worthy storage containers from stores such as West Elm and Pottery Barn. See pages 130–131 for more information about gifting meals.

Here are some more of my favorite online shopping resources for gifting supplies:

- **Aspecialtybox.com:** No matter what kind of box you need, you should be able to find it here.

- **Etsy (etsy.com):** Vintage barware and glasses, vintage serving spoons and knives to attach to gifts, tea towels and other fabrics, bakery boxes, wooden boxes, custom labels

- **Moo (moo.com):** Custom labels and tags

- **Paper Source (papersource.com):** Paper boxes, paper for wrapping and making homemade storage bags (see page 78), crinkle-cut paper, tissue paper, tulle, ribbon and string, washi tape, double-sided tape, mini clothespin clips, gift tags, markers

- **Studio Carta (studiocartashop.com):** Ribbons, washi tape, wrapping and tissue papers

- **Terrain (shopterrain.com):** Kitchen linens, serving utensils, food storage containers

- **The Container Store (containerstore.com):** Food storage containers, baskets

- **VistaPrint (vistaprint.com):** Custom labels and tags

- **The Webstaurant Store (webstaurantstore.com):** Biodegradable food storage containers; disposable pans, platters, and cake plates, bakery boxes

- **Wilton (wilton.com):** Bakery boxes, cellophane bags, foil wrappers and cups, parchment paper, baking pan liners, cake pop sticks

MAKING GIFT TAGS AND RECIPE TAGS

Gift tag and recipe tag language appears with recipes throughout the book, featuring ideas for how to use the gift, serving suggestions, and reheating and finishing instructions for meals. I create gift tags in a variety of ways:

1. Handwrite on premade tags or on cut-out cardstock.

2. Type and print the tag and mount on decorative paper.

3. Photocopy the tags that appear on the recipe pages onto cardstock.

4. Print custom labels and become a food-gifting legend.

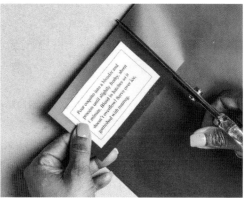

STYLING A PHOTO-WORTHY GIFT BASKET

1 Line the Container

Line with a tea towel, dish towel, cloth napkin, parchment paper, tissue paper, or crinkle-cut paper. As you add items, you'll be able to customize the depth of the base lining by adding crinkle-cut paper to cushion items or make them appear more prominent.

2 Arrange the Contents

Make your homemade items the focal point. A variety of container shapes and materials—bottles and jars, boxes of varying size, cellophane or other bags—makes for a visually interesting basket. Depending on your choices, you can lay things flat, stand them up, or do a combination.

No matter what type of basket I'm crafting, from this I Brought Brunch (page 22) extravaganza to my Cocktail Party (page 113) basket, I follow this guide to build a great-looking basket, every time.

3 Fill in Spaces

Add store-bought items to round out your homemade items and fill in spaces in the container. It's also nice to add a utensil or vessel that would be useful with the gift, such as a coffee scoop, cocktail jigger, cheese knife, decorative serving spoon, or glassware.

4 Add Finishing Touches

Add crinkle fill to cushion glass containers and make items sit higher in the basket. You could tuck in a bold flower or two or a small herb bouquet. Add a big bow to the basket or smaller ribbons or bows to a couple of items. Don't forget a personalized handwritten gift tag!

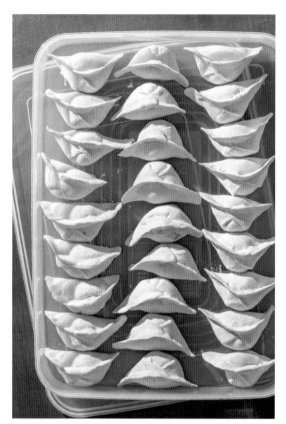

THE GIFT OF A MEAL

The reasons for giving a meal span the spectrum from festive occasions such as a holiday or birthday celebration, to helping out harried and sleepless new parents or caregivers, to bringing soup to nurse a sick friend or provide comfort and nourishment in cases of bereavement.

Although there are lots of ways to dress up a meal gift to make it look pretty, and you'll find plenty of ideas and inspiration in Chapter 3, Board the Meal Train, often packaging up a meal gift will have a lot to do with practicality. You want to choose the right vessel for the job. Each recipe in Chapter 3 gives specific options for how to package the gift, but here are some general guidelines.

Sometimes I give a meal right in the cooking vessel. For example, the Baked Macaroni and Cheese (page 175) can be given either in a disposable aluminum baking pan or in a baking dish that then becomes part of the gift. This recipe is freezer-friendly, ready to go straight from freezer to oven when the recipient is ready for it.

Other times I'll package a meal into storage containers for my recipient to reheat or assemble at serving time. The Best Ground Beef Chili (page 150) is a refrigerator-friendly meal. Usually I'll portion the chili into storage containers and prep and store chili toppings in separate containers so that my recipient(s) can heat and serve it whenever they're ready. Alternatively, you could gift this chili right in the pot you make it in, ready to go onto the stove to reheat.

For the Sichuan Chili–Ginger Chicken Salad (page 140) and the Murgh Makhani (page 152), you give the meal components—vegetables, chicken, toppings—in separate storage containers, and the recipient simply assembles the components right before serving. Alternatively, you could package the chicken salad fully assembled, in a practical or pretty serving bowl with a silicone lid. You could even clean and reuse plastic takeout containers for the salad or some of the other meals in Chapter 3.

Whatever containers you choose, they should be airtight, with secure tops or lids (see page 178 for a tip on how to securely attach a pot lid for transport). If you're wrapping a vessel in plastic wrap for transport, that is not the time to be parsimonious with the wrap! You might want to practice a technique we like to call "hurricane wrap" in the test kitchen (it's also known as "hotel wrap" and "caterer wrap"): Instead of covering just the top with plastic wrap, you tightly wrap the entire container with several layers, creating a secure little cocoon to keep the food fresh and prevent spills. See page 130 to learn how to do this.

To keep a meal cold or frozen during transport, choose a soft-sided or hard-sided cooler or an insulated bag that isn't too much larger than the meal package. This both reduces movement (which prevents spills) and helps to keep the food cool for a longer time. And don't forget to tuck in ice packs. If you're transporting a hot meal, an insulated food carrier is the best way to keep it hot for a couple of hours.

Each of the recipes in Chapter 3 indicates whether it's freezer-friendly, refrigerator-friendly, or both. Of course, most of the meals in the chapter can also be fully cooked and given hot, ready to eat. And every recipe also provides specific guidance for you to pass along to the recipient for finishing the meal as needed. These "gift tags" give instructions for baking, reheating, garnishing, or whatever else is needed to get a delicious, nurturing meal gift on the table with the greatest ease.

PACKING AND SHIPPING FOOD GIFTS

Sending a food gift is my favorite way to let someone far away know that I'm thinking about them. It's easy, as long as you pick the right recipes and package them properly.

It's best to choose foods that are easy to cushion during transit and that can be at room temperature during their entire journey. Although plenty of companies out there send refrigerated and frozen food through the mail, I feel that's something that's best left to professionals.

I do sometimes ship homemade chocolates as a gift, but I'm mindful about the weather. You can't predict the journey your package will take, so it's a little risky to mail anything that might melt in warm weather.

Once you've decided what to include in your mail-away package, there are two critical things to remember. First, seal the food airtight to maintain freshness. Second, pack it with plenty of cushioning to minimize the possibility of the food shifting around and breaking. Your thoughtful gift of Thin and Crispy Chocolate Chip Cookies (page 213) will be all for naught if they arrive broken in pieces and stale, smelling vaguely of a post office warehouse.

Weight is a consideration in shipping costs, so choose lightweight containers to hold your food. I like plastic when possible when shipping gifts, though some gifts, like Classic Strawberry Jam (page 30), need to be packaged in their glass containers (which I wrap in bubble wrap to protect them). I'd rather invest in fast shipping, and I always send food gifts using either overnight or 2-day shipping.

Snugly fill in the areas around the containers with popped popcorn, compostable packing peanuts, or crinkle-cut paper. You could also shred newspaper or old magazines to make your own fill. Seal your box with plenty of packing tape to make the box as airtight as possible. I tend to go for new mailing boxes, since they are sturdier and less likely to be crushed by a careless throw onto a truck than a reused box, but if you have sturdy used boxes on hand that you are comfortable repurposing, go for it.

My Favorite Recipes for Shipping

- Chocolate-Hazelnut Spread (page 28)
- Classic Strawberry Jam (page 20)
- Any of the Spice Blends (pages 44–47)
- Vanilla Extract (page 49)
- Pancake Mix (page 51)
- Hot Chocolate Mix (page 52)
- Any of the Tea Blends (page 57)
- Any of the granolas (pages 60–61)
- Any of the Spiced Nuts (pages 77–78)
- Any of the popcorn seasonings (page 81)
- Any of the party mixes (page 83)
- Southern Cheese Straws (page 86)
- Gruyère, Mustard, and Caraway Cheese Coins (page 107)
- Seeded Pumpkin Crackers (page 108)
- Turkish Bride Soup in a Jar (page 132)
- Mushroom Risotto in a Jar (page 134)
- Earl Grey Baked Oatmeal in a Jar (page 139)
- Brigadeiros (page 192)
- Pistachio-Cherry Torrone (page 197)
- Thin and Crispy Chocolate Chip Cookies (page 213)
- Spicy Mocha Sandwich Cookies with Dulce de Leche (page 215)
- Easy Holiday Sugar Cookies (page 216)
- Nutella Rugelach (page 222)
- Baci di Dama (page 227)
- Any of the biscotti (pages 232–233)
- Ultranutty Pecan Bars (page 239)
- British-Style Currant Scones (page 246)
- Any of the quick breads (pages 248–252)
- Chocolate–Sour Cream Bundt Cake (page 270)

BUILD A PERSONALIZED BASKET

Throughout the chapters you'll find themed basket ideas (and me showing you how to assemble them). But let your imagination run wild and create your own themes, tailored to the special person you're building a basket for! Here are more suggestions to get you going.

Gardener's Basket

- Sweet Zucchini Pickle Chips (page 34)
- Basil Pesto (page 41)
- Caponata (page 91)
- Roasted Tomato–Lime Salsa (page 102)
- Seed packets
- Gardening gloves

Saturday Night Soiree

- Fruits of the Forest Liqueur (page 122)
- Strawberry–Black Pepper Rim Sugar (page 123)
- Sparkling wine
- Marinated Green and Black Olives (page 75)
- Goat Cheese Log with Hazelnut-Nigella Dukkah (page 100)
- Water crackers
- Mixing glass, jigger, and bar spoon

My Kind of Fruit Basket

- Classic Raspberry Jam (page 31)
- Brandied Cherry and Hazelnut Conserve (page 32)
- Stuffed Dates (page 210)
- Pear-Rosemary Muffin Tin Pies (page 291)

I Brought Brunch

- Bloody Mary Mix (page 120) and garnishes
- Bag of ground coffee and/or tin of tea
- Smoked Trout Pâté (Page 92)
- Bagels and cream cheese
- Granola (page 60)
- Banana-Date-Walnut Mini Loaves with Sticky Date Glaze (page 248)
- Egg Tarts (page 286)

Gluten-Free Snack Supply

- Roasted Tomato–Lime Salsa (page 102)
- Whipped Feta Dip (page 97)
- Sichuan Spiced Nuts (page 78)
- Tortilla chips
- Chocolate-Spice Truffles (page 189)

Chilehead Favorites

- Easy Homemade Hot Sauce (page 68)
- Chili Crisp (page 67)
- Taco Seasoning (page 47)
- Thai Panang Curry Paste (page 48)

Elevated Pantry Picks

- Apple-Shallot Chutney (page 33)
- Sweet Zucchini Pickle Chips (page 34)
- Thai Panang Curry Paste (page 48)
- Vanilla Extract (page 49)
- Spiced Chocolate Popcorn Seasoning (page 81)

Don't Forget to Stay Hydrated

- Citrus Burst Black Tea Blend (page 57)
- Star Anise–Orange Cold Brew Coffee Concentrate (page 58)
- Tonic Syrup (page 110)
- Ginger Syrup (page 116)
- Milk of choice
- Seltzer

Pasta Night

- Stuffed Shells with Amatriciana Sauce (page 159)
- Marinated Green and Black Olives (page 75)
- No-Knead Rustic Loaf (page 299) or store-bought breadsticks
- Bottle of red wine

College Care Package

- Chocolate-Hazelnut Spread (page 28)
- Malted Hot Chocolate Mix (page 52)
- Immunitea Herbal Tea Blend (page 57)
- Cheesy Garlic Popcorn Seasoning (page 81)
- Peanut Butter Ganache–Filled Brownies (page 237)
- Sets of colorful plastic bowls, cups, and napkins

Kids' Sleepover Kit

- Sweet and Salty Kettle Corn Party Mix (page 83)
- Fluffy Lemon-Strawberry Marshmallows (page 202)
- Scotcheroos (page 241)
- Cookies and Cream Cake Pops (page 276)

It's a Date

- Blue Cheese Log with Pistachio Dukkah and Honey (page 100)
- Seeded Pumpkin Crackers (page 108)
- 1 (or 2!) bottles of wine
- 2 stemless wineglasses
- Corkscrew

Game Night

- Beet Muhammara (page 98)
- Ultracreamy Hummus with Spiced Walnut Topping (page 94)
- Roasted Tomato–Lime Salsa (page 102)
- Pita chips and tortilla chips
- Saffron–Orange Blossom Spiced Nuts (page 78)

Chili Fest

- Best Ground Beef Chili (page 150)
- Fritos
- Block of cheese and cheese grater
- Whole pineapple or mangos
- Tajin seasoning

One-Handed Snack Basket for New Parents

- Ham Picnic Sandwich with Olive Spread (page 143)
- Popcorn made with Dill Pickle Popcorn Seasoning (page 81)
- Southern Cheese Straws (page 86)
- Blue Cheese and Celery Seed Cheese Coins (page 107)
- Chocolate-Almond Stuffed Dates (page 211)

Winter Doldrums Cure

- Mint Hot Chocolate Mix (page 52)
- Fluffy Peppermint Swirl Marshmallows (page 202)
- Snickers Stuffed Dates (page 211)
- Chocolate-covered espresso beans

more baskets and where to find them

PRESENT
A PANTRY

PANTRY GIFT STORAGE SOLUTIONS

With some exceptions, most of the recipes in this chapter are best presented in some type of jar. For canning recipes such as the Classic Strawberry Jam (page 30), you'll need canning jars. For other gifts, such as the Dark Chocolate Fudge Sauce (page 62), you can use any attractive jar. I make a habit of saving condiment jars and other jars and repurposing them for food gifts. Here are some clever ways to make your repurposed jars look good enough to gift.

HOW TO CHOOSE JARS

- For shelf-stable foods that are meant to be stored for weeks or months, including the Spice Blends (pages 44–47), Pancake Mix (page 51), Hot Chocolate Mix (page 52), and Tea Blends (page 57), airtight containers will extend the shelf life as long as possible.

- For fun ideas for how to package spices and tea blends beyond jars, see page 45.

HOW TO COVER A LID WITH FABRIC

Cut a square of fabric that is 1 to 2 inches wider than the mouth of the jar, or use pre-made jam jar covers.

for canning jars: Place the fabric over the sealed lidded jar, hold it in place, and carefully screw on the outer ring.

for 1-piece lidded jars: After securing the lid, tie twine or ribbon around the fabric to secure it, just below the lid. You could even use colorful rubber bands to attach the fabric.

HOW TO REMOVE WAX FROM SPENT CANDLE JARS

Many fancy candle jars have lids. Instead of throwing them away, I use one of these tricks to clean out the jars for reuse.

Use Oil

1. Pour a thin layer of cooking oil over the wax left in the bottom of the candle jar and let sit for at least 20 minutes. The oil will start to soften and dissolve the wax.

2. Use a butter knife to dislodge the remaining wax and the candle wick base, if necessary. Wipe the jar clean with paper towels, then wash the jar well.

Freeze the Jar

Freeze the jar overnight. Wax shrinks when it freezes, so you'll be able to pop out the frozen wax easily. Wash the jar well.

HOW TO REMOVE LABELS FROM JARS

Make a DIY Gunk Remover

1. Make a paste by stirring together ½ cup baking soda, ¼ cup vegetable oil, and 6 drops citrus essential oil.

2. After peeling off as much of the label as you can, apply a generous amount of the paste to the residue that's left. Let it sit for 10 minutes, and then rub with a damp towel for 1 minute. Wash the jar well.

Use Vinegar

1. Soak a cloth, paper towel, or cotton ball in distilled white vinegar and place it over the sticker for at least 20 minutes, keeping it wet as needed.

2. Remove the label by using a bench scraper or straight-edge razor blade. Wash the jar well.

HOW TO ADD YOUR OWN LABELS TO JARS

Attach it to the glass (this is especially handy if you have trouble removing any last bits of label residue and need to cover them).

Attach a tag to the top of the lid.

Tie a tag around the mouth of the jar with twine.

HOW TO ATTACH ITEMS TO A JAR

See page 118 for instructions on how to tie a decoration, such as a garnish or small serving utensil, onto a jar or bottle.

CHOCOLATE-HAZELNUT SPREAD

makes: 1½ cups   **total time:** 35 minutes

66 As a food stylist, my days tend
to start *very* early, and having a
quick-to-go breakfast or snack option
is top priority: nut butters being my
first choice always. This deeply nutty-
chocolaty, not-too-sweet spread (which
I like to call 'New-tella') outshines
any commercial chocolate-hazelnut
product. It can top toast, banana bread,
or croissants with equal aplomb, or
be swirled into a cup of overnight oats
or bowl of ice cream. And even with
the variety of ways in which one can
enjoy this spread, your lucky recipient
will still just want to eat it with a spoon.
Hazelnut oil is available in larger
grocery stores and gourmet shops.
Walnut oil also works well. Either is
really worth it for this gift, but in a
pinch, you could use vegetable oil."

- - - - - - - - - - - - - - - - - - - -

HOW I GIFT THIS

packaging: Choose a wide-mouthed
glass jar (or jars), or repurpose an old
Nutella jar.

storage: This spread can be stored at
room temperature or in the refrigerator
for about 1 month.

make it a duo: Pair with a store-bought
jar of Biscoff cookie butter.

make it a trio: Match up with
No-Knead Rustic Loaf (page 299) and
a vintage spoon or spreading knife.

2 cups hazelnuts
6 tablespoons baking soda
1 cup (4 ounces) confectioners' sugar
⅓ cup (1 ounce) unsweetened cocoa powder
2 tablespoons hazelnut oil
1 teaspoon vanilla extract
⅛ teaspoon table salt

1. Adjust oven rack to middle position and heat oven to 375 degrees. Fill large bowl halfway with ice and water. Bring 4 cups water to boil. Add hazelnuts and baking soda and boil for 3 minutes. Transfer hazelnuts to ice bath with slotted spoon, drain, and rub skins off with dish towel.

2. Place hazelnuts in single layer on rimmed baking sheet. Roast until fragrant and golden brown, 12 to 15 minutes, rotating sheet halfway through roasting.

3. Process hazelnuts in food processor, scraping down sides of bowl often, until oil is released and smooth and a loose paste forms, about 5 minutes.

4. Add sugar, cocoa, oil, vanilla, and salt and process, scraping down sides of bowl as needed, until fully incorporated and mixture begins to loosen slightly and becomes glossy, about 2 minutes.

CLASSIC STRAWBERRY JAM

makes: four 1-cup jars   total time: 55 minutes

66 One of the many reasons my
   friends look forward to getting
food gifts from me is that they know
I've been planning the bounty well in
advance. I'm jamming and canning
all summer so that they can enjoy
summer faves in the winter. Juicy
seasonal berries or stone fruits turned
into jewel-toned jam is a classic gift
from the kitchen. Even if you've never
made homemade jam before, this
recipe brings it within easy reach.
Choose small, fragrant berries for
the best results. For safety reasons,
use bottled lemon juice, not fresh.
For more information on canning,
see pages 302–305."

HOW I GIFT THIS

packaging: You're going to gift the jar
that you process and store the jam in
(attach a serving spoon, if you like).

storage: Short-term processed jam
can be refrigerated for up to 2 months;
long-term processed jam can be stored
at room temperature for up to 1 year
and refrigerated after opening.

make it a duo: Pair with British-Style
Currant Scones (page 246) or a jar of
peanut butter.

make it a trio: Combine with Seeded
Pumpkin Crackers (page 108) and
a favorite cheese or with No-Knead
Rustic Loaf (page 299) and cultured
butter.

3 pounds strawberries, hulled and cut into ½-inch pieces (10 cups)
3 cups sugar
1¼ cups peeled, cored, and shredded Granny Smith apple
   (1 large apple)
2 tablespoons bottled lemon juice

1. Place 2 small plates in freezer to chill. Set canning rack in large pot, place four
1-cup jars on rack, and add water to cover by 1 inch. Bring to simmer over medium
heat, then turn off heat and cover to keep hot.

2. In Dutch oven, crush strawberries with potato masher until fruit is mostly
broken down. Stir in sugar, apple, and lemon juice and bring to boil, stirring often,
over medium-high heat. Once sugar is completely dissolved, boil mixture, stirring
and adjusting heat as needed, until thickened and registers 217 to 220 degrees,
20 to 25 minutes. (Temperature will be lower at higher elevations; see page 302
for more information.) Remove pot from heat.

3. To test consistency, place 1 teaspoon jam on chilled plate and freeze for
2 minutes. Drag your finger through jam on plate; jam has correct consistency
when your finger leaves distinct trail. If runny, return pot to heat and simmer
for 1 to 3 minutes longer before retesting. Skim any foam from surface of jam
using spoon.

4. Place dish towel flat on counter. Using jar lifter, remove jars from pot, draining
water back into pot. Place jars upside down on towel and let dry for 1 minute. Using
funnel and ladle, portion hot jam into hot jars, leaving ¼-inch headspace. Slide
wooden skewer along inside edge of jar and drag upward to remove air bubbles.

5a. for short-term storage: Let jam cool to room temperature, cover, and
refrigerate until jam is set, 12 to 24 hours.

5b. for long-term storage: While jars are hot, wipe rims clean, add lids, and
screw on rings until fingertip-tight; do not overtighten. Return pot of water with
canning rack to boil. Lower jars into water, cover, bring water back to boil, then
start timer. Cooking time will depend on your altitude: Boil 10 minutes for up to
1,000 feet, 15 minutes for 1,001 to 3,000 feet, 20 minutes for 3,001 to 6,000
feet, or 25 minutes for 6,001 to 8,000 feet. Turn off heat and let jars sit in pot for
5 minutes. Remove jars from pot and let cool for 24 hours. Remove rings, check
seal, and clean rims.

variations

CLASSIC RASPBERRY JAM

Substitute 2 pounds (6½ cups) raspberries for strawberries, reduce peeled and shredded apple to 1 cup, and reduce lemon juice to 1 tablespoon. Cook raspberry mixture in step 2 until thickened and registers 217 to 220 degrees, 10 to 15 minutes.

CLASSIC PEACH JAM

Substitute 2 pounds firm, ripe yellow peaches, halved, pitted, and cut into ½-inch pieces (6 cups) for strawberries. Reduce sugar to 2½ cups and peeled and shredded apple to 1 cup. Increase lemon juice to 3 tablespoons. In step 2, skip mashing fruit; combine peaches, sugar, apple, and lemon juice and let sit for 20 minutes. Then cook mixture as directed until thickened and registers 217 to 220 degrees, 5 to 7 minutes.

BRANDIED CHERRY AND HAZELNUT CONSERVE

makes: two 1-cup jars   **total time:** 40 minutes

" A conserve just sounds like a fancy gift, doesn't it?
Conserves are what I give my friends who host a soiree.
Sweet or savory, they are generally made with a combo of
fruits and nuts and are ideal for accessorizing anything from
a cheese or charcuterie board to a dessert situation with
cookies or ice cream. This blend of cherries, hazelnuts, and
brandy comes together quickly and features an array of
beautiful colors and textures whether you use red or yellow
cherries. Make sure you use bottled lemon juice, not fresh."

HOW I GIFT THIS

packaging: Present this in a nice glass jar with a serving
spoon. Consider reusing a pretty jam or honey jar.

storage: This conserve can be refrigerated for about
2 months.

make it a duo: Create a cheese condiment duo with the
Apple-Shallot Chutney (page 33).

make it a trio: Gift with Mini Chocolate–Sour Cream
Bundt Cakes (page 270) and vin santo.

1½ pounds fresh sweet red or yellow cherries,
     pitted and chopped
½ cup water
1 tablespoon bottled lemon juice
¼ teaspoon table salt
½ cup sugar
⅓ cup hazelnuts, toasted, skinned, and chopped fine
⅓ cup brandy or cognac

1. Bring cherries, water, lemon juice, and salt to boil in
medium saucepan over medium-high heat. Cover, reduce
heat to medium-low, and simmer until cherries are softened,
about 5 minutes.

2. Stir in sugar. Increase heat to medium-high and boil
uncovered, stirring often, until mixture is thickened, 10 to
15 minutes. Off heat, stir in hazelnuts and brandy and let
cool slightly.

3. Portion conserves into two 1-cup jars. Let cool to
room temperature.

APPLE-SHALLOT CHUTNEY

makes: two 1-cup jars   **total time:** 1 hour

❝ Chutney is typically both savory and sweet since it usually contains cooked fruit pieces (and sometimes vegetables) along with vinegar, spices, and sometimes sugar. Its fence-straddling flavor profile makes it versatile for gift-giving since it's so good served with a wide variety of foods, from pork or chicken to crackers and cheese. This chutney has a bit of an autumnal flavor profile from apples and raisins, along with shallots, garlic, thyme, and cider vinegar. Because these ingredients are readily available, though, you can make and give this condiment year-round.❞

HOW I GIFT THIS

packaging: Any small glass jar with a tight-fitting lid will work.

storage: This chutney can be refrigerated for about 2 months.

make it a duo: Pair with a block of cheddar cheese for making gourmet grilled cheese sandwiches.

make it a trio: Pair with a bottle of apple cider or ice wine and a wheel of Brie cheese.

 1 tablespoon extra-virgin olive oil
 3 shallots, sliced ¼ inch thick
 3 garlic cloves, minced
 1½ teaspoons minced fresh thyme or
    ½ teaspoon dried
 ½ teaspoon table salt
 ¼ teaspoon pepper
 ¼ teaspoon ground cinnamon
 1 pound Granny Smith apples, peeled,
    cored, and cut into ½-inch pieces
 2 cups water
 ¼ cup sugar, plus extra as needed
 ¼ cup raisins
 2 tablespoons cider vinegar

1. Heat oil in large saucepan over medium heat until shimmering. Add shallots and cook, stirring often, until softened and well browned, 10 to 12 minutes. Stir in garlic, thyme, salt, pepper, and cinnamon and cook until fragrant, about 1 minute. Stir in apples, water, sugar, and raisins. Cover and cook, stirring occasionally, until apples are just softened, 10 to 15 minutes.

2. Stir in vinegar, increase heat to medium-high, and simmer vigorously, uncovered and stirring often, until mixture is thickened and has reduced to about 2 cups, about 10 minutes. If mixture seems watery, mash several apples against side of pot with rubber spatula to thicken. Season with salt, pepper, and sugar to taste, and let cool slightly.

3. Portion chutney into two 1-cup jars. Let cool to room temperature.

SWEET ZUCCHINI PICKLE CHIPS

makes: four 1-pint jars   **total time:** 40 minutes, plus 3 hours salting

66 When I used to grow in the community garden in Brooklyn, my garden neighbors would grow so many zucchini that I'd inevitably end up with at least half a dozen. I was never a huge fan until I learned that zukes make great pickles. So if you're a gardener like me and my friends and have more zucchini than you know what to do with, making pickles is a special (and welcomed) way to, ahem, off-load them. These sweet-sour pickles are fancied up with shallots. Ball Pickle Crisp is essential to keep the pickles crunchy, so don't skip it! For more information on pickling, see pages 302–305."

HOW I GIFT THIS

packaging: For short-term storage, give the pickles in an airtight glass jar. For long-term storage, you'll give these in their canning jars.

storage: Short-term processed pickles can be refrigerated for up to 1 month; long-term processed pickles can be stored at room temperature for up to 1 year and refrigerated after opening.

big-batch it: Double all of the ingredients and use a larger pot when making the brine; the processing time will remain the same.

make it a basket: Assemble a pickle basket by adding pickled carrots, beets, dilly beans, and so on. Or put together a mini sandwich basket with a baguette, cheese, and kettle chips.

2¾ pounds small zucchini (6 ounces each), trimmed and sliced ¼ inch thick
4 shallots, sliced thin
¼ cup kosher salt
3 cups apple cider vinegar
2 cups sugar
1 cup water
1 tablespoon yellow mustard seeds
¾ teaspoon turmeric
½ teaspoon celery seeds
½ teaspoon Ball Pickle Crisp

1. Toss zucchini and shallots with salt in bowl and refrigerate for 3 hours. Drain vegetables in colander (do not rinse), then pat dry with paper towels.

2. Meanwhile, set canning rack in canning pot, place four 1-pint jars on rack, and add water to cover by 1 inch. Bring to simmer over medium-high heat, then turn off heat and cover to keep hot.

3. Bring vinegar, sugar, water, mustard seeds, turmeric, and celery seeds to boil in large saucepan over medium-high heat; cover and remove from heat.

4. Place dish towel flat on counter. Using jar lifter, remove jars from pot, draining water back into pot. Place jars upside down on towel and let dry for 1 minute. Add ⅛ teaspoon Pickle Crisp to each hot jar, then pack tightly with drained vegetables.

5. Return brine to brief boil. Using funnel and ladle, pour hot brine over vegetables to cover, distributing spices evenly and leaving ½ inch headspace. Slide wooden skewer along inside of jar, pressing slightly on vegetables to remove air bubbles, then add extra brine as needed.

6a. for short-term storage: Let jars cool to room temperature, cover with lids, and refrigerate for at least 1 day.

6b. for long-term storage: While jars are warm, wipe rims clean, add lids, and screw on rings until fingertip-tight; do not overtighten. Before processing jars, heat water in canning pot to temperature between 120 and 140 degrees. Lower jars into water, bring water to 180 to 185 degrees, then cook for 30 minutes, adjusting heat as needed to maintain water between 180 and 185 degrees. Remove jars from pot and let cool for 24 hours. Remove rings, check seal, and clean rims.

variation

SWEET AND SPICY ZUCCHINI PICKLE CHIPS

Add 3 red jalapeño chiles, stemmed and sliced into rings, to zucchini mixture before salting in step 1. Divide 8 garlic cloves, peeled and quartered, between jars before packing with vegetables.

UNDER THE ITALIAN SUN

66 Italians know how to make the most of their summer vacations. There's so much coastline that it's easy to spend time lounging on the beach, then take a swim to work up an appetite for a proper lunch or dinner. And Italians certainly don't stop eating pasta in the summertime—they make simple fresh tomato sauces and herb pestos, both to eat right away and to preserve for the winter. This basket is very much in that spirit. Your lucky recipient can nibble on olives and maybe sip some wine while tossing pasta with a vibrant sauce made with either peak-season tomatoes or fresh, fragrant basil."

HOW I GIFT THIS

I start building a basket around my chosen homemade items, then expand to include complementary store-bought items, or maybe more homemade ingredients. Here I focus on two recipes that I can make well in advance, the tomato sauce and the pesto, then I add the olives. The size of the container will depend on what else I want to include. A harvest basket is nice for a smaller gift, while a wooden wine crate is great as a larger container that can include everything on the list. Cushion the jars as needed with crinkle-cut paper. Tying a bow on the store-bought pasta (and the bread, if you include it) adds a festive touch.

START WITH

Summer Tomato Sauce (page 38)

Basil Pesto (page 41)

Marinated Green and Black Olives (page 75)

Dried or fresh pasta

IF YOU WANT, ADD

No-Knead Rustic Loaf (page 299)

Bottle of wine

Basil plant

Seed packets

Fresh tomatoes

SUMMER TOMATO SAUCE

makes: four 1-pint jars   total time: 2 hours

" There's a short list of fresh seasonal foods that I miss when their time has come and gone; at the top of that list stands tomatoes. This sauce lets me offer up a bright taste of summer that my recipients can open on some dreary January night. It uses a whopping 10 pounds of tomatoes, so it's a great choice if you're a gardener or belong to a CSA. While rustic tomato sauces can include the skins, I find them distracting, so I peel the tomatoes before cooking them with garlic and basil. Adding red wine vinegar to each jar keeps the sauce's pH in the sweet spot for storage purposes. I like to use plum tomatoes, though other types work too. For more information on canning, see pages 302–305."

HOW I GIFT THIS

packaging: For short-term storage, give the sauce in an airtight glass jar. For long-term storage, you'll give it in the canning jars.

storage: Short-term processed sauce can be refrigerated for up to 1 month; long-term processed sauce can be stored at room temperature for up to 1 year and refrigerated after opening.

make it a trio: Give with fresh or dried pasta (1 pint is enough to sauce 8 ounces pasta) and a basil plant.

10 pounds tomatoes, cored, peeled, and cut into 1½-inch pieces
4 garlic cloves, minced
⅓ cup tomato paste
⅓ cup chopped fresh basil
1 tablespoon table salt
1 teaspoon sugar
½ cup red wine vinegar

1. Set canning rack in large pot, place four 1-pint jars on rack, and add water to cover by 1 inch. Bring to simmer over medium-high heat, then turn off heat and cover to keep hot.

2. Working in 4 batches, process tomatoes in blender until almost smooth, 10 to 15 seconds; transfer to Dutch oven. Stir in garlic, tomato paste, basil, salt, and sugar and bring to boil over medium-high heat. Boil, stirring often and reducing heat as needed, until sauce has thickened and measures slightly more than 2 quarts, 1¼ to 1½ hours.

3. Place dish towel flat on counter. Using jar lifter, remove jars from pot, draining water back into pot. Place jars upside down on towel and let dry for 1 minute. Add 2 tablespoons vinegar to each hot jar. Using funnel and ladle, portion hot sauce into hot jars, leaving ½ inch headspace. Slide wooden skewer along inside of jar to remove air bubbles and add more sauce as needed.

4a. for short-term storage: Let jars cool to room temperature. Cover and refrigerate.

4b. for long-term storage: While jars are hot, wipe rims clean, add lids, and screw on rings until fingertip-tight; do not overtighten. Return pot of water with canning rack to boil. Lower jars into water, cover, bring water back to boil, then start timer. Cooking time will depend on your altitude: Boil 35 minutes for up to 1,000 feet, 40 minutes for 1,001 to 3,000 feet, 45 minutes for 3,001 to 6,000 feet, or 50 minutes for 6,001 to 8,000 feet. Turn off heat and let jars sit in pot for 5 minutes. Remove jars from pot and let cool for 24 hours. Remove rings, check seal, and clean rims.

PEELING TOMATOES

Use a serrated peeler or this blanching method to remove tomato skins.

1. Remove core and score small X in bottom of each tomato.

2. Add not more than 6 tomatoes (any more and the water temperature drops too low) to large pot of boiling water; boil until skins loosen, 15 to 60 seconds. Using slotted spoon, transfer tomatoes to ice bath to cool, 2 minutes.

3. Remove tomatoes from ice bath and remove loosened skins. Return water to boil and proceed with next batch.

BASIL PESTO

makes: 1¾ cups   total time: 30 minutes

66 In my world, pesto lives alongside my everyday condiments in the fridge because it so easily transforms basic ingredients into simple but elegant meals. Pesto is useful in so many ways that it just makes for the perfect gift, and its beautiful fragrance will make your recipient think fondly of you every time they use it. This homemade pesto stays a beautiful vibrant green thanks to the blanching step (which locks in basil's color) and is miles above anything store-bought. To make sure this gift is special, I use high-quality extra-virgin olive oil and Italian pine nuts. When shopping for basil, look for a 4-ounce plastic container of leaves with stems. If you don't have a scale to measure the Parmesan, the amount of processed Parmesan should be about ½ cup plus 2 tablespoons."

HOW I GIFT THIS

packaging: Spoon this into a wide-mouth jar with a one-piece screw-top lid (a two-piece lid will get oily).

storage: The pesto can be refrigerated for about 2 days or frozen for about 1 month. To prevent browning, press plastic wrap flush to the surface or top with a thin layer of olive oil.

make it a basket: For a garden basket, add Sweet Zucchini Pickle Chips (page 34), Summer Tomato Sauce (page 38), and one of the jams on pages 30–31.

½ cup pine nuts
¾ cup extra-virgin olive oil, divided
4 ounces fresh basil leaves and stems
¾ teaspoon table salt, plus salt for blanching basil
1¼ ounces Parmesan cheese
2 garlic cloves, peeled

1. Cook pine nuts and 1 tablespoon oil in 8-inch skillet over medium heat, stirring often, until pine nuts are light golden, 3 to 6 minutes. Spread pine nuts out on plate and let cool for 15 minutes.

2. Meanwhile, bring 2 quarts water to boil in medium saucepan. Remove and discard basil stems from leaves (you should have 4 cups leaves, or 3 ounces by weight). Add basil leaves and 1½ teaspoons salt to boiling water and cook until basil is wilted and bright green, 5 to 10 seconds. Using spider skimmer or slotted spoon, transfer basil directly to salad spinner and spin to remove excess water. Spread basil on clean dish towel to dry. (If you don't have a salad spinner, drain basil on clean dish towel and thoroughly pat dry with paper towels.)

3. Process Parmesan in food processor until finely ground, about 30 seconds; transfer to medium bowl. Process pine nuts, basil, garlic, salt, and remaining oil in now-empty processor until smooth, about 1 minute, scraping down sides of bowl as needed. Transfer pesto to bowl with Parmesan and stir to combine.

---

gift tag

5 Ways to Use Pesto

- Dilute with cooking water to sauce 1 pound pasta.

- Slather on crusty artisan bread.

- Mix with sour cream or yogurt to make a dip.

- Dollop into a steaming bowl of vegetable soup.

- Spoon over eggs or grilled chicken or fish.

HAPPY HOUSEWARMING

66 I've moved houses enough times to know that although it can be chaotic, it also offers the opportunity for a fresh start. At some point as you're packing up all your stuff, you start to look at items with a more critical eye: Do I really need to bring this to my new home? Is this too old to be worth packing and carrying? Although obviously I cook a lot, I'm just as guilty as anyone else of having jars of indeterminate age in my spice cabinet. That's why I love to give this housewarming basket to anyone moving into a new home. Not only is it a thoughtful way to freshen up that cupboard, but it's also the chance to potentially expand their spice repertoire with some globe-trotting gourmet blends."

HOW I GIFT THIS

Though I've offered my suggestions for what to start with, you could give any combination of the spice recipes in this chapter. If you like, supplement the homemade items with store-bought spices, a nice finishing salt, and tools for making the most of these blends: measuring spoons, a mini whisk, or a jar scraper. I like to nestle everything into a clear plastic storage tub, with or without a lid, for something attractive yet practical that can be reused for kitchen or pantry storage. You can line the tub with colorful tissue or crinkle-cut paper or dish towels. Make sure you label the individual jars so that your recipient can immediately tuck them away for later use.

START WITH

One of the Dukkahs (page 44)

Shichimi Togarashi (page 47)

Herbes de Provence (page 46)

Taco Seasoning (page 47)

Thai Panang Curry Paste (page 48)

IF YOU WANT, ADD

Advieh (page 46)

Vanilla Extract (page 49)

Store-bought spices

Coarse or flake finishing salt

Jar scraper

Measuring spoons

Mini whisk

Dish towels

SPICE BLENDS

HOW I GIFT THESE

packaging: I like to repurpose attractive spice jars or tins or even small condiment jars when gifting spice blends. The blends also all work nicely packed in shaker jars with large holes (look for ones with an inner or an outer lid to keep the jar airtight).

big-batch it: It's easy to scale up any of these spice blends if you're putting together several gifts.

PISTACHIO DUKKAH

makes: ½ cup   total time: 15 minutes

66 If you're a traveler like me, you know that friends love gifts that reflect your adventures. I love sharing how I came to know about a food or how a dish has inspired me to travel to a new place like Egypt! Dukkah, with its mix of toasted nuts, seeds, freshly ground spices, and sometimes legumes, is traditionally sprinkled on bread dipped in olive oil, often for an afternoon street snack. It's also great with beans, grains, and salads. If you don't own a spice grinder, you can use a mini food processor."

storage: The dukkah can be refrigerated for about 3 months.

make it a duo: Pair with a bottle of extra-virgin olive oil.

make it a basket: To the olive oil, add Whipped Feta Dip (page 97), Ultracreamy Hummus (page 94), and pita.

   1½ teaspoons coriander seeds, toasted
   ¾ teaspoon cumin seeds, toasted
   ½ teaspoon fennel seeds, toasted
   2 tablespoons sesame seeds, toasted
   3 tablespoons shelled pistachios, toasted and chopped fine
   ½ teaspoon flake sea salt
   ½ teaspoon pepper

Process coriander seeds, cumin seeds, and fennel seeds in spice grinder until finely ground, about 30 seconds. Add sesame seeds and pulse until coarsely ground, about 4 pulses; transfer to small bowl. Stir in pistachios, salt, and pepper.

HAZELNUT-NIGELLA DUKKAH

makes: ½ cup   total time: 15 minutes

66 This dukkah is a bit warmer and more intense than the pistachio dukkah, thanks to the hazelnuts and nigella seeds. Used throughout the Middle East, North Africa, and South Asia, nigella seeds have piney notes and an herby-oniony flavor. You can find them at spice shops and specialty markets. If you don't have a spice grinder, you can use a mini food processor."

storage: The dukkah can be refrigerated for about 3 months.

make it a basket: Put together a selection of spice blends and homemade condiments from this chapter for a stock-your-spice-cabinet basket.

   1 teaspoon fennel seeds, toasted
   1 teaspoon coriander seeds, toasted
   1½ tablespoons raw sunflower seeds, toasted
   1 tablespoon sesame seeds, toasted
   1½ teaspoons nigella seeds
   3 tablespoons hazelnuts, toasted, skinned, and chopped fine
   1½ teaspoons paprika
   ½ teaspoon flake sea salt

Process fennel seeds and coriander seeds in spice grinder until finely ground, about 30 seconds. Add sunflower seeds, sesame seeds, and nigella seeds and pulse until coarsely ground, about 4 pulses; transfer to small bowl. Stir in hazelnuts, paprika, and salt.

PRETTY WAYS TO PACKAGE SPICE BLENDS

In addition to using repurposed jars from my pantry, some of my favorite ways for packaging homemade spice blends include small tins, lidded salt cellars, and mortars and pestles.

HERBES DE PROVENCE

makes: ½ cup   **total time:** 5 minutes

66 Herbes de Provence is my quintessential 'new cook' gift. I usually gift it to folks who don't really cook a lot or who might feel intimidated in the kitchen. All I have to do is share the good gospel of the blend's versatility and—just like that—a more confident cook arises. The aromatic blend evokes the romance of the garrigue, those shrubby, fragrant evergreen areas found in the South of France. Home cooks of that region use this in traditional dishes like ratatouille, and with chicken dishes and vegetable soups; it's also lovely sprinkled on goat cheese or roasted potatoes. It can be made with a variety of herbs and spices; if you'd like to make a more floral blend, add 2 teaspoons dried lavender."

storage: The herbes de Provence can be stored at room temperature for about 1 month.

make it a duo: Pair with dried lavender sprigs or a lavender plant, with instructions for adding the flowers to the blend.

make it a trio: Pair with a bottle of French olive oil and a goat cheese log for sprinkling with the spice.

2 tablespoons dried thyme
2 tablespoons dried marjoram
2 tablespoons dried rosemary
2 teaspoons fennel seeds

Combine all ingredients in bowl.

ADVIEH

makes: ½ cup   **total time:** 10 minutes

66 This warm spice blend is a staple in Persian cooking, where it's often layered into rice dishes. (It also makes an amazing steak rub.) The ingredients can be tailored to the particular dish and the cook's preferences. This version includes fragrant dried rosebuds, cinnamon, and peppercorns, along with cumin and cardamom. Be sure to use food-grade dried rosebuds, which you can find at spice shops and specialty markets."

storage: The advieh can be stored at room temperature for about 1 month.

make it a duo: Pair with a bag of long-grain white rice or Feta Cheese Log with Advieh and Olive Oil (page 100).

1 (3-inch) cinnamon stick, broken into pieces
1 tablespoon cumin seeds, toasted
1 teaspoon cardamom pods
½ teaspoon black peppercorns
¼ ounce (½ cup) dried rosebuds, stems removed
½ teaspoon flake sea salt

Process cinnamon stick in spice grinder until finely ground, about 30 seconds. Add cumin seeds, cardamom pods, and peppercorns and process until coarsely ground, about 15 seconds. Add rosebuds and pulse until coarsely ground and pieces of petal are no larger than ⅛ inch, about 5 pulses. Transfer to small bowl and stir in salt.

SHICHIMI TOGARASHI

makes: ½ cup   **total time:** 10 minutes

❝ As an ovarian cancer thriver, it's been important for
me to eat in a way that brings me joy and comfort while
in treatments; umami boosts have always saved the day for
me. Enjoying a warm bowl of ramen with all the fixings,
including shichimi togarashi, makes my day, and I love to
share that with friends. The complexity of this Japanese
spice blend is utterly intriguing. It's pungent and spicy from
chile heat, aromatic from additional spices, and fragrant
from orange zest. I also love sprinkling this finishing spice on
simple rice dishes or grilled extra-firm tofu, but there are
countless other uses for this magical umami mixture."

storage: The shichimi togarashi can be stored at room
temperature for about 1 month.

make it a basket: Add short-grain rice or dried
ramen noodles, nori, Japanese pickles, and a bottle
of small-batch tamari.

1½ teaspoons grated orange zest
 4 teaspoons sesame seeds, toasted
 1 tablespoon paprika
 2 teaspoons pepper
 ½ teaspoon garlic powder
 ½ teaspoon ground ginger
 ¼ teaspoon cayenne pepper

Microwave orange zest in small bowl, stirring occasionally,
until dry and no longer clumping together, about 2 minutes.
Stir in sesame seeds, paprika, pepper, garlic powder, ginger,
and cayenne.

┌─ gift tag ─────────────────────────────┐

5 Ways to Use Shichimi Togarashi

- Sprinkle on popcorn.

- Sprinkle into cooked rice or ramen soup.

- Shake over cooked eggs.

- Top avocado toast.

- Use as a seafood seasoning.

└──┘

TACO SEASONING

makes: ½ cup (equivalent to 2 store-bought packets)
total time: 5 minutes

❝ Simplicity, ingredients from the pantry, and a high flavor
return on minimal effort make this taco blend a home
run for any Tex-Mex food fan on your gift list. A big bonus is
that it's free of the preservatives and excess sodium found in
store-bought packets. Chili powder creates the robust flavor
base, so use your favorite. The cornstarch will add saucy body
to the juices in a skillet of ground meat, simmering into an
ideal taco filling."

storage: The taco seasoning can be stored at room
temperature for about 1 month.

make it a trio: Pair with a package of hard taco shells
or soft corn tortillas and the Roasted Tomato–Lime Salsa
(page 102) or your favorite salsa.

¼ cup chili powder
 4 teaspoons ground cumin
 4 teaspoons cornstarch
 2 teaspoons paprika
 2 teaspoons table salt
 1 teaspoon granulated garlic
 1 teaspoon onion powder
 1 teaspoon dried oregano

Combine all ingredients in bowl.

┌─ gift tag ─────────────────────────────┐

5 Ways to Use Taco Seasoning Besides Tacos

- Use as a spice rub on protein.

- Add to a Texas-style chili or black bean chili.

- Sprinkle on popcorn or unsalted potato chips.

- Stir into ranch dressing.

- Sprinkle over roasted or grilled vegetables.

└──┘

THAI PANANG CURRY PASTE

makes: ½ cup   **total time:** 15 minutes

" Most people are familiar with green, yellow, and red Thai curries, but I like to give something a little different for a curry paste gift. Panang curry is a slightly sweeter, less spicy version of Thai red curry paste. Even in Thailand, many home cooks start with store-bought curry paste, so making this from scratch is really special—the flavors are so bright and fresh. The makrut lime leaves are worth seeking out, but you can substitute 1 (3-inch) strip each of lemon and lime zest."

HOW I GIFT THIS

packaging: Give this in a wide-mouthed jar so it can be easily stirred and spooned out.

storage: The curry paste can be refrigerated for about 1 week.

big-batch it: It's easy to scale up this recipe if you're putting together several gifts.

make it a trio: Team the paste with a bottle of sriracha sauce and a bottle of Thai soy sauce.

½ ounce (about 20) bird chiles, stemmed
1 teaspoon coriander seeds
½ teaspoon cumin seeds
2 lemongrass stalks, trimmed to bottom 6 inches and sliced thin
6 tablespoons water
8 garlic cloves, peeled and smashed
2 tablespoons packed dark brown sugar
2 makrut lime leaves
1 tablespoon tomato paste
1 teaspoon grated fresh ginger

1. Process bird chiles, coriander seeds, and cumin seeds in spice grinder until finely ground, about 30 seconds; transfer to blender.

2. Microwave lemongrass and water in covered bowl until steaming, about 2 minutes; transfer to blender with spices. Add garlic, sugar, lime leaves, tomato paste, and ginger and process until smooth paste forms, about 4 minutes, scraping down sides of blender jar as needed.

---

gift tag

5 Ways to Use Thai Panang Curry Paste

- Thin with coconut milk or broth to make a sauce for noodles.

- Whisk into yogurt to make a dip for vegetables.

- Stir together with rice vinegar or lime juice and vegetable oil to make a dressing.

- Thin with vegetable oil and brush on vegetables, chicken, or fish before grilling.

- Stir into a clean-out-your-fridge stir-fry.

VANILLA EXTRACT

makes: 1 cup   **total time:** 10 minutes, plus 6 weeks steeping

> 66 Growing vanilla vines, pollinating their beautiful orchid blossoms, and curing the resulting vanilla pods (the only edible fruit that comes from any orchid) is an intensive labor of love that happens in only a select few tropical locales on earth. If all that isn't reason enough to gift a precious bottle of homemade vanilla extract, I don't know what is. This is truly a special-occasion extract. You will need a 1-pint Mason jar with a lid. Heating the jar before adding the hot liquid ensures that the jar won't crack."

HOW I GIFT THIS

packaging: I divide this special extract into four 4-ounce bitters bottles for precise measuring—and for multiple gifts.

storage: The vanilla extract can be stored at room temperature for about 3 months.

make it ahead: This extract needs to steep for at least 6 weeks before it's ready to use.

8 vanilla beans
1 cup vodka

1. Cut vanilla beans in half lengthwise. Using tip of paring knife or spoon, scrape out seeds and transfer to small saucepan. Cut vanilla bean pods into 1-inch pieces and add to saucepan. Add vodka, cover, and cook over medium-low heat until mixture is hot and steaming, about 2 minutes. (Do not open lid while pot is over flame or alcohol will ignite.)

2. Fill one 1-pint Mason jar with hot tap water to warm. Drain jar, then pour vanilla mixture into jar and let cool completely. Cover and let sit in dark place until flavors meld, at least 6 weeks or up to 10 weeks, shaking jar occasionally.

3. Line fine-mesh strainer with double layer of coffee filters and set over 2-cup liquid measuring cup. Strain extract through filters, then transfer to clean bottles; discard solids.

---

gift tag

5 Ways to Use Vanilla Extract That Aren't Baking

- Macerate fresh berries with a few drops.
- Squeeze a few drops into cream before whipping.
- Drizzle a few drops over plain yogurt or vanilla ice cream.
- Use in cocktails.
- Add a few drops to coffee or tea.

PANCAKE MIX

makes: 12 cups (enough for 6 dozen pancakes)   **total time:** 10 minutes

66 This is a fantastic and easy big-batch gift on its own,
but it also makes an amazing special gift if you've been
invited to someone's home for the weekend. You can treat
your hosts to a pancake breakfast made with a wholesome
homemade mix, or leave all the fixings with them so they
can enjoy fluffy pancake nirvana whenever they want—and
think fondly of you. Heck, you might want to give batches
of this mix to yourself so that you never have to resort to
boxed pancakes again."

HOW I GIFT THIS

packaging: I like to divide the whisked mix evenly into six
airtight containers. One 2-cup container is enough for
one batch of pancakes, so even if you give more than one
container to your recipient, you can let them know that
each one is just the right amount for breakfast.

storage: The pancake mix can be stored at room
temperature for about 2 months.

make it a trio: Gift with a cast-iron skillet or griddle and
a ¼-cup scoop for the batter.

make it a basket: Add maple syrup, chocolate chips, dried
or fresh fruit, juice, shredded coconut, good butter, and a
wooden spoon.

10½ cups (52½ ounces) all-purpose flour
 1⅓ cups (9⅓ ounces) sugar
   5 teaspoons table salt
   6 tablespoons baking powder
   1 tablespoon baking soda

Whisk flour, sugar, and salt together in large bowl until well
combined. Strain baking powder and baking soda through
fine-mesh strainer into flour mixture then whisk until very
well combined, about 1 minute.

---

recipe card

Pancakes

Whisk 1½ cups milk, 2 large eggs, and ¼ cup vegetable
oil in a large bowl, then stir in 2 cups mix (the batter
should look lumpy). Let sit for 10 minutes. Spray a
12-inch nonstick skillet with vegetable oil spray, then
heat over medium heat until hot, about 1 minute. For
each pancake, spread ¼ cup batter into a small round
in the skillet and cook until surface bubbles begin to
pop, 2 to 3 minutes. Flip the pancakes and cook until
golden, 1 to 2 minutes. Makes 12 pancakes.

HOT CHOCOLATE MIX

makes: 3 cups (enough for 12 servings)　　**total time:** 10 minutes

66 This isn't your childhood hot cocoa. This better-than-boxed mix has the deep flavor and luxurious body of European sipping chocolate, but its richness is restrained enough that you can still indulge in a full mug's worth, American-style. It's the best of both worlds and a very grown-up treat. Any type of cocoa powder will work; the key is supplementing it with some unsweetened bar chocolate and a combination of nonfat dry milk powder and cornstarch. The latter two ingredients add lots of creamy body for a thicker, smoother beverage. Salt and vanilla extract are classic additions that heighten the chocolate goodness, so don't skip them."

- -

HOW I GIFT THIS

packaging: Pack the mix in Mason jars, repurposed tea tins, ceramic lidded mugs, or a thermos (it's a great gift for the campers in your life).

storage: The hot chocolate mix can be stored at room temperature for about 2 months.

big-batch it: The recipe is easily doubled or tripled.

make it a duo: Pair with Fluffy Vanilla Marshmallows (page 201), a bottle of Vanilla Extract (page 49), or some peppermint schnapps.

make it a trio: Gift with a milk frother and some peppermint candy sticks to use as stirrers.

1 cup (7 ounces) sugar
6 ounces unsweetened chocolate, chopped fine
1 cup (3 ounces) unsweetened cocoa powder
½ cup (1½ ounces) nonfat dry milk powder
5 teaspoons cornstarch
1 teaspoon vanilla extract
¾ teaspoon kosher salt

Process all ingredients in food processor until ground to powder, 30 to 60 seconds.

variations
MALTED HOT CHOCOLATE MIX
Substitute malted milk powder for nonfat dry milk powder and reduce sugar to ¾ cup.

MEXICAN HOT CHOCOLATE MIX
Add 1 teaspoon ground cinnamon, ¾ teaspoon ancho chile powder, and pinch cayenne pepper to processor with other ingredients.

MINT HOT CHOCOLATE MIX
Substitute mint extract for the vanilla.

MOCHA HOT CHOCOLATE MIX
Add ⅓ cup instant espresso powder to processor with other ingredients.

gift tag

For each serving, heat 1 cup milk in a small saucepan over medium heat until steaming. Whisk in ¼ cup mix and heat, whisking constantly, until the hot chocolate is simmering, 2 to 3 minutes.

Hi Friend,
To make one serving hot cocoa, heat
1 cup milk in a small saucepan over
medium heat until steaming. Whisk in 1/4 cup mix and continue to heat,
whisking constantly until hot chocolate is
simmering, 2 to 3 minutes longer.

AFTERNOON TEA

" The British tradition of afternoon tea is indulgent and oh-so civilized. I consider it a can't-miss ritual when visiting England, but it's also a festive event to share in gift form. Afternoon tea (also known as 'low tea') can be as simple as a quick break for scones and a cuppa, or as elaborate as starting with little sandwiches made with cucumber, smoked salmon, or egg salad, moving on to scones with clotted cream and jam, and ending with some dainty desserts. This basket falls somewhere in the middle of that spectrum; it focuses on the sweets, but with such panache that it will transport your recipient to the clinking, softly clattering delights of a London tearoom."

HOW I GIFT THIS

Naturally, this basket must start with a tea blend (or two)! Scones and a quick bread add some substance to the tea break, and then a special confection like macarons, presented in a windowed bakery box for maximum impact, finishes the tea session with style. There are lots of additional possibilities to consider: clotted cream or lemon curd for the scones, tea cups and accessories, berries or other fruit, and more sweets. Fresh flowers are an especially nice touch. A wide, shallow container that can double as a tea tray, such as a shallow wicker basket or wooden tray, is a great choice. Line it with crinkle-cut paper or a tea towel to cushion items.

START WITH

One or more of the Tea Blends (page 57)

British-Style Currant Scones (page 246)

Cranberry-Orange Pecan Bread (page 252)

Macarons (page 229)

IF YOU WANT, ADD

Almond Biscotti (page 232)

Clotted cream

Lemon curd

Fresh fruit

Tea cups

Tea infuser

Fresh flowers

TEA BLENDS

HOW I GIFT THESE

packaging: Package tea blends in airtight containers: I reuse tea tins or source test tube–style glass containers, which show off the different blends well.

storage: These tea blends can be stored at room temperature for about 3 months.

big-batch it: These are easily scaled up if you're putting together several gifts.

make it a trio: Give all three tea blends.

make it a basket: To the blends, add teacups, honey, and a honey dripper.

IMMUNITEA HERBAL TEA BLEND

makes: 1 cup (enough for 16 servings)
total time: 5 minutes

66 The herbal components in this tea blend are perfect for anyone who's feeling under the weather. Elderberry and rose hips make a fruity-floral base, similar to hibiscus but with deeper flavor. The echinacea, an herbaceous flower that can help boost the immune system, lends savory, hay-like notes, and lemon balm finishes this soothing tea with a light, citrusy flavor. Look for dried echinacea labeled 'cut and sifted.'"

make it a duo: Pair with the Chicken and Ramen Soup (page 164) to bolster someone who's unwell.

- 7 tablespoons dried rose hips
- ¼ cup dried elderberries
- 3 tablespoons dried lemon balm
- 3 tablespoons cut and sifted dried echinacea

Combine all ingredients in bowl.

COZY AND CALM HERBAL TEA BLEND

makes: 1 cup (enough for 16 servings)
total time: 5 minutes

66 This blend is equally welcome at afternoon tea as it is as a wind-down evening cuppa. It makes a wonderful gift for an expectant or new mother. Chamomile and lavender add sweet floral flavor and aromas to balance the grassy passionflower and earthy valerian root. Dried passion-flower and valerian root can be purchased at specialty tea shops, health stores, and online."

make it a duo: Pair with the Pistachio-Orange Stuffed Dates (page 211) for a relaxing snack.

- 6 tablespoons dried chamomile
- 5 tablespoons dried lavender
- 2 tablespoons dried passionflower
- 2 tablespoons dried valerian root

Combine all ingredients in bowl.

CITRUS BURST BLACK TEA BLEND

makes: 1 cup (enough for 16 servings)
total time: 5 minutes

66 One of the all-time classic tea pairings is bright lemon with earthy black tea. In this blend, lemon verbena adds a lemon curd–like richness to black tea leaves thanks to its herbal-tangy sweetness. Dried orange peel bolsters the citrus with a slight floral note, while coriander seeds, which also have a citrusy flavor, add savoriness. A boldly flavored tea such as Assam is ideal; you could also use Irish or English breakfast tea."

make it a duo: Pair with Shortbread Cookies (page 220) or British-Style Currant Scones (page 246).

- ⅔ cup dried lemon verbena
- ⅓ cup coriander seeds
- ⅓ cup dried orange peel
- ⅓ cup black tea leaves

Pulse lemon verbena in spice grinder until coarsely ground and pieces are no larger than ½ inch, about 3 pulses. Add coriander seeds and orange peel and pulse until coarsely ground and pieces of lemon verbena are no larger than ¼ inch, about 4 pulses. Transfer to small bowl and stir in black tea.

gift tag

Add 1 tablespoon tea blend to a tea infuser or tea sachet. Steep with 1 cup boiling water in a teacup, covered, for 10 minutes. Remove the tea infuser and serve.

COLD BREW COFFEE CONCENTRATE

makes: 4 cups (enough for 6 to 8 servings)   **total time:** 30 minutes, plus 25 hours resting and chilling

66 Cold brew coffee has passionate fans and carries a premium price in coffee shops—making this concentrate a welcome gift for your cold brew crew. It's also great for college students or anyone else who requires caffeine for brain power! The appeal of cold brew lies in its milder acidity and lower bitterness compared to iced coffee made from hot-brewed coffee. A 24-hour hands-off steep delivers amazing flavor, and pouring the finished concentrate through a fine-mesh strainer before bottling guarantees that it's grit-free."

HOW I GIFT THIS

packaging: I love to put this into a glass growler or a vintage stopper-top bar bottle.

storage: This concentrate can be refrigerated for about 1 week.

make it a duo: Pair with a bag of Cocoa-Coconut Granola (page 61) for a morning wake-up. Or go in an evening direction and pair with a bottle of Coffee Liqueur (page 125).

make it a trio: Complement with a bottle of Spiced Syrup (page 115) or a store-bought flavored syrup and a fun to-go cup or two.

make it a basket: Add to the Let's Fika basket (page 263).

8 ounces medium-roast coffee beans, ground coarse (3 cups)
4 cups filtered water, room temperature

1. Stir coffee and water together in 2-quart jar or narrow pitcher. Allow raft of ground coffee to form, about 10 minutes, then stir again to recombine. Cover with plastic wrap and let steep at room temperature for 24 hours.

2. Set fine-mesh strainer over large bowl. Pour concentrate into strainer and using back of ladle or rubber spatula, gently stir concentrate to help filter through strainer, extracting as much liquid as possible. Discard grounds.

3. Set now-empty strainer over second large bowl and line with large coffee filter. Strain concentrate for a second time through lined strainer, gently stirring concentrate to help filter through strainer. (This may take up to 10 minutes.) Transfer to airtight container. Refrigerate until chilled, at least 1 hour.

variations
PUMPKIN-SPICED COLD BREW COFFEE CONCENTRATE
Add 2 teaspoons toasted and cracked allspice berries, 4 toasted and cracked cinnamon sticks, and 12 toasted whole cloves to coffee and water mixture in step 1.

STAR ANISE–ORANGE COLD BREW COFFEE CONCENTRATE
Add 1 toasted star anise pod and 1 tablespoon grated orange zest to coffee and water mixture in step 1.

gift tag

Dilute this concentrate as desired, depending on how strong you like your coffee. A 1:1 ratio of concentrate to water is really nice, but experiment to find your custom cup.

GRANOLA

makes: 9 cups   **total time:** 1 hour, plus 1 hour cooling

66 Homemade granola is a crowd-pleaser, and it's so easy to make in large quantities and different flavors for gift-giving. This one starts with a flavorful, healthful base of traditional oats and adds earthy quinoa and mellow millet. The sky's the limit in terms of how to give this: as part of a mailed care package, a breakfast basket, a stocking stuffer, a bon voyage snack for someone going on a road, airplane, or camping trip . . . The granola bakes into one big sheet that you break into shards after it's cooled. You'll want to firmly pack the granola mixture into the rimmed baking sheet before baking, and don't touch it once it's in the oven. Don't use quick oats. I like the convenience of prewashed quinoa here; the rinsing removes the quinoa's bitter protective coating. Millet doesn't come prewashed, though, so you'll have to rinse that (or you could substitute an equal quantity of additional quinoa for the millet)."

HOW I GIFT THIS

packaging: Pack the granola into cellophane bags, Mason jars with a serving spoon attached, or a decorative tin that you can divide into compartments if giving more than one flavor.

storage: All of these granolas can be stored at room temperature for about 2 weeks.

mail it: If you're mailing this or giving it to a camper, break it into large pieces. The chunks will naturally break into smaller pieces during transit.

big-batch it: This easily scales up to make even more granola. You could also divide the granola base in half or thirds at the end of step 3, then stir in add-ins for one or two of the variations (don't forget to cut the add-ins by half or a third). Bake each smaller batch on a quarter-size rimmed baking sheet.

⅔ cup millet
¼ cup maple syrup
¼ cup light brown sugar
2 teaspoons vanilla extract
½ teaspoon table salt
½ cup refined coconut oil, melted
5 cups old-fashioned rolled oats
⅔ cup prewashed white quinoa
2 tablespoons chia seeds (optional)
2 cups dried fruit and/or toasted nuts, chopped (optional)

1. Adjust oven rack to upper-middle position and heat oven to 325 degrees. Line rimmed baking sheet with parchment paper.

2. Rinse millet under cold running water in a fine-mesh strainer for 1 minute. Shake excess water and transfer to clean dish towel to dry for 10 minutes.

3. Whisk maple syrup, brown sugar, vanilla, and salt together in large bowl. Whisk in oil until fully emulsified. Fold in millet, oats, quinoa, and chia seeds, if using, until thoroughly coated.

4. Transfer oat mixture to prepared sheet and spread into even layer. Using back of spatula, evenly compress oat mixture until very compact. Bake until lightly browned, about 45 minutes, rotating pan halfway through baking. Remove granola from oven and cool to room temperature on wire rack, about 1 hour. Break cooled granola into pieces of desired size. Fold in dried fruit and/or nuts, if using.

variations

COCOA-COCONUT GRANOLA

Add 1½ cups sweetened shredded coconut, ½ cup cacao nibs, and ⅓ cup Dutch-processed cocoa powder to oat mixture in step 3. Substitute 4 ounces chopped bittersweet chocolate for optional dried fruit and nuts. If you like, amp up the coconut flavor by using unrefined coconut oil.

PEANUT BUTTER–BANANA GRANOLA

Add ⅓ cup peanut butter powder and 1 teaspoon cinnamon to oat mixture in step 3. Use 1½ cups chopped dry-roasted peanuts and 1½ cups crushed banana chips for optional dried fruit and nuts.

GREEN GRANOLA

Add 1½ cups (8 ounces) raw pepitas, ½ cup hemp hearts, 2 tablespoons spirulina powder, and 1½ teaspoons ground ginger to oat mixture in step 3. If you like, amp up the savory flavor by using extra-virgin olive oil instead of coconut oil.

DARK CHOCOLATE FUDGE SAUCE

makes: 2 cups   total time: 20 minutes

" This one is for all the chocolate lovers on your list. The luxurious sauce gets its deep chocolate goodness from two kinds of chocolate and its velvety texture from the butter stirred in at the end. I prefer to use Dutch-processed cocoa powder (the test kitchen's favorite is Droste), but other cocoa powders will work. Your recipient can drizzle, dip, or dollop in any way that makes their heart happy—this luscious sauce lives in a judgment-free zone."

HOW I GIFT THIS

packaging: Pour the sauce into a wide-mouthed jar with a one-part screwtop to minimize drips.

storage: The sauce can be refrigerated for about 1 month.

make it a duo: Pair with the Dulce de Leche (opposite).

make it a basket: Add to a DIY sundae basket with the Dulce de Leche, Cinnamon-Ginger Spiced Nuts (page 77), shredded coconut, assorted sprinkles, maraschino cherries, waffle cone bowls, and even the ice cream.

1¼ cups (8¾ ounces) sugar
⅔ cup whole or 2 percent low-fat milk
¼ teaspoon table salt
⅓ cup (1 ounce) unsweetened cocoa powder, sifted
3 ounces unsweetened chocolate, chopped fine
4 tablespoons unsalted butter, cut into 8 pieces and chilled
1 teaspoon vanilla extract

1. Heat sugar, milk, and salt in medium saucepan over medium-low heat, whisking gently, until sugar has dissolved and liquid starts to bubble around edges of saucepan, 5 to 6 minutes. Reduce heat to low, add cocoa, and whisk until smooth.

2. Remove saucepan from heat, stir in chocolate, and let stand for 3 minutes. Whisk sauce until smooth and chocolate is fully melted. Add butter and whisk until fully incorporated and sauce thickens slightly. Whisk in vanilla.

variations
DARK CHOCOLATE-ORANGE FUDGE SAUCE
Bring the milk and 8 (3-inch) strips orange zest to simmer in medium saucepan over medium heat. Remove saucepan from heat, cover, and let stand for 15 minutes. Strain milk mixture through fine-mesh strainer into bowl, pressing on zest to extract liquid; discard zest. Return milk to saucepan and proceed with recipe, reducing cooking time to 3 to 4 minutes.

DARK CHOCOLATE-PEANUT BUTTER FUDGE SAUCE
Increase salt to ½ teaspoon. Whisk in ¼ cup peanut butter with vanilla until fully incorporated in step 2.

gift tag
Gently heat the sauce in the microwave (don't let it exceed 110 degrees), stirring every 10 seconds, until just warmed and pourable. This reheats well multiple times!

DULCE DE LECHE

makes: 3⅓ cups   **total time:** 2¾ hours

" Creamy, glossy, butterscotch-y dulce de leche is more popular throughout Latin America than peanut butter is in the United States. While traditional from-scratch versions of this caramelized milk jam can start with fresh milk and take hours, modern adaptations bring this sweet treat within easy reach by using sweetened condensed milk. With an oven and a little time and patience, you'll be on your way to impressing friends and family with its toasty caramel-like goodness."

HOW I GIFT THIS

packaging: Pour into a wide-mouthed jar with a one-part screwtop to minimize drips.

storage: The dulce de leche can be refrigerated for about 1 month.

make it a duo: Pair with the Dark Chocolate Fudge Sauce (opposite) or with Easy Holiday Sugar Cookies (page 216) or Shortbread Cookies (page 220).

add to a basket: Tuck into the Pancake Mix basket on page 51.

2 (14-ounce) cans sweetened condensed milk
1 teaspoon vanilla extract
¼ teaspoon table salt

1. Adjust oven rack to middle position and heat oven to 350 degrees. Pour condensed milk into 13 by 9-inch baking pan. Cover pan tightly with aluminum foil. Pour 1 inch boiling water into large roasting pan and carefully set baking pan inside (water should come about halfway up sides of baking pan). Bake, topping up roasting pan with boiling water every 45 minutes, until condensed milk is brown and has jiggly, flan-like consistency, 2¼ to 2½ hours.

2. Carefully transfer cooked condensed milk (it will look broken and grainy) to fine-mesh strainer set over bowl. Stir and press solids with back of small ladle or spoon. Stir in vanilla and salt.

---

gift tag

Gently heat the sauce in the microwave (don't let it exceed 110 degrees), stirring every 10 seconds, until just warmed and pourable. This doesn't reheat well, so heat only as much as you need.

5 Ways to Use Dulce de Leche

- Schmear on buttered toast.

- Use to sweeten anything from coffee to milk shakes to vinaigrettes.

- Dip pretzels into it.

- Use as a filling in cookie sandwiches or between cake layers.

- Eat with a spoon!

DULCE DE LECHE
(PAGE 63)

DARK CHOCOLATE
FUDGE SAUCE
(PAGE 62)

CHILI CRISP

makes: 1½ cups   total time: 45 minutes, plus 12 hours resting

"" China's household chili sauce was created in the 1990s by a woman named Tao Huabi. Her now world-famous brand is Lao Gan Ma, which translates as 'Old Godmother.' And when it comes to food and food gifts, who doesn't want to rely on the wisdom of mothers? Seems like a pretty wise idea to me. There are now countless versions of chili crisp available, but I like to give a flavorful homemade version to anyone who likes a little spice in their life. The Sichuan chili flakes here are milder and more finely ground than red pepper flakes; Aleppo pepper or Korean red pepper flakes (gochugaru) are good alternatives. You'll find monosodium glutamate in the spice aisle under the brand name Ac'cent."

HOW I GIFT THIS

packaging: You'll want a wide-mouthed non-embossed glass jar with a tight-fitting lid to avoid leaking and staining.

storage: The chili crisp can be refrigerated for about 3 months.

make it a trio: Combine with a bag of heirloom rice and a tin of sardines or smoked salmon.

make it a basket: Give this with the Chinese Pork Dumplings (page 181), soy sauce, black vinegar, and chopsticks.

½ cup salted dry-roasted peanuts, chopped
½ cup Sichuan chili flakes
2 tablespoons Sichuan peppercorns, crushed
1½ teaspoons kosher salt
¼ teaspoon monosodium glutamate (optional)
1 cup vegetable oil
2 large shallots, sliced thin
4 large garlic cloves, sliced thin
1 (1-inch) piece ginger, unpeeled, sliced into ¼-inch-thick rounds and smashed
3 star anise pods
10 green cardamom pods, crushed
2 cinnamon sticks
2 tablespoons toasted sesame oil

1. Combine peanuts, chili flakes, peppercorns, salt, and monosodium glutamate, if using, in heatproof bowl; set fine-mesh strainer over bowl. Cook vegetable oil and shallots in medium saucepan over medium-high heat, stirring frequently, until shallots are deep golden brown, 10 to 14 minutes. Using slotted spoon, transfer shallots to second bowl. Add garlic to vegetable oil and cook, stirring constantly, until golden brown, 2 to 3 minutes. Using slotted spoon, transfer garlic to bowl with shallots.

2. Add ginger, star anise, cardamom, and cinnamon sticks to vegetable oil. Reduce heat to medium and cook, stirring occasionally, until ginger is dried out and mixture is very fragrant, 15 to 20 minutes. Strain ginger oil through fine-mesh strainer into bowl with chili powder mixture (which may bubble slightly); discard solids in strainer. Stir well to combine. Once cool, stir shallots, garlic, and sesame oil into ginger–chili powder mixture. Transfer to airtight container and let stand for at least 12 hours.

┌─ gift tag ──────────────────────

Ways to Use Chili Crisp

- Stir into cooked rice or Chinese noodles.

- Spoon over grilled tofu or tempeh.

- Spread onto an egg sandwich.

- Add a spoonful to stir-fried broccoli.

- Serve as a dipping sauce with dumplings.

- Believe it or not—spoon over vanilla ice cream!

EASY HOMEMADE HOT SAUCE

makes: 1 cup   total time: 15 minutes, plus 4 days brining

" Chileheads are always searching for new hot sauces to try, and you'll get big props for sure if you give them a homemade bottle. Give this on Father's Day, Memorial Day, the Fourth of July—or at any summer party gathering. The recipe includes half of the seeds from the Fresno chiles to make a medium-spicy hot sauce, but you can customize the heat level by either using all of the seeds or leaving them all out. You could also use red jalapeños instead of Fresnos. I always wear rubber gloves when handling chiles. The left-over brine is a little cook's bonus for you: Refrigerate it and use it in marinades, dressings, cocktails, or even on its own as a condiment to spice up soups or braised greens."

- -

HOW I GIFT THIS

packaging: Put into a glass jar or a repurposed hot sauce bottle (remove the stopper insert, since this is a chunky sauce). Have some fun—give your hot sauce a name and make customized labels!

storage: The hot sauce can be refrigerated for about 3 months.

big-batch it: You can easily scale this up to make multiple gifts; just be sure to use a 1-quart Mason jar and 1-quart zipper-lock bag for each batch. I often do this and give the sauce in 4-ounce bottles.

make it a duo: Pair with Chili Crisp (page 67) or Taco Seasoning (page 47).

1 tablespoon table salt for brining
8 ounces Fresno chiles, stemmed and halved lengthwise
4 ounces (1 cup) coarsely chopped red bell pepper
1 tablespoon sugar
½ teaspoon table salt
2 tablespoons extra-virgin olive oil

1. Whisk 2 cups water and 1 tablespoon salt together in 4-cup liquid measuring cup until salt is dissolved. Remove seeds from half of Fresnos. Place Fresnos and bell pepper in 1-quart Mason jar, pressing peppers firmly into bottom of jar.

2. Pour brine into jar with peppers, making sure liquid covers peppers. Fill 1-quart zipper-lock bag with ⅓ cup water, press out air, and seal bag. Place bag of water on top of peppers in jar to keep them submerged in brine. Affix jar lid but only partially tighten, leaving lid loose enough to allow air to escape as mixture ferments.

3. Let jar sit at room temperature away from direct sunlight for 4 days. Check container daily, skimming residue from surface and ensuring that peppers remain submerged. (After 2 or 3 days, brine will become cloudy and bubbles will rise to surface when jar is moved.)

4. Drain peppers in fine-mesh strainer, reserving brine for another use, if desired. Process peppers, sugar, and salt in food processor until coarsely pureed, about 1 minute, scraping down sides of bowl as needed. Add oil and pulse until combined, about 2 pulses.

FUN WITH HOT SAUCE LABELS

Homemade hot sauce demands that you come up with a fun name, so I like to give my gifts an equally fun label. Here are some options.

1. Buy colorful waterproof labels to write on with permanent marker.

2. Use an embossing label maker for a retro touch.

3. Any number of websites allow you to custom-design and order personalized labels for your food gift creations.

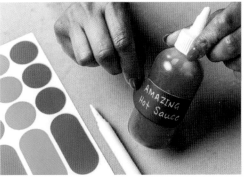

GIVE A SNACK OR A SIP

PACKING UP SNACKS AND SIPS

This just might be the most varied chapter in this book. Giving any of the gifts here makes me feel like I'm bringing the party along with me—and the delighted reactions of my recipients definitely reinforce that feeling. Here are some tips for delivering these potentially messy gifts with style and grace.

HOW TO PACKAGE OILY OR STICKY FOOD GIFTS

Plain Jars

Nonembossed glass jars work best for oily items like Marinated Green and Black Olives (page 75) and Bacon Jam (page 89), since they are nonporous and easy to clean. A tight-fitting one-piece lid or simple canning lid is helpful here, too.

Tight-Sealing Bottles

For infusions like the syrups and liqueurs in this chapter, look for bottles with tight-sealing tops. I especially like swing-top bottles (also called flip-top bottles or Grolsch-style bottles). Or repurpose an old liquor bottle from your bar (see page 27 for how to remove the label). I generally avoid bottles with real corks for gifting liqueurs because they get too sticky.

HOW TO KEEP CRISP FOODS CRISP

To extend the storage life of anything crisp, such as Spiced Nuts (page 77), Firecracker Party Mix (page 83), and Pimento Cheese Coins (page 107), slip a silica packet into the container.

HOW TO LABEL CONTAINERS THAT CONTAIN OILY FOODS

Precut Labels

Oil-resistant precut labels are readily available online. Permanent markers work best to write on these types of labels.

Contact Paper

Contact paper is oil-resistant, making it a great choice for more creative custom labels. Permanent markers work best to write on contact paper.

Packing Tape

You could also use paper and cover it completely with clear packing tape.

HOW TO GARNISH DIPS FOR THE BEST PRESENTATION

Toppings

If the dip has a topping, like the Ultracreamy Hummus with the Spiced Walnut Topping (pages 94–95), either give the topping in a separate container or make a well in the middle of the hummus as a "bowl" for the topping. Give toasted nuts in a separate jar so they stay crunchy.

Herbs

If you want to give herbs as a dip garnish, pick whole leaves from the stems for herbs like cilantro and thyme. Give chives whole. Alternatively, you could give an herb bouquet (see page 130); this is nice for any fresh herb but especially important for basil, which oxidizes quickly.

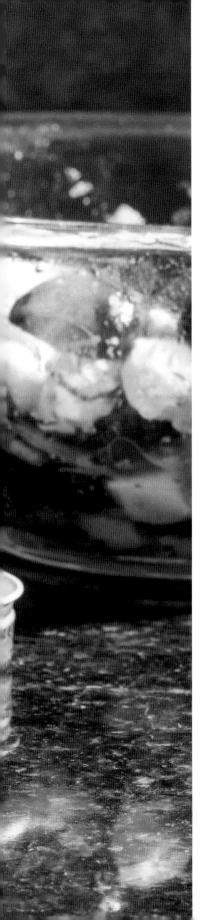

MARINATED GREEN AND BLACK OLIVES

makes: about 2½ cups   **total time:** 10 minutes, plus 4 hours marinating

" I'm always amazed at the abundant offerings of olives at the grocery store olive bar, and while I'm tempted to 'shortcut' and buy them, it doesn't exactly qualify as a homemade food gift. But it's almost effortless to customize a fresher and far more flavorful olive blend for gifting. The most important step is to start with good olives and extra-virgin olive oil. Olives packed in brine and with pits have better flavor than pitted olives. You can use any variety or varieties of black or green olives that you want. Adding different herbs, and even cheese, personalizes your gift even more. If you can't find pearl mozzarella balls, you can substitute baby mozzarella balls (bocconcini), cut in half."

HOW I GIFT THIS

packaging: Package the olives in screw-top glass jars or decorated deli containers. Wrapping the lid in newspaper looks good and also absorbs any little oil drips.

storage: The olives can be refrigerated for about 4 days.

make it a duo: Pair with a baguette.

make it a trio: Combine with Gruyère, Mustard, and Caraway Cheese Coins (page 107) and a bottle of white wine.

add to a basket: Include in the Summer Supper basket (page 145), the Cocktail Party basket (page 113), or the Crackers and Cheese basket (page 105).

1 cup brine-cured green olives with pits
1 cup brine-cured black olives with pits
¾ cup extra-virgin olive oil
1 shallot, minced
2 teaspoons grated lemon zest
2 teaspoons minced fresh thyme
2 teaspoons minced fresh oregano
1 garlic clove, minced
½ teaspoon red pepper flakes
½ teaspoon table salt

Pat olives dry with paper towels. Toss with oil, shallot, lemon zest, thyme, oregano, garlic, pepper flakes, and salt in bowl. Cover and refrigerate for at least 4 hours.

variations
MARINATED OLIVES WITH PEARL MOZZARELLA
Reduce amount of black and green olives to ½ cup each and add 8 ounces (2 cups) fresh pearl mozzarella balls (perlini). Substitute 1 tablespoon shredded fresh basil for oregano.

MARINATED GREEN OLIVES WITH FETA
Omit black olives and fresh thyme and add 8 ounces feta cheese, cut into ½-inch cubes (2 cups). Substitute orange zest for lemon zest.

SPICED NUTS

makes: about 3 cups   total time: 1 hour, plus 30 minutes cooling

" Spiced nuts are a supremely versatile food gift since
they're as much at home being served with cocktails
as they are packed into a backpack for a camping trip or
brought along on a road trip. Making them from scratch lets
you customize the flavors and is a lot more economical than
buying tiny yet crazy-expensive bags from a fancy nut shop.
The base coating on all of these nuts—a mixture of egg white,
water, and salt—coats the nuts evenly, helps the sugar and
spices cling tightly, and dries in the oven to a delicately
crunchy crust that stores beautifully for several weeks. If you
can't find superfine sugar, process granulated sugar in a food
processor for 1 minute."

HOW I GIFT THIS

packaging: These look great in a glass jar with a clip-top lid or
packed into decorative paper bags or nut cones (see page 78
for how to make a bag). You could even package them in a
repurposed glass or plastic supermarket nut container.

storage: The spiced nuts can be stored at room temperature
for about 3 weeks.

make it a duo: Pair the Cinnamon-Ginger nuts with a
wheel of Brie or with the spices used in the nut mix, the
Saffron-Orange nuts with a wedge of Manchego cheese,
and the Sichuan nuts with a favorite beer.

add to a basket: Add to the Cocktail Party basket (page 113).

CINNAMON-GINGER SPICED NUTS

⅔ cup superfine sugar
2 teaspoons ground cinnamon
1 teaspoon ground ginger
1 teaspoon ground coriander
1 large egg white
1 tablespoon water
1 teaspoon table salt
1 pound raw whole almonds, cashews,
    walnuts, and/or shelled pistachios

1. Adjust oven rack to middle position and heat oven to
275 degrees. Line rimmed baking sheet with parchment paper.
Mix sugar, cinnamon, ginger, and coriander in small bowl.

2. Whisk egg white, water, and salt in large bowl. Add nuts
and toss to coat. Sprinkle sugar mixture over nuts, toss to
coat, then spread evenly over prepared sheet. Bake until nuts
are dry and crisp, about 50 minutes, stirring occasionally. Let
cool completely on sheet, about 30 minutes. Break nuts apart.

SAFFRON-ORANGE BLOSSOM SPICED NUTS

  1 tablespoon hot tap water
  ¼ teaspoon crumbled saffron threads
  1 large egg white
  1 tablespoon orange blossom water
  1 teaspoon table salt
  1 pound raw whole almonds, cashews, walnuts, and/or shelled pistachios
  ½ cup superfine sugar

1. Adjust oven rack to middle position and heat oven to 275 degrees. Line rimmed baking sheet with parchment paper. Combine hot water and saffron and let steep for 5 minutes.

2. Whisk saffron mixture, egg white, orange blossom water, and salt in large bowl. Add nuts and toss to coat. Sprinkle sugar over nuts, toss to coat, then spread evenly over prepared sheet. Bake until nuts are dry and crisp, about 50 minutes, stirring occasionally. Let cool completely on sheet, about 30 minutes. Break nuts apart.

SICHUAN SPICED NUTS

  ¼ cup superfine sugar
  1 tablespoon Sichuan chili flakes
  2 teaspoons ground Sichuan peppercorns
  ½ teaspoon five-spice powder
  ½ teaspoon white pepper
  1 large egg white
  1 tablespoon water
  1½ teaspoons table salt
  1 pound raw whole peanuts, almonds, cashews, walnuts, and/or shelled pistachios

1. Adjust oven rack to middle position and heat oven to 275 degrees. Line rimmed baking sheet with parchment paper. Mix sugar, chili flakes, peppercorns, five-spice powder, and pepper in small bowl.

2. Whisk egg white, water, and salt in large bowl. Add nuts and toss to coat. Sprinkle sugar mixture over nuts, toss to coat, then spread evenly over prepared sheet. Bake until nuts are dry and crisp, about 50 minutes, stirring occasionally. Let cool completely on sheet, about 30 minutes. Break nuts apart.

FOLDING PAPER INTO A BAG

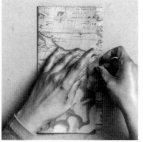

1. Cut rectangle of paper twice the size of desired bag size. Place on surface, exterior side facing down and long side facing you. Fold short sides in toward middle, overlapping them, and tape together.

2. Fold up bottom of paper, making it about twice as wide as you want bag base to be and pressing firmly to establish crease.

3. Open bottom fold of bag base and flatten each corner inward to make triangle.

4. Fold both long sides of bag base in toward middle, overlapping them, and tape together.

5. After filling bag, fold over open top of bag and either clip to seal or punch two holes through folded top and tie ribbon through them to enclose.

CHEESY GARLIC POPCORN SEASONING

makes: ¼ cup (enough for 14 cups popped corn)   total time: 10 minutes

66 Popcorn seasoning blends are awesome kids' gifts (you'll be their favorite aunt, uncle, or what have you) and are also great to mail to your favorite college student, but you can bring out the kid in anyone, of any age, by giving any (or all) of these homemade blends. Don't forget to include a recipe card with the test kitchen's foolproof method for stovetop popcorn that pops more of the kernels than you ever thought possible. You can use any variety of cheese powder you like; cheddar is the most commonly available flavor."

HOW I GIFT THIS

packaging: Store in a shaker-type jar for easy sprinkling or a latch-top glass jar.

storage: These seasoning blends can be stored at room temperature for about 1 month.

big-batch it: This recipe is easily scaled up.

make it a duo: Pair one seasoning with a bag of artisan popcorn kernels.

make it a trio: Give all three seasoning blends, of course! Or gift a handmade three-way container of popped and seasoned corn, like the tins you see at the holidays, along with a scoop.

make it a basket: Combine all three blends with popcorn kernels, a silicone microwave popper or air popper, and serving bags or bowls.

2 tablespoons cheese powder or nutritional yeast
2 teaspoons garlic powder
1½ teaspoons dried parsley
1 teaspoon dried basil
½ teaspoon table salt

Grind cheese powder, garlic powder, parsley, basil, and salt in spice grinder to fine powder.

variations

SPICED CHOCOLATE POPCORN SEASONING
Grind 1 tablespoon unsweetened cocoa powder, 1 tablespoon confectioners' sugar, 1 teaspoon ground cinnamon, ¼ teaspoon cayenne pepper, and ¼ teaspoon table salt in spice grinder to fine powder.

DILL PICKLE POPCORN SEASONING
Grind 1 tablespoon ground coriander, 2 teaspoons dried dill weed, 1½ teaspoons white vinegar powder, 1 teaspoon garlic powder, 1 teaspoon onion powder, ¾ teaspoon table salt, and ½ teaspoon dry mustard in spice grinder to fine powder.

---

recipe card

Seasoned Popcorn

Heat 3 tablespoons vegetable oil and 3 popcorn kernels in a large saucepan over medium heat until the kernels pop. Off the heat, add ⅓ cup popcorn kernels, cover, and let sit for 30 seconds. Return the pan to medium-high heat and cook with the lid slightly ajar until the popping slows to about 2 seconds between pops. Pour into a large bowl and toss with 2 tablespoons melted unsalted butter. Add ¼ cup popcorn seasoning in two additions, tossing after each addition to coat. Makes 14 cups.

FIRECRACKER PARTY MIX

makes: about 10 cups   total time: 1 hour, plus 30 minutes cooling

" Bring one of these casual, personalized snack mixes to your next group movie night or card game night, mail one to a hungry college student or homesick summer camper, or give a bag to a traveling friend as a bon voyage airplane or road-trip snack. Crunchy and salty, each party mix packs a huge flavor punch and features loads of different shapes and textures— which guarantees a snack-repeat, snack-repeat kind of situation."

HOW I GIFT THIS

packaging: This is a natural for packing into a fun tin or large snack bowl for one large gift. Or pack into smaller jars for multiple gifts.

storage: These party mixes can be stored at room temperature for about 2 weeks.

divide it: Try making two different flavors at once! This makes a lot as it is, so I halve the ingredients and bake each half-batch in a quarter-size rimmed baking sheet.

make it a duo: Pair with one of the spiced nuts (pages 77–78).

add to a basket: Include in the Snack Care Package (page 84) or add to the Cocktail Party basket (page 113).

5 cups Corn Chex cereal
2 cups sesame sticks
1 cup wasabi peas
1 cup chow mein noodles
1 cup honey-roasted peanuts
6 tablespoons unsalted butter, melted
2 tablespoons soy sauce
1 teaspoon ground ginger
¾ teaspoon garlic powder
¼ teaspoon cayenne pepper

1. Adjust oven rack to middle position and heat oven to 250 degrees. Combine cereal, sesame sticks, peas, chow mein noodles, and peanuts in large bowl. Whisk melted butter, soy sauce, ginger, garlic powder, and cayenne together in separate bowl, then drizzle over cereal mixture and toss until well combined.

2. Spread mixture on rimmed baking sheet and bake, stirring every 15 minutes, until golden and crisp, about 45 minutes. Let cool to room temperature, about 30 minutes.

variations
FISHERMAN'S FRIEND PARTY MIX
Substitute 2 cups oyster crackers for sesame sticks, 1 cup Pepperidge Farm Cheddar Goldfish for wasabi peas, 1 cup Pepperidge Farm Pretzel Goldfish for chow mein noodles, and 1 cup lightly crushed Melba toast rounds for peanuts. Substitute 2 tablespoons hot sauce for soy sauce and add 1 tablespoon lemon juice and 1 tablespoon Old Bay seasoning to melted butter mixture in step 1. Omit ginger, garlic powder, and cayenne.

BBQ PARTY MIX
Substitute 2 cups corn chips for sesame sticks, 1 cup Melba toast rounds for wasabi peas, 1 cup pretzel sticks for chow mein noodles, and 1 cup smoked almonds for peanuts. Substitute ¼ cup barbecue sauce for soy sauce, 1 teaspoon chili powder for ground ginger, and ½ teaspoon dried oregano for garlic powder.

SWEET AND SALTY KETTLE CORN PARTY MIX
Substitute 2 cups Corn Pops cereal for sesame sticks, 2 cups popped popcorn for wasabi peas, 1 cup Corn Nuts for chow mein noodles, and omit peanuts. Substitute 2 tablespoons maple syrup for soy sauce, 1 teaspoon table salt for ground ginger, ¼ teaspoon pepper for cayenne, and omit garlic powder.

SNACK CARE PACKAGE

66 At first glance, you might assume that this mail-away basket is maybe for a kid at sleepaway camp or a ravenous college student. That's definitely true, but take another look and tell me truly: Is there anything in this basket that a grown-up wouldn't want? I know that I'd be thrilled to receive this gift in the mail, as would most of my friends, so don't be afraid to admit it if you feel the same way. And of course, you can always customize the flavors by using some of the recipe variations, or add additional store-bought elements that you know are your recipient's favorites."

HOW I GIFT THIS

There are a lot of practical considerations to take into account when mailing gifts; see page 20 for tips on packing and mailing gift baskets. But that doesn't mean your gift can't still look attractive when the recipient opens the box. Since you'll need plenty of packing materials to cushion the contents and keep them from shifting during transit, consider the filler as part of the visual presentation. Wrap anything delicate in a colorful dish towel or other fabric, or maybe tinted bubble wrap. Have some fun and use popped popcorn or bright crinkle-cut paper as the box filler. Don't forget to add a gift tag, labels, and maybe a couple of bows or ribbons, for a wow factor as soon as the box is opened.

START WITH

Dill Pickle Popcorn Seasoning (page 81)

Firecracker Party Mix (page 83)

Pimento Cheese Coins (page 107)

Thin and Crispy Chocolate Chip Cookies (page 213)

IF YOU WANT, ADD

Bag of popcorn kernels

Additional popcorn seasonings

Silicone microwave popcorn popper or paper lunch bags for popping the corn

Spiced Nuts (page 77)

Granola (page 60)

K-cups or other coffee pods

Assorted candy

Vitamin C packets

SOUTHERN CHEESE STRAWS

makes: 48 straws   **total time:** 1 hour

66 Cheese straws look dainty but taste bold. These crumbly, buttery treats have a cult following in the South but deserve to be known far and wide. The elegantly elongated crackers are often made and given during the Christmas season, but they will bring cheer any time of year. Extra-sharp cheddar cheese accented by paprika and cayenne pepper makes them irresistible alongside a glass of sweet tea—or a frosty mint julep or martini. When rolling and cutting the dough, flour the counter and the top of the dough as needed to prevent sticking."

HOW I GIFT THIS

packaging: The straws package nicely stacked in cellophane bags and tied with a ribbon, or in a bakery box. I also like to stand them up in a nice glass that can be used for serving them. Just keep in mind that they are delicate.

storage: The cheese straws can be stored at room temperature for about 1 week.

make it a duo: Pair with the Bloody Mary Mix (page 120).

add to a basket: Add to the Afternoon Tea basket (page 54) or the Cocktail Party basket (page 113).

8 ounces extra-sharp cheddar cheese, shredded (2 cups)
1½ cups (7½ ounces) all-purpose flour
8 tablespoons unsalted butter, cut into 8 pieces and chilled
¾ teaspoon table salt
¾ teaspoon paprika
½ teaspoon baking powder
¼ teaspoon cayenne pepper
3 tablespoons ice water

1. Adjust oven rack to middle position and heat oven to 350 degrees. Line rimmed baking sheet with parchment paper. Process cheddar, flour, butter, salt, paprika, baking powder, and cayenne in food processor until mixture resembles wet sand, about 20 seconds. Add ice water and process until dough ball starts to form, about 25 seconds.

2. Turn out dough onto lightly floured counter. Knead briefly until dough fully comes together, 2 to 3 turns. Using your hands, pat dough into rough 4-inch square. Roll dough into 10-inch square, about ¼ inch thick, flouring counter as needed to prevent sticking.

3. Position dough so an edge is parallel to edge of counter. Using rounded side of fork, drag tines across entire surface of dough to make decorative lines.

4. Using pizza cutter or chef's knife, trim away and discard outer ½ inch of dough to make a neat square. Cut dough into 3 equal pieces perpendicular to decorative lines. Working with 1 section of dough at a time, cut into ½-inch-wide strips in direction of lines.

5. Evenly space cheese straws on prepared sheet, about ½ inch apart. Bake until edges of straws are light golden brown, 30 to 35 minutes, rotating sheet halfway through baking. Let straws cool completely on sheet.

BACON JAM

makes: 1¼ cups   **total time:** 1½ hours

" I believe that no food has a better balance of sweet, salty, smoky, and meaty than bacon. And turning it into an umami-infused jam with onion, garlic, maple syrup, and cider vinegar makes it downright swoonable—I mean, spoonable. In fact, you might want to double this batch, because once you taste it, you won't want to give it away. It just has so very many uses, so let your imagination run wild. Use regular rather than thick-cut bacon in this recipe."

HOW I GIFT THIS

packaging: I like to reuse a jam jar or other wide-mouthed jar for this chunky, savory jam.

storage: This jam can be refrigerated for about 4 days.

make it a duo: Pair with the Pancake Mix (page 51) or some fancy English muffins.

make it a trio: Group with No-Knead Rustic Loaf (page 299) and a wedge of cheddar or gouda.

add to a basket: Add to the Crackers and Cheese basket (page 105).

1 pound bacon, cut crosswise into ½-inch-wide strips
2 cups thinly sliced onions
4 sprigs fresh thyme
2 garlic cloves, smashed and peeled
4 cups water
⅓ cup cider vinegar
⅓ cup maple syrup
⅛ teaspoon cayenne pepper

1. Cook bacon in 12-inch nonstick skillet over medium heat until crispy, 15 to 18 minutes. Using slotted spoon, transfer bacon to paper towel–lined plate; set aside. Pour off all but 2 tablespoons fat from skillet.

2. Heat fat left in skillet over medium heat until shimmering. Add onions, thyme sprigs, and garlic and cook until onion is softened and browned, 5 to 7 minutes. Stir in water, vinegar, maple syrup, cayenne, and reserved bacon. Increase heat to medium-high and bring to boil. Cook, stirring occasionally, until nearly all liquid has evaporated and mixture begins to sizzle loudly, 22 to 28 minutes.

3. Remove from heat and let cool for 15 minutes. Discard thyme sprigs. Transfer bacon mixture to food processor and pulse until minced, 15 to 20 pulses. Transfer to 2-cup container.

---

gift tag

This jam is best served warm, so microwave the quantity you're going to use briefly to warm it up first, stirring as needed.

Ways to Use Bacon Jam

- Add to a breakfast sandwich.
- Top a burger.
- Use as a dip with apple wedges.
- Stir into green peas or wilted spinach.
- Stir into a vinaigrette.
- Spoon onto a baked potato.
- Stir into banana pancake batter.

CAPONATA

makes: 3 cups   **total time:** 1 hour

" Caponata, the classic sweet-and-sour Sicilian eggplant relish, is delicious enough to eat straight out of the bowl. Eggplant has a bit of a fussy reputation, since it can absorb oil like a sponge when fried (as it is for caponata), but the test kitchen's method of microwaving it first on a bed of coffee filters is a brilliant technique that collapses the eggplant's cells. This lets you brown it in only a tiny bit of oil, and enables the cooked eggplant to absorb all the flavors of the other luscious ingredients: anchovies, olives, raisins, and celery. If you don't have coffee filters, try food-safe, undyed paper towels. Remove the eggplant from the microwave immediately so that the steam can escape."

HOW I GIFT THIS

packaging: Give the caponata in a glass or plastic serving container, with the toasted pine nuts alongside in a separate container for sprinkling on before serving.

storage: The caponata and the toasted nuts can be refrigerated for about 1 week; bring to room temperature before serving.

make it a duo: Pair with No-Knead Rustic Bread (page 299) or a baguette.

make it a trio: Team with Basil Pesto (page 41) and a bag of artisan pasta.

1½ pounds eggplant, cut into ½-inch pieces
½ teaspoon table salt
¾ cup V8 juice
¼ cup red wine vinegar, plus extra for seasoning
¼ cup chopped fresh parsley
2 tablespoons packed brown sugar
3 anchovy fillets, rinsed and minced
1 large tomato, cored, seeded, and chopped
¼ cup raisins
2 tablespoons minced black olives
6–7 teaspoons extra-virgin olive oil, divided
1 celery rib, chopped fine
1 red bell pepper, stemmed, seeded, and chopped fine
1 small onion, chopped fine
¼ cup pine nuts, toasted

1. Toss eggplant with salt in bowl. Line plate with double layer of coffee filters and lightly spray with vegetable oil spray. Spread eggplant in even layer on coffee filters. Microwave until eggplant is dry and shriveled to one-third of its original size, 8 to 15 minutes (eggplant should not brown). Transfer eggplant immediately to paper towel–lined plate.

2. Whisk V8 juice, vinegar, parsley, sugar, and anchovies together in bowl. Stir in tomato, raisins, and olives.

3. Heat 1 tablespoon oil in 12-inch nonstick skillet over medium-high heat until shimmering. Add eggplant and cook, stirring occasionally, until edges are browned, 4 to 8 minutes, adding 1 teaspoon more oil if skillet appears dry; transfer to bowl.

4. Add remaining 1 tablespoon oil to now-empty skillet and heat over medium-high heat until shimmering. Add celery, bell pepper, and onion and cook, stirring occasionally, until softened and edges are spotty brown, 6 to 8 minutes.

5. Reduce heat to medium-low and stir in eggplant and V8 juice mixture. Bring to simmer and cook until liquid is thickened and coats vegetables, 4 to 7 minutes. Season with extra vinegar to taste. Transfer to 3-cup container and let cool completely. Sprinkle with pine nuts before serving.

SMOKED TROUT PÂTÉ

makes: 2 cups   total time: 15 minutes, plus 30 minutes resting

66 It will seem as though you spent a lot of time preparing
    this elegant party snack, but it comes together in a flash,
making it great for when you want to give a fancy gift, fast.
You're really just mashing together ingredients and then
packing the spread into a nice container or two, ideally one
that your recipient can just open and serve. The pâté's rich,
smoky, salty flavors are punched up by bright lemon, heady
horseradish, and green chile, making this an irresistible
kitchen gift."

HOW I GIFT THIS

packaging: This packages well in an airtight, sturdy
deli container or a Weck-style canning jar.

storage: The pâté can be refrigerated for about 3 days;
bring to room temperature before serving.

make it a duo: Pair with sturdy crackers or a tin of
smoked trout.

make it a trio: Combine with bagels and cream cheese.

make it a basket: Put together an elegant snack basket
with the pâté, bagel chips, assorted tinned seafood, a bottle
of fino or palo cortado sherry, and a nice spreading knife.

 8 ounces smoked trout
 4 ounces cream cheese, cut into 4 pieces and softened
 ¼ cup sour cream
 2 tablespoons mayonnaise
 1 scallion, sliced thin
 4 teaspoons minced jalapeño chile
 4 teaspoons lemon juice
 1 tablespoon prepared horseradish
 ¾ teaspoon pepper
 ½ teaspoon Tabasco sauce
 ¼ teaspoon table salt

Using your hands, finely shred trout in medium bowl,
discarding skin and bones. Add cream cheese, sour cream,
mayonnaise, scallion, jalapeño, lemon juice, horseradish,
pepper, Tabasco, and salt. Stir and mash vigorously with
fork until thoroughly combined. Set aside for 30 minutes
to allow flavors to blend. Transfer to 2-cup container.

ULTRACREAMY HUMMUS

makes: 3¾ cups   total time: 40 minutes

66 After one sample taste (remember, it's supposed to be a gift) of this deluxe, velvety-smooth hummus, you'll understand why this recipe earned its place here. Its luxuriously creamy texture is like no hummus you've ever bought at the store. Small tricks are game-changers, from simmering the canned chickpeas with baking soda until their grainy skins slide right off, to steeping minced garlic in lemon juice and salt to mellow its bite. Tahini that is lighter in color is best here—it means it hasn't been roasted as long (which can lead to bitterness). You can gift this hummus with or without the Spiced Walnut Topping, but the topping makes it more special."

HOW I GIFT THIS

packaging: I like to pack the hummus and topping right into serving containers, like nice lidded glass dishes or jars or large ramekins with lids.

storage: The hummus and the topping can be refrigerated in separate containers for about 1 week.

make it a basket: Add Marinated Green and Black Olives (page 75), a bottle of olive oil, a jar of za'atar, pita chips, and a couple of serving spoons.

2 (15-ounce) cans chickpeas, rinsed
½ teaspoon baking soda
4 garlic cloves, peeled
⅓ cup lemon juice (2 lemons), plus extra for seasoning
1 teaspoon table salt
¼ teaspoon ground cumin
½ cup tahini, stirred well
2 tablespoons extra-virgin olive oil

1. Combine chickpeas, baking soda, and 6 cups water in medium saucepan and bring to boil over high heat. Reduce heat and simmer, stirring occasionally, until chickpea skins begin to float to surface and chickpeas are creamy and very soft, 15 to 25 minutes.

2. While chickpeas cook, mince garlic using garlic press or rasp-style grater. Measure out 1 tablespoon garlic and set aside; discard remaining garlic. Whisk lemon juice, salt, and reserved garlic together in small bowl and let sit for 10 minutes. Strain garlic-lemon mixture through fine-mesh strainer set over bowl, pressing on solids to extract as much liquid as possible; discard solids.

3. Drain chickpeas in colander and return to saucepan. Fill saucepan with cold water and gently swish chickpeas with your fingers to release skins. Pour off most of water into colander to collect skins, leaving chickpeas behind in saucepan. Repeat filling, swishing, and draining 3 or 4 times, until most skins have been removed (this should yield about ¾ cup skins); discard skins. Transfer chickpeas to colander to drain.

4. Process chickpeas, garlic-lemon mixture, ¼ cup water, and cumin in food processor until smooth, about 1 minute, scraping down sides of bowl as needed. Add tahini and oil and process until hummus is smooth, creamy, and light, about 1 minute, scraping down sides of bowl as needed. (Hummus should have pourable consistency similar to yogurt. If too thick, loosen with water, adding 1 teaspoon at a time.) Season with salt and extra lemon juice to taste. Transfer to 4-cup container.

gift tag

Serve the hummus and walnut topping at room temperature. The hummus will thicken slightly over time in the refrigerator, so stir in warm water, 1 tablespoon at a time, to restore creaminess. Any leftover walnut topping makes an amazing sandwich spread!

SPICED WALNUT TOPPING

makes: ¾ cup   **total time:** 10 minutes

The topping should remain coarse-textured, so don't overprocess it.

- ¾ cup extra-virgin olive oil
- ⅓ cup walnuts
- ¼ cup paprika
- ¼ cup tomato paste
- 2 garlic cloves, peeled
- 1 teaspoon ground turmeric
- ½ teaspoon ground cumin
- ½ teaspoon ground allspice
- ½ teaspoon table salt
- ¼ teaspoon cayenne pepper

Process all ingredients in clean, dry workbowl until uniform coarse puree forms, about 30 seconds, scraping down sides of bowl halfway through processing. Transfer to 1-cup container.

Take a Dip!

WHIPPED FETA DIP

makes: 2 cups   total time: 15 minutes

66 Salty and rich, yet unbelievably
light in texture and so quick to
make, this is a simple anytime gift
that I enjoy giving to my cheese-loving
friends—especially if I've been invited
to their house for cocktails. Since this
dip is salty from the feta, if you give
it with chips of any kind, I suggest
choosing an unsalted variety. The cow's
milk feta produces a firmer dip that
holds up better at room temperature, so
don't substitute sheep's milk feta here."

- -

HOW I GIFT THIS

packaging: I pack the dip right into the
serving vessel(s), such as a nice glass
storage container or individual-serving
cups.

storage: This dip can be refrigerated
for about 3 days; bring to room
temperature before serving.

make it a trio: Combine with either
the Marinated Green and Black Olives
(page 75) or the Beet Muhammara
(page 98) and some pita bread.

make it a platter: If you know your
recipient will be serving this right away,
assemble individual plastic crudités
cups with sliced vegetables so guests
get their own fun servings. Plan on
¼ cup dip per serving. (This works best
if you aren't traveling too far with the
dip and can just cover the platter with
plastic wrap.)

1½ teaspoons lemon juice
¼   teaspoon minced garlic
8   ounces cow's-milk feta cheese
3   tablespoons milk
2   tablespoons plus 2 teaspoons extra-virgin olive oil, divided
2   teaspoons minced fresh oregano

1. Combine lemon juice and garlic in small bowl and set aside. Break feta into
rough ½-inch pieces and place in medium bowl. Add water to cover, then swish
briefly to rinse. Transfer to fine-mesh strainer and drain well.

2. Transfer feta to food processor. Add milk and reserved lemon juice mixture
and process until feta mixture resembles ricotta cheese, about 15 seconds. With
processor running, slowly drizzle in 2 tablespoons oil. Continue to process until
mixture has Greek yogurt–like consistency (some small lumps will remain), 1½ to
2 minutes, stopping once to scrape down bottom and sides of bowl. Add oregano
and pulse to combine. Transfer to 2-cup container and drizzle with remaining
2 teaspoons oil.

variations

WHIPPED FETA AND ROASTED RED PEPPER DIP
Omit oregano. Substitute red wine vinegar for lemon juice. Reduce milk to
2 tablespoons. With milk, add ¼ cup chopped jarred roasted red peppers,
½ teaspoon smoked paprika, and pinch cayenne pepper.

WHIPPED FETA DIP WITH DILL AND PARSLEY
Substitute 1 tablespoon minced fresh dill (or mint, if desired) and 1 tablespoon
minced fresh parsley for oregano.

BEET MUHAMMARA

makes: 2 cups   total time: 30 minutes

66 'Look at this gorgeous color!' will be the first thing your recipient says upon opening this vibrantly colored, deeply flavorful gift. Beets make a beautiful (to behold and taste) addition to muhammara, the smoky red pepper dip that's enjoyed throughout the Middle East. The multi-dimensional beets bring out the best in all the traditional ingredients, heightening the sweetness of the red peppers and pomegranate molasses and bolstering the earthiness of the walnuts. You can use the large holes of a box grater or a food processor fitted with a shredding disk to shred the beets."

HOW I GIFT THIS

packaging: I pack this dip right into the serving vessel, such as a nice glass storage container.

storage: The muhammara can be refrigerated for about 3 days.

make it a duo: Pair with a baguette, pita bread, or pita chips.

make it a trio: Put together a dip trio including Ultracreamy Hummus (page 94) and Whipped Feta Dip (page 97).

8 ounces beets, trimmed, peeled, and shredded
1 cup jarred roasted red peppers, rinsed and patted dry
1 cup walnuts, toasted
1 scallion, sliced thin
2 tablespoons extra-virgin olive oil, plus extra for drizzling
2 tablespoons pomegranate molasses
2 teaspoons lemon juice
¾ teaspoon table salt
½ teaspoon ground cumin
⅛ teaspoon cayenne pepper
2 tablespoons minced fresh parsley

1. Microwave beets in covered bowl, stirring often, until beets are tender, about 4 minutes. Transfer to fine-mesh strainer set over bowl and let drain for 10 minutes.

2. Process drained beets, peppers, walnuts, scallion, oil, pomegranate molasses, lemon juice, salt, cumin, and cayenne in food processor until smooth, about 1 minute, scraping down sides of bowl as needed. Season with salt to taste. Transfer to 2-cup container, drizzle with extra oil, and sprinkle with parsley.

---

gift tag

5 Ways to Use Beet Muhammara

- Serve as a dip for crudités, crackers, or pita chips.

- Spread on bread or into sandwiches.

- Top grilled chicken, fish, pork, or vegetables.

- Stir into Greek yogurt.

- Stir into cooked lentils or chickpeas.

BLUE CHEESE LOG WITH PISTACHIO DUKKAH AND HONEY

serves: 8 to 10   **total time:** 25 minutes, plus 1½ hours freezing

66 I love giving these cheese logs during the end-of-year holiday time. Not only are they very easy to make, but everyone I know seems to be in need of last-minute fancy snacks at that time of year. Gifting these to your crew will make you a save-the-day hero. They are each very different in flavor, but equally delicious."

- -

HOW I GIFT THIS

packaging: Wrap the cheese log securely in parchment paper, tying it with twine and tucking an herb sprig into the bow for decoration. Or source a vintage corn-on-the-cob dish to nestle the wrapped cheese log into. Package the honey or olive oil separately for the recipient to drizzle on before serving.

storage: These garnished cheese logs can be refrigerated for about 3 days.

big-batch it: This recipe is easily scaled up.

make it a duo: Give a jar of honey with the blue cheese log, pomegranate molasses or date syrup with the feta log, or chili oil or maple syrup with the goat cheese log.

4 ounces (1 cup) soft, mild blue cheese
8 ounces cream cheese
1 small garlic clove, minced
½ teaspoon pepper
⅓ cup Pistachio Dukkah (page 44)
2 tablespoons honey

1. Process blue cheese, cream cheese, garlic, and pepper in food processor until smooth, scraping down sides of bowl as needed, about 1 minute.

2. Lay 18 by 11-inch sheet of plastic wrap on counter with long side parallel to counter edge. Transfer cheese mixture to center of plastic and shape into approximate 9-inch log with long side parallel to counter edge. Fold plastic over log and roll up. Pinch plastic at ends of log and roll on counter to form tight cylinder. Tuck ends of plastic underneath and freeze log until completely firm, 1½ to 2 hours.

3. Unwrap cheese log and let sit until outside is slightly tacky to the touch, about 10 minutes. Spread dukkah into even layer on large plate and roll cheese log in dukkah to coat evenly, pressing gently to adhere. Package honey in small jar.

variations
GOAT CHEESE LOG WITH HAZELNUT-NIGELLA DUKKAH
Substitute 1½ cups goat cheese for blue cheese and decrease cream cheese to 6 ounces. Substitute ⅓ cup Hazelnut-Nigella Dukkah (page 44) for Pistachio Dukkah, and extra-virgin olive oil for honey.

FETA CHEESE LOG WITH ADVIEH AND OLIVE OIL
Substitute feta cheese for blue cheese, ¼ cup Advieh (page 46) for Pistachio Dukkah, and extra-virgin olive oil for honey. Add additional ¼ cup extra-virgin olive oil to food processor with feta.

Happy New Year!

Happy New Year!

ROASTED TOMATO-LIME SALSA

makes: four 1-cup jars   **total time:** 1 hour

> 66 You can add salsa to the top of your list of things that are better made from scratch. This one has the spicy, smoky-sweet, intense flavor of traditional salsa asada, or roasted salsa. Since you can process this for long-term storage, it's a great way to use home-grown tomatoes and chile peppers in the summertime for gifting anytime of year. For safety reasons, make sure to use bottled lime juice, not fresh, in this recipe. For more information on canning, see pages 302–305."

HOW I GIFT THIS

packaging: You'll be giving the salsa in the jars you used for processing it.

storage: Short-term processed salsa can be refrigerated for up to 1 month; long-term processed salsa can be stored at room temperature for up to 1 year and refrigerated after opening.

big-batch it: To double the recipe, double all the ingredients. Broil the vegetables in 4 batches in step 2 and increase the cooking time in step 3 to 20 to 25 minutes, until the salsa measures slightly more than 8 cups.

make it a duo: Pair with the Easy Homemade Hot Sauce (page 68), the Chicken Enchiladas (page 156), or the Best Ground Beef Chili (page 150).

2½ pounds tomatoes, cored and halved
1 onion, sliced into ½-inch-thick rounds
5 red jalapeño or Fresno chiles, stemmed and halved lengthwise
6 garlic cloves, peeled
⅓ cup bottled lime juice
2½ teaspoons table salt
2 teaspoons sugar
2 teaspoons chopped fresh cilantro
1 teaspoon ground cumin

1. Set canning rack in large pot, place four 1-cup jars in rack, and add water to cover by 1 inch. Bring to simmer over medium-high heat, then turn off heat and cover to keep hot.

2. Adjust oven rack 4 inches from broiler element and heat broiler. Line rimmed baking sheet with aluminum foil. Place tomatoes, cut side down, and onion on prepared sheet. Broil until tomatoes are well charred, about 15 minutes; transfer tomatoes and onions to separate bowls. Place chiles, cut side down, and garlic on now-empty sheet and broil until chiles are well charred, about 8 minutes.

3. Transfer chiles, garlic, half of tomatoes, and half of onions to food processor and process until a thick puree, about 10 seconds; transfer to Dutch oven. Transfer remaining broiled tomatoes and onions to now-empty food processor and pulse into ½-inch pieces, 2 or 3 pulses; add to pot. Stir in lime juice, salt, sugar, cilantro, and cumin. Boil over medium-high heat, stirring often, until salsa has thickened slightly and measures slightly more than 4 cups, about 10 minutes.

4. Place dish towel flat on counter. Using jar lifter, remove jars from pot, draining water back into pot. Place jars upside down on towel and let dry for 1 minute. Using funnel and ladle, portion hot salsa into hot jars, leaving ½-inch headspace. Slide wooden skewer along inside of jar to remove air bubbles, adding more salsa as needed.

5a. for short-term storage: Let jars cool to room temperature. Cover and refrigerate.

5b. for long-term storage: While jars are hot, wipe rims clean, add lids, and screw on rings until fingertip-tight; do not overtighten. Return pot of water with canning rack to boil. Lower jars into water, cover, bring water back to boil, then start timer. Cooking time will depend on your altitude. Boil 15 minutes for up to 1,000 feet, 20 minutes for 1,001 to 3,000 feet, 25 minutes for 3,001 to 6,000 feet, or 30 minutes for 6,001 to 8,000 feet. Turn off heat and let jars sit in pot for 5 minutes. Remove jars from pot and let cool for 24 hours. Remove rings, check seal, and clean rims.

CRACKERS AND CHEESE

" A cheese basket is a pretty common food gift, and we've probably all given one to somebody at some point. But if you order a basket from a cheese shop, fancy food store, or online purveyor, you'll pay a serious premium. And if you buy a ready-made cheese plate from a supermarket, you'll be getting something that's pretty ordinary at best. Putting together a custom basket lets you really tailor the contents to your recipient. Make the crackers and buy the cheese, or buy the crackers and make one of the cheese logs in this chapter, or make everything! You've got lots of choices here, all of them good. (BTW, I've never met a person who wasn't hugely impressed when presented with from-scratch crackers.)"

HOW I GIFT THIS

A shallow tray (that can also double as a cheese-serving tray) showcases the varied goodies. This photo shows what I consider to be the ultimate crackers and cheese basket—you don't have to do it all to make a wonderful gift! The cheese and the crackers are the focal point. From there, you can add something savory like olives, something sweet like conserve, and/or something crunchy like nuts. To arrange everything, cushion the bottom with crinkle-cut paper. Pack fragile items like crackers in long rectangular boxes (both to protect them and to keep them crisp) and fit them into the tray first, then fill in with cheeses and any other items. Small items like nuts can go in little containers. You can fill in any empty spaces with fruit, a little honey jar, small cookies, or other items.

START WITH

Seeded Pumpkin Crackers (page 108)

Gruyère, Mustard, and Caraway Cheese Coins (page 107)

Fancy cheeses

Marinated Green and Black Olives (page 75)

Brandied Cherry and Hazelnut Conserve (page 32) or store-bought jam or marmalade

IF YOU WANT, ADD

Pistachio-Spice Biscotti (page 233)

Baci di Dama (page 227)

Store-bought crackers

Fresh or dried fruit

Spiced Nuts (page 77) or store-bought

Jar of honey

Cheese knife

GRUYÈRE, MUSTARD, AND CARAWAY CHEESE COINS

makes: 80 crackers   **total time:** 40 minutes, plus 1½ hours chilling and cooling

> **"** Maybe you've never attempted homemade crackers, but I'm here to tell you: If you've ever made slice-and-bake cookies, then you can make these easy, cheesy, buttery, just-a-little-spicy crackers. Best of all, they make a giant batch of dough that you can roll into logs and stash in your freezer for several weeks, ready to thaw, slice, and bake for whatever occasion warrants a gift of food. (And you can still pretend that you just whipped up the homemade crackers at a moment's notice.)"

HOW I GIFT THIS

packaging: I like to pack these in an airtight jar, box, or cookie tin so they stay nice and crisp.

storage: These crackers can be stored at room temperature for about 1 week.

make it a duo: Pair with the Bacon Jam (page 89), caramelized onion jam, red pepper jelly, a stick of salami, or a bottle of red wine.

add to a basket: These are great additions to the Crackers and Cheese basket (page 105).

8 ounces Gruyère cheese, shredded (2 cups)
1½ cups (7½ ounces) all-purpose flour
1 tablespoon cornstarch
1 teaspoon caraway seeds
½ teaspoon table salt
¼ teaspoon paprika
¼ teaspoon cayenne pepper
8 tablespoons unsalted butter, cut into 8 pieces and chilled
¼ cup whole-grain mustard

1. Process Gruyère, flour, cornstarch, caraway seeds, salt, paprika, and cayenne in food processor until combined, about 30 seconds. Scatter butter pieces over top and process until mixture resembles wet sand, about 20 seconds. Add mustard and process until dough forms ball, about 10 seconds. Transfer dough to counter and divide in half. Roll each half into 10-inch log, wrap in plastic wrap, and refrigerate until firm, at least 1 hour. (Dough can be refrigerated for up to 3 days or frozen for up to 1 month; if frozen, thaw completely before continuing with step 2.)

2. Adjust oven racks to upper-middle and lower-middle positions and heat oven to 350 degrees. Line 2 rimmed baking sheets with parchment paper. Unwrap logs and slice into ¼-inch-thick coins, giving dough logs quarter turn after each slice to keep logs round. Place coins on prepared sheets, spaced ½ inch apart.

3. Bake until light golden around edges, 22 to 28 minutes, switching and rotating sheets halfway through baking. Let coins cool completely on sheets, about 30 minutes, before serving.

variations

BLUE CHEESE AND CELERY SEED CHEESE COINS
Substitute 1 cup crumbled blue cheese plus 1 cup shredded extra-sharp cheddar for Gruyère. Substitute celery seeds for caraway seeds. Increase paprika to 2 teaspoons and cayenne to ½ teaspoon. Omit mustard.

PIMENTO CHEESE COINS
Substitute extra-sharp cheddar for Gruyère. Substitute garlic powder for caraway seeds. Increase paprika to 1 tablespoon and cayenne to ½ teaspoon. Substitute 3 tablespoons water for mustard.

SEEDED PUMPKIN CRACKERS

makes: 50 crackers   **total time:** 2 hours, plus 5½ hours chilling and cooling

66 These vibrantly flavored, visually striking crackers are inspired by biscotti, another crunchy delight made by forming dough into a loaf that's baked, then sliced into individual pieces and baked a second time. Here you season pumpkin puree with orange zest and baharat, a Middle Eastern and North African spice blend. Once the dough comes together, you fold in sesame seeds, pistachios, and dried apricots. Then after the first bake, freeze the loaves to firm them up before slicing thinly for the second bake. And here's a major payoff: You need only slice and bake the number of crackers you want to package and give at any given time, reserving the rest of the frozen loaves for another gifting occasion. This recipe is best made in two 5½ by 3-inch loaf pans. You can use one 8½ by 4½-inch loaf pan instead; bake the loaf for the same amount of time and then slice the frozen loaf down the center before slicing crosswise. The crackers will continue to crisp as they cool."

HOW I GIFT THIS

packaging: Give these in an airtight jar or cookie tin or a windowed bakery box to show off how pretty they are.

storage: These crackers can be stored at room temperature for about 5 days.

make it DIY: Give the whole loaf after the first bake, with a recipe card including instructions for the recipient to slice and bake the crackers.

make it a trio: With these dramatic-looking crackers, I go for a dramatic cheese, like Morbier with its layer of ash, and a 10-year tawny port.

make it a basket: Package with a fancy goat cheese, assorted tinned fish, and one of the Spiced Nuts on pages 77–78.

1 cup (5 ounces) all-purpose flour
1 teaspoon baking powder
¼ teaspoon baking soda
1 cup canned unsweetened pumpkin puree
1 teaspoon baharat
½ teaspoon table salt
¼ cup (1¾ ounces) sugar
2 tablespoons vegetable oil
2 large eggs
1 tablespoon grated orange zest
⅓ cup dried apricots, chopped
⅓ cup sesame seeds
⅓ cup shelled pistachios, toasted and chopped
2 tablespoons coarse sea salt

1. Adjust oven rack to middle position and heat oven to 350 degrees. Grease two 5½ by 3-inch loaf pans. Whisk flour, baking powder, and baking soda together in large bowl; set aside. Combine pumpkin puree, baharat, and table salt in 10-inch skillet. Cook over medium heat, stirring occasionally, until reduced to ¾ cup, 6 to 8 minutes; transfer to medium bowl. Stir in sugar and oil and let cool slightly, about 5 minutes.

2. Whisk eggs and orange zest into pumpkin mixture then fold into reserved flour mixture until combined (some small lumps of flour are OK). Fold in apricots, sesame seeds, and pistachios. Scrape batter into prepared pans, smoothing tops with rubber spatula. Bake until skewer inserted in center comes out clean, 45 to 50 minutes, switching and rotating pans halfway through baking.

3. Let loaves cool in pans on wire rack for 20 minutes. Remove loaves from pans and let cool completely on rack, about 1½ hours. Transfer cooled loaves to zipper-lock bag and freeze until firm, about 3 hours. (Loaves can be frozen for up to 1 month before slicing.)

4. Heat oven to 300 degrees and line rimmed baking sheet with parchment paper. Using serrated knife, carefully slice each frozen loaf as thin as possible (about ¼ inch thick). Arrange slices in single layer on prepared sheet and sprinkle with sea salt. Bake until dark golden, 25 to 30 minutes, flipping crackers and rotating sheet halfway through baking. Transfer sheet to wire rack and let crackers cool completely, about 30 minutes.

TONIC SYRUP

makes: 16 ounces   **total time:** 50 minutes, plus 12 hours resting

66 When it comes to gin and tonics, you'd better believe that the tonic water is just as important as the gin. This homemade tonic syrup bests any store-bought tonic water, so if you know someone who's tried all the fancy tonics—well, this is the gift for them. Not only does it make an elevated version of a classic gin and tonic, but you can give your recipient a recipe for a sophisticated modern update (see the recipe card). Rather than being clear, like commercial versions, tonic water made from this syrup has a lovely amber color from the quinine. You can purchase cinchona bark chips online or in specialty spice shops; look for ¼-inch chips. You can purchase food-grade citric acid online or in grocery stores that sell canning supplies."

HOW I GIFT THIS

packaging: This is sticky, so store in a leakproof bottle or jar with a tight-fitting lid.

storage: The syrup can be refrigerated for about 2 months.

big-batch it: This recipe is easily scaled up.

make it a trio: Complement with a bottle of gin and a bottle of old-fashioned aromatic bitters.

16 ounces water
2 tablespoons (½ ounce) cinchona bark chips
5 (3-inch) strips lemon zest plus 1 tablespoon juice
4 (2-inch) strips lime zest plus 1½ teaspoons juice
1 lemongrass stalk, trimmed to bottom 6 inches and chopped coarse
Pinch table salt
1 cup sugar
2 tablespoons citric acid

1. Bring water, cinchona bark chips, lemon zest and juice, lime zest and juice, lemongrass, and salt to simmer in medium saucepan over medium-high heat. Reduce heat to low, cover, and cook, stirring occasionally, for 30 minutes.

2. Off heat, stir in sugar and citric acid until dissolved. Cover and let sit for at least 12 hours or up to 24 hours.

3. Set fine-mesh strainer over medium bowl and line with triple layer of cheesecloth. Strain syrup through prepared strainer, pressing on solids to extract as much syrup as possible; discard solids.

---

recipe card

Shake this syrup before using.

Tonic Water
Combine 1 part syrup with 4 parts chilled seltzer.

New-Fashioned Gin and Tonic
Add 2 ounces London dry gin, 1½ teaspoons syrup, and ⅛ teaspoon old-fashioned aromatic bitters to a mixing glass, then fill it three-quarters full with ice. Stir until just combined and chilled, about 15 seconds. Strain into a chilled old-fashioned glass half-filled with ice. Garnish with a strip of lime peel, if you like. Serves 1.

COCKTAIL PARTY

" The next time someone is kind enough to invite you over for drinks, accept graciously and then surprise them by bringing this gift along. Your recipient can choose to open it up right away, or maybe they'll invite you back to share some of the goodies. Either way, it's a win-win for everybody. This is also a great gift for the end-of-year holiday season, when festive food and drink are free-flowing. Cocktails are elegant, so I like to be elegant in my choices of what to include here. The Tonic Syrup lets you make elevated gin and tonics (or vodka tonics, if that's more your jam). The trout pâté and cheese straws are smoky, creamy, salty, cheesy, and just a touch fancy—perfect complements to perfectly chilled cocktails."

HOW I GIFT THIS

For a luxe presentation and to continue the theme of elegance, I try to source a vintage ice bucket or champagne bucket from a flea market or vintage store and line it with a bar towel. Alternatively, you could use a woven basket in a shape that mimics an ice bucket. If you can find a vintage cocktail tray, that could work too, though you might want to wrap it in cellophane or fabric to keep items secure.

START WITH

Tonic Syrup (page 110)

Gin or vodka

Smoked Trout Pâté (page 92)

Bagel chips or other sturdy crackers

Southern Cheese Straws (page 86)

IF YOU WANT, ADD

Saffron–Orange Blossom Spiced Nuts (page 78)

Simple Syrup (page 115)

Seltzer

Cocktail shaker and jigger

Bar spoon

Lemons, limes, and channel knife for making garnishes

SIMPLE SYRUP

makes: 8 ounces   **total time:** 15 minutes

" Simple syrup is an extremely easy and economical gift to give anyone from a cocktail lover to a mocktail aficionado. It's an often-overlooked pantry staple: I know that when I have a jar in my refrigerator door, I use it in all kinds of ways. But do I ever think to actually make it ahead of time to have it on hand? No. And commercial versions are expensive in a that's-just-silly sort of way. I really appreciate the simple thoughtfulness of this gift."

HOW I GIFT THIS

packaging: The syrups are sticky, so store in a leakproof bottle or jar with a tight-fitting lid.

storage: These syrups can be refrigerated for about 1 month.

big-batch it: This recipe is easily scaled up.

make it a duo: Pair the Simple Syrup or Spiced Syrup with the Cold Brew Coffee Concentrate (page 58). Pair the Citrus Syrup with one of the Tea Blends (page 57).

add to a basket: Add to the Cocktail Party basket (page 113).

¾ cup sugar
5 ounces warm tap water

Whisk sugar and warm water together in bowl until sugar has dissolved. Let cool completely, about 10 minutes.

variations

HERB SYRUP

Select ½ cup fresh herb leaves (basil, dill, mint, or tarragon), or 12 fresh thyme sprigs, or 1 fresh rosemary sprig. Heat sugar and water in small saucepan over medium heat, whisking often, until sugar has dissolved, about 5 minutes; do not boil. Stir in herb and let cool completely, about 30 minutes. Strain syrup through fine-mesh strainer into airtight container; discard solids.

CITRUS SYRUP

Grate 2 teaspoons grapefruit, lemon, lime, or orange zest. Heat sugar, water, and zest in small saucepan over medium heat, whisking often, until sugar has dissolved, about 5 minutes; do not boil. Let cool completely, about 30 minutes. Strain syrup through fine-mesh strainer into airtight container; discard solids.

SPICED SYRUP

Combine 1 cinnamon stick, 8 allspice berries, lightly crushed, and 4 whole cloves. Heat sugar, water, and spice mix in small saucepan over medium heat, whisking often, until sugar has dissolved, about 5 minutes; do not boil. Let cool completely, about 30 minutes. Strain syrup through fine-mesh strainer into airtight container; discard solids.

---

gift tag

Shake this syrup before using.

5 Ways to Use Simple Syrup

- Drizzle or brush over freshly baked cake.
- Stir into hot or cold coffee or tea or lemonade.
- Drizzle over fruit salad.
- Use to sweeten whipped cream.
- Use in cocktails, of course!

GINGER SYRUP

makes: 8 ounces   total time: 25 minutes, plus 12½ hours resting and cooling

66 Ginger syrup is a wonderful
   refrigerator-door gift; your
recipient can turn it into ginger ale
by adding seltzer, use it to add zip
to lemonade or iced tea, drizzle over
vanilla ice cream, and of course use in
cocktails. Since ginger helps to settle
the stomach, this also makes a nice
gift for someone who is ill. The syrup
has plenty of fresh ginger for a
warming heat, plus some dried ginger
for a little extra kick and lemon juice
to brighten the flavor."

HOW I GIFT THIS

packaging: This is sticky, so store
in a leakproof bottle or jar with a
tight-fitting lid.

storage: The syrup can be refrigerated
for about 1 month.

big-batch it: This recipe is easily
scaled up.

make it a duo: Pair with a bottle
of black rum (such as Gosling's) or
a chai tea blend.

add to a basket: Include in the
Get Well Soon basket (page 163).
Or put together a cocktail basket
with the syrup, vodka, crystallized
ginger, limes, a mint bouquet, a jigger,
and a pair of Moscow mule mugs.

8   ounces fresh ginger, unpeeled, chopped coarse
¾   cup sugar
5   ounces water
½   teaspoon ground ginger
2   teaspoons lemon juice

1. Process fresh ginger in food processor until finely chopped, about 30 seconds,
scraping down sides of bowl as needed.

2. Heat sugar and water in small saucepan over medium heat, whisking often,
until sugar has dissolved, about 5 minutes; do not boil. Off heat, stir in chopped
ginger and ground ginger and let cool to room temperature, about 30 minutes.
Cover and refrigerate for at least 12 hours or up to 24 hours.

3. Set fine-mesh strainer over medium bowl and line with triple layer of cheesecloth that overhangs edges. Transfer ginger mixture to prepared strainer and let
drain until liquid no longer runs freely, about 10 minutes. Pull edges of cheesecloth
together to form pouch, then firmly squeeze pouch to extract as much syrup from
pulp as possible; discard pulp. Stir in lemon juice.

---

recipe card

Shake this syrup before using.

Ginger Ale
Combine 1 part syrup with 4 parts chilled seltzer.

Moscow Mule
Fill a chilled collins glass or mule mug halfway with ice. Add 2 ounces vodka,
1½ ounces ginger syrup, and ½ ounce lime juice and stir to combine. Add
5 ounces seltzer and, using a bar spoon, gently lift the vodka mixture from
the bottom of the glass to the top to combine. Top with additional ice and
garnish with a lime slice and mint sprig. Serves 1.

Dark and Stormy
Fill a chilled collins glass halfway with ice. Add 1½ ounces syrup, ½ ounce
lime juice, and 2 ounces black rum and stir to combine. Add 5 ounces
seltzer and, using a bar spoon, gently lift the ginger mixture from the
bottom of the glass to the top to combine. Top with additional ice. Serves 1.

COQUITO

makes: about 6½ cups   **total time:** 10 minutes, plus 1 hour chilling

66 During the holiday season, many families with Latin American heritage make their own home version of this celebratory drink to share with family and friends. 'Coquito,' which means 'little coconut' in Spanish, originated in Puerto Rico, and it makes a great (and egg-free) gift alternative to eggnog. It packs loads of creamy coconut richness and warm spices, with golden rum adding spirited punch. All your recipient needs to do is blend the drink briefly right before serving, to recombine and give the cocktail a wonderful frothiness. I like using Coco López brand cream of coconut, which can be found in the soda and drink-mix aisle of the grocery store."

HOW I GIFT THIS

packaging: Give this in whatever size bottles you like, from party favor–size up to carafe-size. It's especially fun to give single-serving bottles.

storage: The coquito can be refrigerated for about 3 days.

make it a duo: Add a jar of ground nutmeg or a whole nutmeg with a grater. Or pair with the Cold Brew Coffee Concentrate (page 58).

   1 (15-ounce) can cream of coconut
   1 (14-ounce) can coconut milk
   1 (12-ounce) can evaporated milk
 10 ounces gold rum
   1 teaspoon vanilla extract
  ½ teaspoon ground cinnamon
  ¼ teaspoon ground nutmeg

Whisk all ingredients together in large pitcher until combined. Refrigerate for at least 1 hour.

HOW TO ATTACH A DECORATION

1. Lay ribbon parallel to counter edge and place decoration on center of ribbon, perpendicular to it.

2. Bring ribbon together and tie in knot to secure.

3. Wrap ribbon around top of bottle, tie in knot to secure, then tie in bow.

gift tag
Pour coquito into a blender and process until slightly frothy, about 1 minute. Blend in batches so it doesn't overflow! Serve over ice, garnished with nutmeg.

BLOODY MARY MIX

makes: four 1-pint jars   **total time:** 1¼ hours

" Ready to serve or store after gifting, this homemade Bloody Mary mix will be greeted with cheers by any brunch-loving folks in your life. Poured into single-serving bottles, it also makes a great party favor for a bachelorette weekend. It's fresh and feisty, with a serious kick from Worcestershire sauce, horseradish, and hot sauce. You can give it as is, or customize it however you like, adding as many garnishing options as you want to build out a gift of any level. Include long skewers to corral all those garnishes. For safety reasons, be sure to use bottled lemon juice, not fresh-squeezed juice, in this recipe. For more information on canning, see pages 302–305. For more information on peeling tomatoes, see page 39."

HOW I GIFT THIS

packaging: If you're giving short-term processed mix, you can tailor the size of the jar to the size of the gift you want to give. If you process this for long-term storage, you'll be giving the mix in the jars you used for processing it.

storage: Short-term processed mix can be refrigerated for at least 3 months; long-term processed mix can be stored at room temperature for up to 1 year and refrigerated after opening.

make it a trio: Add a jar of horseradish and a couple of lemons.

make it a basket: Give a big bottle of the mix along with a bottle of vodka. Tuck them, along with garnishes—hot sauce, olives, cornichons, grape tomatoes, lemons, and limes—into a crate. If you like, add a pepper grinder, some stalks of celery, and a jigger. Don't forget skewers!

gift tag

For every 8 ounces Bloody Mary Mix, stir in 2 ounces vodka. Garnish however your heart desires!

9 pounds tomatoes, cored, peeled, and cut into 1½-inch pieces
⅔ cup bottled lemon juice, plus extra for seasoning
2½ tablespoons Worcestershire sauce
2 tablespoons prepared horseradish, plus extra for seasoning
2½ teaspoons table salt
2½ teaspoons pepper
1 teaspoon hot sauce

1. Set canning rack in large pot, place four 1-pint jars in rack, and add water to cover by 1 inch. Bring to simmer over medium-high heat, then turn off heat and cover to keep hot.

2. Working in batches, process tomatoes in blender until smooth, about 30 seconds; transfer to bowl. Strain mixture through fine-mesh strainer into Dutch oven, pressing firmly on solids with ladle to extract as much juice as possible; discard solids. Bring juice to boil over medium-high heat. Boil, stirring often and reducing heat as needed, until juice has thickened and measures slightly more than 2 quarts, 10 to 30 minutes.

3. Stir in lemon juice, Worcestershire sauce, horseradish, salt, pepper, and hot sauce. Season with additional lemon juice, horseradish, salt, and pepper to taste and return to brief boil; remove from heat.

4. Place dish towel flat on counter. Using jar lifter, remove jars from pot, draining water back into pot. Place jars upside down on towel and let dry for 1 minute. Using funnel and ladle, portion hot mix into hot jars, leaving ½-inch headspace. Slide wooden skewer along inside of jar to remove air bubbles and add more mix as needed.

5a. for short-term storage: Let jars cool to room temperature, cover, and refrigerate.

5b. for long-term storage: While jars are hot, wipe rims clean, add lids, and screw on rings until fingertip-tight; do not overtighten. Return pot of water with canning rack to boil. Lower jars into water, cover, bring water back to boil, then start timer. Cooking time will depend on your altitude:

Boil 40 minutes for up to 1,000 feet, 45 minutes for 1,001 to 3,000 feet, 50 minutes for 3,001 to 6,000 feet, or 55 minutes for 6,001 to 8,000 feet. Turn off heat and let jars sit in pot for 5 minutes. Remove jars from pot and let cool for 24 hours. Remove rings, check seal, and clean rims.

FRUITS OF THE FOREST LIQUEUR

makes: 16 ounces   **total time:** 10 minutes, plus 1 week steeping

66 This luxurious, garnet-hued, intensely flavored berry liqueur is inspired by such iconic commercial liqueurs as Chambord (made from black raspberries) and crème de cassis (made from black currants). But now you can gift a personalized version, and for a fraction of the price. Freeze-dried berries, which bring bright, bold flavors, are available year-round, making this a gift that you can give anytime. You could use just one kind of berry (blackberries or blue-berries work best), but a liqueur made with a combination is more intriguing. I love pairing this liqueur with a rim sugar also made using freeze-dried berries. You'll need a pint-size glass jar with a tight-fitting lid to make this recipe."

HOW I GIFT THIS

packaging: This is sticky, so store in a leakproof bottle or jar with a tight-fitting lid.

storage: The liqueur can be stored at room temperature for about 1 year. The rim sugar can be stored at room tempera-ture for about 1 month.

big-batch it: This recipe is easily scaled up.

make it DIY: Instead of making the liqueur yourself, layer the freeze-dried berries in a pint-size Mason jar and include a bottle of vodka and a bottle of the simple syrup, along with the recipe for the liqueur.

make it a duo: Pair with the Strawberry–Black Pepper Rim Sugar and the recipe for the Royal Berry. Or pair with a bottle of Frangelico and the recipe for Nuts and Berries.

make it a basket: Include a bottle of the liqueur, a jar of the Strawberry–Black Pepper Rim Sugar, a bottle of sparkling wine, two coupe or flute glasses, and the recipe for the Royal Berry.

1 ounce freeze-dried blackberries, blueberries, and/or raspberries
½ ounce freeze-dried strawberries
12 ounces vodka
4 ounces Simple Syrup (page 115)

1. Place blackberries, strawberries, and vodka in pint-size glass jar. Cover tightly and shake to combine. Store jar in cool, dark place for 1 week, shaking mixture once every other day.

2. Set fine-mesh strainer in medium bowl and line with triple layer of cheesecloth. Strain vodka mixture through prepared strainer, pressing on solids to extract as much liquid as possible; discard solids. Return infused vodka to clean jar and add simple syrup. Cover and gently shake to combine.

---

recipe card

Shake this liqueur before serving.

Royal Berry
Wet the outside rim of a coupe or flute glass and coat with Strawberry–Black Pepper Rim Sugar. Add 1 blackberry or raspberry to the bottom of the glass. Add 1½ ounces liqueur, then pour in 4 ounces sparkling wine. Using a bar spoon, gently lift the liqueur from the bottom of the glass to the top to combine. Serves 1.

Nuts and Berries
Combine 1½ ounces liqueur and 1½ ounces Frangelico in a rocks glass and stir until combined. Add ice, then top with 2 ounces half-and-half and stir until combined and chilled, about 30 seconds. Serves 1.

STRAWBERRY–BLACK PEPPER RIM SUGAR

makes: about 1 cup
total time: 5 minutes
Leftovers make an intriguing popcorn sprinkle or sugar cookie topping.

- 1¼ cups (1 ounce) freeze-dried strawberries
- ¾ cup (5¼ ounces) sugar
- 1 teaspoon pepper

Working in batches, process strawberries in spice grinder until finely ground, about 30 seconds. Transfer to small bowl and whisk in sugar and pepper.

COFFEE LIQUEUR

makes: 16 ounces   **total time:** 10 minutes, plus 1 week steeping

66 Making your own rich and earthy coffee liqueur, with hints of chocolate, whispers of vanilla, and a trace of toasted nuttiness, is a cinch. The simple infusion takes minutes to assemble, steeps for a week, and then keeps for a year, so you can make it anytime to have on hand for gifting (if you can resist drinking it yourself, that is). It's the perfect buzz for any coffee lover in your life. For a more intensely flavored liqueur, substitute dark-roast coffee beans for the medium-roast; light-roast beans won't work well. You can substitute 1½ teaspoons cocoa powder for the cacao nibs, but the resulting liqueur will be slightly cloudy. You will need a pint-size glass jar with a tight-fitting lid to make this recipe."

HOW I GIFT THIS

packaging: This is sticky, so store in a leakproof bottle or jar with a tight-fitting lid.

storage: The liqueur can be stored at room temperature for about 1 year.

big-batch it: This recipe is easily scaled up.

make it a duo: Pair with the Dark Chocolate Fudge Sauce (page 62) or the Chocolate-Coffee-Hazelnut Bread (page 252).

make it a basket: Gather the components to make either the Vodka Espresso Martinis or Rum Espresso Martinis: the appropriate spirits along with espresso beans, a cocktail shaker and strainer, and a pair of martini glasses.

½ cup medium-roast coffee beans
1½ teaspoons cacao nibs
¼ vanilla bean, halved lengthwise
8 ounces vodka
4 ounces brandy
4 ounces Simple Syrup (page 115)

1. Place coffee beans, cacao nibs, vanilla bean, vodka, and brandy in pint-size glass jar. Cover tightly and shake to combine. Store jar in cool, dark place for 1 week, shaking mixture once every other day.

2. Set fine-mesh strainer in medium bowl and line with triple layer of cheesecloth. Strain vodka mixture through prepared strainer; discard solids. Return infused vodka mixture to clean jar and add simple syrup. Cover and gently shake to combine.

---

recipe card

Shake this liqueur before serving.

Vodka Espresso Martini
Use 1½ ounces vodka; 1 ounce brewed espresso, chilled; and ¾ ounce coffee liqueur.

Rum Espresso Martini
Use 1½ ounces aged rum; 1 ounce brewed espresso, chilled; ¾ ounce Bénédictine; and ½ ounce coffee liqueur.

For either cocktail, add the ingredients to a cocktail shaker, then fill with ice. Shake until combined and chilled, about 15 seconds. Strain into a chilled cocktail glass and garnish with espresso beans. Serves 1.

SWEET VERMOUTH

makes: 32 ounces   total time: 40 minutes, plus 12½ hours steeping

66 Sweet vermouth can make or break cocktails ranging from Manhattans to Negronis. This homemade vermouth is a little bit of a labor of love, but it's not difficult to make and is oh-so special, with herbal, floral, bitter, warm spice, and fruity notes. An easy stovetop caramel enriches the sweetness and the color. The hibiscus flowers bring it closer to the hue of commercial vermouths, but they are optional. I like Pinot Grigio here, but you can substitute your favorite unoaked dry white wine. You can purchase dried wormwood, chamomile flowers, hibiscus flowers, and quassia bark chips online or in specialty spice shops; look for chips that are about ¼ inch in size. For an accurate measurement of boiling water, bring a full kettle of water to a boil and then measure out the desired amount. You will need a quart-size glass jar with a tight-fitting lid to make this recipe."

HOW I GIFT THIS

packaging: This is sticky, so store in a leakproof bottle or jar with a tight-fitting lid.

storage: The vermouth can be refrigerated for about 3 months.

big-batch it: This recipe is easily scaled up.

make it a duo: Pair with the Gruyère, Mustard, and Caraway Cheese Coins (page 107), the Cinnamon-Ginger Spiced Nuts (page 77), or one of the biscotti (pages 232–233).

make it a basket: Give all the fixings for Manhattans: the sweet vermouth, bourbon or rye, cocktail cherries, and assorted bitters. You can make it a full-size basket, or give small quantities in mini baskets to make multiple gifts. Gild the lily by adding a jigger, bar spoon, rocks glasses, and/or a mixing glass.

6 ounces vodka
½ cup golden raisins, chopped
2 (3-inch) strips orange zest
1 bay leaf
1 teaspoon dried wormwood
1 teaspoon dried chamomile flowers
6 juniper berries, lightly crushed
½ teaspoon quassia bark chips
½ teaspoon coriander seeds
½ teaspoon dried sage
½ teaspoon dried thyme
¼ teaspoon black peppercorns
4 whole cloves
2 green cardamom pods
½ star anise pod
2 teaspoons dried hibiscus flowers (optional)
6 ounces boiling water, divided
¾ cup sugar
20 ounces Pinot Grigio

1. Combine vodka, raisins, orange zest, bay leaf, wormwood, chamomile flowers, juniper berries, quassia bark chips, coriander seeds, sage, thyme, peppercorns, cloves, cardamom pods, and star anise pod in quart-size glass jar. Cover and store jar in cool, dark place for at least 12 hours or up to 24 hours.

2. Set fine-mesh strainer in medium bowl and line with triple layer of cheesecloth. Strain vodka mixture through prepared strainer, pressing on solids to extract as much liquid as possible; discard solids. Set aside.

3. If using hibiscus, combine flowers and 4 ounces boiling water in bowl and let steep for 5 minutes. Strain through fine-mesh strainer into separate bowl, pressing on solids to extract as much liquid as possible.

4. Combine sugar and 2 ounces boiling water in medium saucepan. Bring to boil over medium-high heat and cook, without stirring, until mixture is amber-colored around edges of saucepan. Reduce heat to low and continue to cook, swirling saucepan occasionally, until caramel is evenly dark amber, 3 to 5 minutes. Off heat, carefully whisk in either hibiscus tea or remaining 4 ounces boiling water (mixture will bubble and steam) until syrup is smooth. Immediately transfer caramel to large bowl and let cool completely, about 30 minutes.

5. Add infused vodka, wine, and caramel to clean jar, cover, and gently shake to combine.

---
recipe card

Shake this vermouth before using.

Manhattan

Add 2 ounces bourbon or rye, ¾ ounce sweet vermouth, and ⅛ teaspoon bitters of your choice to a mixing glass, then fill three-quarters full with ice. Stir until combined and chilled, about 30 seconds. Strain into a chilled cocktail glass and garnish with a maraschino cherry. Serves 1.

BOARD THE MEAL TRAIN

HOW TO GIVE A MEAL

Most of the meals in this chapter can be given for either the refrigerator or the freezer or both. Of course, they can also be given fully cooked and hot, for enjoying right away. Some of the recipes make big batches that can be divided however you like, such as the Best Ground Beef Chili (page 150) and the Vegetarian Curried Lentil Soup (page 167). Other recipes have instructions for how to divide them. For example, the Baked Macaroni and Cheese (page 175) and the Stuffed Shells with Amatriciana Sauce (page 159) are designed to be one gift baked in a 13 by 9-inch baking dish, but instructions are also given for dividing these recipes into two gifts, each made in an 8-inch baking dish.

HOW TO HURRICANE WRAP A CASSEROLE DISH FOR STORAGE

This style of wrapping is often called "hotel wrap" in professional kitchens, but in our test kitchen it has the nickname of "hurricane wrap." Whatever you call it, it keeps food airtight for freezer, refrigerator, and room-temperature storage.

1. Lay out a long sheet of plastic wrap and wrap it tightly around the casserole dish, overlapping the wrap to make layers.

2. Lay out a second long sheet of plastic wrap, turn the dish 90 degrees, and repeat the wrapping and overlapping with the second sheet of plastic wrap.

HOW TO GIVE AN HERB BOUQUET

With delicate herbs like basil and cilantro, it's best to give a bunch of fresh herbs to let your recipient finish the dish just before serving.

Wrap the stems of the herbs in a damp paper towel; then wrap the bottom of the herb bunch in parchment paper and tie with twine.

HOW TO PACKAGE TINY AMOUNTS OF FINISHING ELEMENTS

For dry items like spices, seeds, and nuts, you can purchase very small zipper-lock plastic bags, waxed paper bags, cellophane bags, or tiny storage containers. Liquids are best given in tiny glass jars or food storage containers.

HOW TO TRANSPORT COLD OR HOT MEALS

Disposable Dishes

Place disposable pans in a box or on a baking sheet for bottom stability. If necessary, line the baking sheet with a silicone baking mat to keep the pan from sliding around.

Frozen or Refrigerated Meals

If the meal is frozen or refrigerated, pack it in an insulated cold carrier, cooler, or tote bag with ice packs.

Hot Meals

If the meal is hot, place it in an insulated food carrier.

Hot Meals DIY

If you don't have a carrier for hot meals, nestle the pan in a cardboard box insulated and cushioned with a large towel.

---

meal planner

This list will help you decide which meal to give as a gift, depending on whether you want a refrigerator meal or a freezer meal. A few recipes are even shelf-stable! Specific storage guidelines are given with each recipe.

Shelf-Stable

- Turkish Bride Soup in a Jar (page 132)
- Mushroom Risotto in a Jar (page 134)
- Earl Grey Baked Oatmeal in a Jar (page 139)

Refrigerator- and Freezer-Friendly

- Vegetarian Curried Lentil Soup (page 167)
- Hearty Beef Stew (page 168)
- Hearty Meat Lasagna (page 172)
- Baked Macaroni and Cheese (page 175)
- Meatballs and Marinara (page 177)

Refrigerator-Friendly

- Sichuan Chili–Ginger Chicken Salad (page 140)
- Turkey Picnic Sandwich with Sun-Dried Tomato Spread (page 142)
- Overnight Kale Salad with Roasted Sweet Potatoes and Pomegranate Vinaigrette (page 146)
- Italian Pasta Salad (page 149)
- Best Ground Beef Chili (page 150)
- Murgh Makhani (page 152)
- Easy Pulled Pork (page 154)
- Chicken Enchiladas (page 156)
- Stuffed Shells with Amatriciana Sauce (page 159)
- Chicken and Ramen Soup (page 164)

Freezer-Friendly

- Chicken Pot Pie (page 170)
- Chinese Pork Dumplings (page 181)

TURKISH BRIDE SOUP IN A JAR

serves: 4 to 6   **total time:** 10 minutes

66 The traditional Turkish soup called ezogelin corbasi is
richly flavorful. Since the majority of the components—
lentils, bulgur, and spices—are already shelf-stable, with just
a few swaps it's transformed into a pantry meal in a jar.
It's a great idea for new parents, someone doing a kitchen
renovation, or anyone who has little time to cook. Tomato
powder is important here, so don't skip it; you can reconstitute
leftover powder to use as you would tomato paste. Bouillon
cubes can be used if bouillon powder is unavailable; substitute
7 cubes and crumble them into smaller pieces so they will
dissolve easily. Lemon, fresh mint, and yogurt are nice
toppings, so if you know your recipient might be cooking the
meal soon, giving the soup with these items will make the gift
even more special."

HOW I GIFT THIS

packaging: While this looks great layered in a Mason jar,
you can package it (layered or not) in any airtight container.

storage: The jar can be stored at room temperature for
about 3 months.

make it a duo: Pair with Mushroom Risotto in a Jar
(page 134).

   1 cup red lentils, picked over for debris
   ½ cup medium-grind bulgur
   2 tablespoons plus 1 teaspoon chicken or
       vegetable bouillon powder
   4 teaspoons tomato powder
   4 teaspoons paprika
   1 teaspoon ground dried Aleppo pepper
   ½ cup dried onion flakes
   1 tablespoon dried mint, crumbled

Add lentils, bulgur, bouillon powder, tomato powder,
paprika, and Aleppo pepper to 4-cup airtight container.
Place onion and mint into separate small packages,
then add both to container with lentil mixture.

---
recipe card

Turkish Bride Soup

Cook the onion flakes with ¼ cup extra-virgin olive oil
and 1 cup water in a large pot over medium-high heat
until the onion flakes are golden, about 8 minutes.
Stir in the lentil mixture and cook until fragrant, about
1 minute. Add 7½ cups water and bring to a boil. Reduce
the heat to medium-low, partially cover, and cook until
the lentils are broken down and the bulgur is tender,
about 20 minutes. Off the heat, stir in the dried mint
and let soften. Drizzle olive oil over each portion, if you
like. Top with yogurt and fresh mint and serve with
lemon wedges, if you've got them. Serves 4 to 6.

MUSHROOM RISOTTO IN A JAR

serves: 4 to 6   total time: 15 minutes

66 Like me, a lot of my friends are glampers, campers, and travelers who love to create a homey feel when away, so presenting a complete meal in a jar in its cooking vessel (in this case, a saucepan) is an extra-special way to gift it. Dried porcini and shiitakes are the most commonly available dried mushrooms, but any dried mushroom can be used in place of the shiitakes. Bouillon cubes can be used if bouillon powder is unavailable; substitute 1½ cubes for the 1½ teaspoons powder; crumble cubes into smaller pieces so they will dissolve easily. Grated Parmesan and minced parsley or chives are nice toppings to the risotto, so if you know the recipient might be cooking the meal soon, giving the risotto with these items will make this meal even more special."

HOW I GIFT THIS

packaging: While this looks great layered in a Mason jar, you can package it (layered or not) in any airtight container.

storage: The jar can be stored at room temperature for about 3 months.

make it a duo: Pair with a wedge of Parmesan cheese or a container of grated Parmesan.

make it a basket: Line a lightweight enameled saucepan with a dish towel and nestle in the risotto, a set of camping utensils, and the recipe card.

1 ounce dried porcini mushrooms, broken into ½-inch pieces, divided
1½ cups arborio rice
1 tablespoon dried onion flakes
1½ teaspoons chicken or vegetable bouillon powder
1½ teaspoons dried minced garlic
1½ teaspoons dried thyme
1 teaspoon table salt
¾ teaspoon pepper
1 ounce dried shiitake or mixed mushrooms, broken into ½-inch pieces

Grind one-quarter of porcini mushroom pieces to fine powder in spice grinder. Add to 4-cup airtight container along with rice, onion, bouillon, garlic, thyme, salt, and pepper. Place remaining porcini and shiitake mushrooms into separate package, then add to container with rice mixture.

---

recipe card

Mushroom Risotto

Rinse the mushroom pieces. Melt 4 tablespoons unsalted butter and 2 tablespoons extra-virgin olive oil in a medium saucepan over medium heat. Add the rice mixture and mushrooms and cook, stirring often, for 2 minutes. Stir in 4½ cups water and bring to a simmer. Cover, reduce heat to medium-low, and cook until almost all the liquid has been absorbed, about 15 minutes, stirring twice during cooking. Increase the heat to medium and gradually add 2 cups warm water, ½ cup at a time, stirring constantly, until the risotto is creamy but loose, about 5 minutes. Cover, remove from the heat, and let sit for 5 minutes. Stir in 2 tablespoons unsalted butter and 2 teaspoons white wine vinegar (optional). Season with salt to taste and top with grated Parmesan and minced parsley or chives, if you've got them. Serves 4 to 6.

SUNDAY BREAKFAST

"The notion of Sunday breakfast conjures different feelings, associations, and memories for everybody, but it brings up in my mind leisurely mornings in comfy clothes with no particular place you have to be, definitely with some background music going, and plenty of choices on the table for nibbling. In giving this gift, I like to bring those Sunday morning vibes to anyone who needs them. And couldn't we all use more Sunday morning vibes in our lives? You can easily keep this gift low-key with just a few items, or splash out and keep right on adding things to make a spread everyone will want to linger all morning over. This is an especially great gift whenever you are a weekend houseguest. It also makes a fun present to be enjoyed the (late) morning after a holiday such as New Year's, Thanksgiving, or Christmas— a little hair of the dog, anyone?"

HOW I GIFT THIS

This cheerful offering deserves a unique container, like a wooden storage bin that your recipient can reuse later in the kitchen (or in practically any other room in the house). With its deep sides and open front, this bin showcases all the foods really well. You can stack the Bloody Mary Mix bottle toward the high back, along with a stack of bagels and container of cream cheese tied up nicely in a plastic bag. Nesting storage containers will keep fruit fresh, if you're including that. Tuck in smaller jars of Bloody Mary garnishes up front.

START WITH

Earl Grey Baked Oatmeal in a Jar (page 139)

Green Granola (page 61)

Bagels and cream cheese

Bloody Mary Mix (page 120)

Bloody Mary garnishes of your choice

IF YOU WANT, ADD

Bacon Jam (page 89)

Yogurt

Fresh or dried fruit

Bag of ground coffee

Dairy of choice for coffee

Vodka

EARL GREY BAKED OATMEAL IN A JAR

serves: 4 to 6   **total time:** 10 minutes

66 When I'm a houseguest over the holidays, I bring this along as a gift for the 'chef' who cooks the entire holiday meal and shouldn't have to shoulder breakfast too. Sometimes I even do the baking as part of my gift! You can use any dried (or freeze-dried) fruit. For freeze-dried, break larger fruits into smaller pieces before measuring. You can also substitute 4 bags of Earl Grey tea for the loose-leaf. Don't substitute quick or instant oats. You could toast the nuts yourself and adjust the recipe card accordingly, but their shelf life will be shorter. If you know your recipient might be baking this soon, berries, yogurt, and maple syrup are nice toppings to include to make this gift even more special."

HOW I GIFT THIS

packaging: While this looks great layered in a Mason jar, you can package it (layered or not) in any airtight container.

storage: The jar can be stored at room temperature for about 3 months.

make it a duo: Pair with one of the Tea Blends (page 57) or Cold Brew Coffee Concentrate (page 58).

make it a basket: Build a brunch basket with Peanut Butter–Banana Granola (page 61), Blueberry-Lemon-Cardamom Bread (page 251), and Bloody Mary Mix (page 120).

2 cups old-fashioned rolled oats
3 tablespoons sugar
2 tablespoons ground flaxseeds
1½ tablespoons Earl Grey tea leaves
½ teaspoon table salt
¼ teaspoon ground cardamom
½ cup dried cherries, chopped
½ cup slivered almonds

Add oats, sugar, flaxseeds, tea, salt, cardamom, and cherries to 4-cup airtight container. Place almonds in separate package, then add to container with oat mixture.

— recipe card ————

Earl Grey Baked Oatmeal

Toast the nuts on a small baking sheet on the middle rack at 375 degrees, stirring occasionally, until golden, about 8 minutes. Combine the oat mixture with 2 cups milk of your choice and 2 tablespoons melted butter. Transfer to a greased 8-inch square baking pan and bake until the edges are deep golden brown and the middle is just set, 30 to 35 minutes. Let cool in the pan on a wire rack for 10 minutes. Sprinkle with the nuts and serve with fresh fruit, yogurt, or a drizzle of maple syrup, if you've got it. Serves 4 to 6.

SICHUAN CHILI-GINGER CHICKEN SALAD

serves : 4 to 6   **total time:** 1¼ hours

66 Anyone who needs a flavorful and bright meal in a flash—for any reason—will appreciate a gift of this chicken salad. All they need to do is assemble the components on a platter and dig in. I like to use Sichuan chili flakes, but Korean red pepper flakes, called gochugaru, are a good alternative. The Sichuan peppercorns don't add more heat, but they do add a unique tingling sensation and earthy, citrusy flavor. Rice vinegar can be substituted for black vinegar, if desired."

HOW I GIFT THIS

packaging: Consider putting each component into a set of stacking bowls, or gift the components in nesting bowls all packed into a beautiful salad bowl with salad tongs.

storage: The dressed chicken and prepared vegetables and herbs can be refrigerated separately for about 2 days.

make it a duo: Chili crisp (store-bought or the homemade version on page 67) and Sichuan chili flakes are great accompaniments, and both are long-lasting staples for your recipient's pantry.

make it a trio: Add Ginger Syrup (page 116) and bottles of seltzer for making drinks.

chicken
- 4 (6- to 8-ounce) boneless, skinless chicken breasts, trimmed
  Table salt for cooking chicken

dressing
- ¼ cup vegetable oil
- 1 garlic clove, peeled and smashed
- 1 (½-inch) piece ginger, peeled and sliced in half
- 2 tablespoons Sichuan chili flakes
- 2 tablespoons soy sauce
- 1 tablespoon Chinese black vinegar
- 1 tablespoon toasted sesame oil
- 2 teaspoons sugar
- 1–2 teaspoons ground Sichuan peppercorns

vegetables
- ½ head napa cabbage, sliced thin (6 cups)
- 1½ cups coarsely chopped fresh cilantro leaves and stems, divided
- 6 scallions, sliced in half lengthwise, then sliced thin on bias, divided
- 1 celery rib, sliced thin on bias
- 2 teaspoons toasted sesame seeds

1. for the chicken: Cover chicken with plastic wrap and pound thick ends gently with meat pounder until ¾ inch thick. Discard plastic wrap. Whisk 4 quarts cool water with 2 tablespoons salt in Dutch oven. Arrange chicken in steamer basket, making sure not to overlap. Submerge steamer basket in pot. Heat over medium heat, stirring occasionally to even out hot spots, until water registers 175 degrees, 15 to 20 minutes. Cover pot and remove from burner. Let stand until chicken registers 160 degrees, 17 to 22 minutes.

2. for the dressing: While chicken cooks, combine vegetable oil, garlic, and ginger in bowl. Microwave until oil is hot and bubbling, about 2 minutes. Stir in chili flakes and let cool for 10 minutes. Strain oil mixture through fine-mesh strainer into large bowl; discard solids. Whisk soy sauce, vinegar, sesame oil, sugar, and 1 teaspoon peppercorns into strained oil. Add up to 1 teaspoon additional peppercorns to taste.

3. Transfer chicken to cutting board and let cool for 10 to 15 minutes. Shred chicken lengthwise into long, thin strips. Add chicken to bowl with dressing, toss to coat, and season with salt to taste. Pack chicken in airtight container.

4. for the vegetables: Pack cabbage, 1 cup chopped cilantro, two-thirds scallions, and celery together in airtight container. Pack remaining ½ cup chopped cilantro, remaining scallions, and sesame seeds together in airtight container. Refrigerate.

─ **gift tag** ─────────────────

Toss the cabbage mixture and a pinch of salt
in a bowl, then arrange it in an even layer on
a large platter. Mound the chicken on top and
sprinkle with the cilantro-scallion mixture.

TURKEY PICNIC SANDWICH WITH SUN-DRIED TOMATO SPREAD

serves: 4   **total time:** 40 minutes, plus 3 hours resting, cooling, and pressing

❝ The next time you're invited along for a picnic in the park, a day at the beach, or even a hike in the hills, let them know you'll bring the sustenance. You might not think of a sandwich as an obvious food gift, but this one is specially designed to be made ahead of time to allow the flavors to develop and meld together with the crusty pizza-dough bread. For the turkey version and its variations, a supersavory sandwich spread acts as a delicious 'glue' to hold everything together. Letting the pizza dough sit at room temperature for 1 hour makes it easier to shape. If you don't have a Dutch oven, you can use a baking sheet or skillet loaded with hefty canned goods to press the sandwich.❞

- - - - - - - - - - - - - - - - - - - -

HOW I GIFT THIS

packaging: You'll wrap the whole large filled loaf in plastic before pressing it. You could give it that way, but I like to cut the sandwich into quarters and wrap each quarter in parchment or waxed paper, tying them closed with twine.

storage: The pressed sandwich can be refrigerated for about 1 day; bring to room temperature before serving.

make it a trio: Give with kettle chips and sparkling lemonade.

add to a basket: Include in the Summer Supper basket (page 145).

sandwich
- 1 pound store-bought pizza dough
- 1 teaspoon extra-virgin olive oil
- 4 ounces sliced Muenster cheese
- 8 ounces thinly sliced deli turkey
- ½ cup fresh parsley leaves
- 1¼ cups jarred roasted red peppers, drained and patted dry

spread
- ¾ cup oil-packed sun-dried tomatoes, drained and patted dry
- ¼ cup sliced almonds, toasted
- ¼ cup capers, rinsed
- 1 teaspoon lemon juice
- 1 small garlic clove, minced
- ¼ teaspoon table salt
- ¼ teaspoon red pepper flakes
- 6 tablespoons extra-virgin olive oil

1. for the sandwich: Line rimmed baking sheet with parchment paper and grease parchment. Place dough on prepared sheet. Cover loosely with greased plastic wrap and let rest at room temperature for 1 hour.

2. Adjust oven rack to upper-middle position and heat oven to 425 degrees. Keeping dough on sheet, use your hands to shape dough into rough 7-inch square (edges may be rounded; this is OK). Brush top of dough with oil. Bake until light golden brown, 13 to 15 minutes. Let cool completely on sheet, about 1 hour.

3. for the spread: Meanwhile, process tomatoes, almonds, capers, lemon juice, garlic, salt, and pepper flakes in food processor until finely chopped, about 20 seconds, scraping down sides of bowl as needed. Transfer to bowl and stir in oil.

4. Slice bread in half horizontally. Spread tomato mixture on cut sides of bread, about ½ cup per piece (use all of it). Layer Muenster, turkey, parsley, and red peppers on bread bottom. Cap with bread top and wrap sandwich tightly in double layer of plastic. Place Dutch oven on top of sandwich and let sit at room temperature for 1 hour. Refrigerate.

variations

CAPICOLA PICNIC SANDWICH WITH ARTICHOKE SPREAD

Substitute provolone for Muenster, hot capicola for turkey, and 1 thinly sliced small fennel bulb for roasted red peppers. For spread, substitute 1 (14-ounce) can artichoke hearts, drained and patted dry, for sun-dried tomatoes; ¼ cup chopped jarred hot cherry peppers for almonds; and 1 teaspoon chopped fresh thyme for capers.

HAM PICNIC SANDWICH WITH OLIVE SPREAD

Substitute sliced mozzarella for Muenster, Black Forest ham for turkey, and 1 cup shredded carrots for red peppers. For spread, substitute pitted kalamata olives for sun-dried tomatoes and ½ cup fresh parsley leaves for almonds.

- CAPICOLA
  SANDWICH
- KALE SALAD W.
  SWEET POTATOES
  + RADICCHIO
- ITALIAN PASTA
  SALAD

Enjoy!

SUMMER SUPPER

66 Summer contains a lot of joys, and eating outdoors is right up there near the top of the list, IMO. This summer supper basket makes a perfect picnic gift, whether that picnic is going to happen in someone's backyard over Memorial Day or treating Dad for Father's Day, at the beach for the Fourth of July, or at the local park to celebrate an August birthday. The food is really customizable here: There are two other flavor variations on the sandwich to consider, you can include the kale salad or the pasta salad or both, or you can choose a different cookie from the Sweeten Someone's Day chapter for dessert. Don't forget to include a variety of beverages. You can also dress this basket up or down according to how many accessories you enclose, from simple plates and napkins all the way up to a picnic blanket."

HOW I GIFT THIS

I look at this as an event-oriented kind of gift, so I tend to give it when I'm going to be part of the celebration and I know it's going to be consumed right away. That way, I can fully assemble the sandwiches and salads. For an all-out presentation, I source a vintage picnic basket. These are sometimes better for looks than for usability, so you could also choose a more modern picnic basket or backpack or a cooler. Make sure the salads and vinaigrette are in tight-sealing containers and the cookies are protected from breaking. I wrap the sandwiches in parchment paper tied with twine so that everyone can just reach in and grab one.

START WITH

Capicola Picnic Sandwich with Artichoke Spread (page 143)

Overnight Kale Salad with Roasted Sweet Potatoes and Pomegranate Vinaigrette (page 146)

Thin and Crispy Chocolate Chip Cookies (page 213)

IF YOU WANT, ADD

Marinated Green and Black Olives (page 75)

Italian Pasta Salad (page 149)

Fresh seasonal fruit

Cans of wine, hard seltzer, and/or nonalcoholic seltzer

Picnic plates, utensils, and plenty of napkins

Picnic blanket

Bug spray

OVERNIGHT KALE SALAD WITH ROASTED SWEET POTATOES AND POMEGRANATE VINAIGRETTE

serves: 4   total time: 1¼ hours

66 I bet I know what you're thinking.
First a sandwich, then a salad as a food gift? Believe it—especially when it's this overnight kale salad. We all know by this point in the millennium that kale benefits from being 'massaged' and left to sit with its dressing for a while to soften and soak up flavor. This salad really ups the ante from an obligatory kale salad to a gift-worthy offering by adding roasted sweet potatoes, pomegranate seeds, toasted pecans, and shaved Parmesan. The elegant dressing uses pomegranate molasses and honey for a salad you'll never find in a fast-casual chain."

HOW I GIFT THIS

packaging: If you're packing this into a picnic basket for same-day enjoyment, you can assemble the salad. Otherwise, pack the components into separate containers as directed.

storage: The kale salad, the extra vinaigrette, and the finishing elements can be refrigerated separately for about 1 day.

add to a basket: Include in the Summer Supper basket (page 145).

1½ pounds sweet potatoes, peeled, quartered lengthwise, and sliced crosswise ½ inch thick
1 tablespoon plus ⅓ cup extra-virgin olive oil, divided
¾ teaspoon table salt, divided
¾ teaspoon pepper, divided
2 tablespoons water
1½ tablespoons pomegranate molasses

1 shallot, minced
1 tablespoon honey
1 tablespoon cider vinegar
12 ounces kale, stemmed and sliced into 1-inch-wide strips
½ head radicchio (5 ounces), cored and sliced thin
⅓ cup pomegranate seeds
½ cup pecans, toasted and chopped
1 ounce Parmesan cheese, shaved

1. Adjust oven rack to middle position and heat oven to 400 degrees. Toss sweet potatoes with 1 tablespoon oil, ½ teaspoon salt, and ½ teaspoon pepper until evenly coated. Arrange in single layer in rimmed baking sheet and roast until bottom edges of potatoes are browned, about 15 minutes. Flip potatoes and continue to roast until second side is spotty brown, 10 to 15 minutes. Transfer potatoes to large plate and let cool to room temperature, about 20 minutes.

2. Meanwhile, whisk water, pomegranate molasses, shallot, honey, vinegar, remaining ¼ teaspoon salt, and remaining ¼ teaspoon pepper together in medium bowl. Whisking constantly, drizzle in remaining ⅓ cup oil.

3. Vigorously knead and squeeze kale with hands until leaves are uniformly darkened and slightly wilted, about 5 minutes. Toss kale, roasted potatoes, and radicchio with ⅓ cup vinaigrette in large bowl. Transfer remaining vinaigrette to small container. Add pomegranate seeds to small container and pecans and Parmesan to another container. Refrigerate.

> **gift tag**
>
> Bring the kale salad and the vinaigrette to room temperature. Whisk the vinaigrette, then toss with the kale salad, pomegranate seeds, and chopped pecans and Parmesan. Season with salt and pepper to taste.

ITALIAN PASTA SALAD

serves: 4 to 6   **total time:** 50 minutes

66 Pasta salad is a decidedly Italian American invention and a favorite at summertime cookouts—which is exactly when I like to give a gift of this intensely flavored salad. The flavor inspiration comes from antipasto platters: salami, mozzarella, olives, sun-dried tomatoes, pepperoncini, capers, and basil. The corkscrew-shaped fusilli has plenty of little pockets for capturing the dressing. The trick to getting the right pasta texture in a pasta salad is to cook the pasta a little longer than you would if you were eating it hot, because the pasta firms up as it cools. I like to use a small, individually packaged, dry Italian-style salami such as Genoa or soppressata in this salad, but you could also use unsliced deli salami."

HOW I GIFT THIS

packaging: Package the pasta salad and the arugula in separate containers to combine before serving. Basil oxidizes quickly, so it's best to gift a whole bunch and let your recipient prep the basil before serving.

storage: The pasta salad can be refrigerated for about 3 days.

add to a basket: Add to the Summer Supper basket (page 145).

gift tag

Bring the pasta salad to room temperature. Chop 1 cup basil. Toss pasta salad with arugula and chopped basil. Season with salt and pepper to taste.

1 pound fusilli
  Table salt for cooking pasta
¼ cup extra-virgin olive oil
3 garlic cloves, minced
3 anchovy fillets, rinsed, patted dry, and minced
¼ teaspoon red pepper flakes
1 cup pepperoncini, stemmed, plus 2 tablespoons brine
2 tablespoons capers, rinsed
½ cup oil-packed sun-dried tomatoes, sliced thin
½ cup pitted kalamata olives, quartered
8 ounces salami, cut into ⅜-inch pieces
8 ounces fresh mozzarella cheese, cut into ⅜-inch pieces and patted dry
2 ounces (2 cups) baby arugula
1 bunch basil (enough for 1 cup chopped)

1. Bring 4 quarts water to boil in large pot. Add pasta and 1 tablespoon salt and cook, stirring often, until pasta is tender throughout, 2 to 3 minutes past al dente. Drain pasta and rinse under cold water until chilled. Drain well and transfer to large bowl.

2. Meanwhile, combine oil, garlic, anchovies, and pepper flakes in liquid measuring cup. Cover and microwave until bubbling and fragrant, 30 to 60 seconds. Set aside.

3. Slice half of pepperoncini into thin rings and set aside. Transfer remaining pepperoncini to food processor. Add capers and pulse until finely chopped, 8 to 10 pulses, scraping down sides of bowl as needed. Add pepperoncini brine and warm oil mixture and process until combined, about 20 seconds.

4. Add dressing to pasta and toss to combine. Add tomatoes, olives, salami, mozzarella, and reserved pepperoncini and toss well. Package arugula and basil separately. Refrigerate.

BEST GROUND BEEF CHILI

serves: 8 to 10   **total time:** 3 hours

66 Y'all know I'm a Midwest girl and that casseroles, stews, and soups are my jam. Chili is at the top of my list here and this is truly a blue-ribbon chili, rich with ancho chiles, chipotle chiles, ground beef, pinto beans, and loads of herbs and spices. And it makes a nice big batch, too, so you can turn this into multiple gifts with ease—or bring the whole pot to a Super Bowl party. You can just give the chili on its own, but how fun it is to really complete the meal and add to the gift by packing up a kit of all the toppings for serving."

HOW I GIFT THIS

packaging: I package everything in glass storage containers, nestling the toppings into muffin cups and then into their own storage container. A bouquet of cilantro tops it off!

storage: The chili can be refrigerated for about 3 days. Assemble the toppings when you're ready to give the gift.

divide it: This is easily split in half for two gifts.

make it a duo: Add a bottle of Easy Homemade Hot Sauce (page 68) or Roasted Tomato–Lime Salsa (page 102).

make it a basket: The toppings listed in the ingredient list are just a starting point, so customize them based on what you think your recipient will enjoy.

2 tablespoons plus 2 cups water, divided
1 teaspoon table salt
¾ teaspoon baking soda
2 pounds 85 percent lean ground beef
3 ounces (6 to 8) dried ancho chiles, stemmed, seeded, and torn into ½-inch pieces (1½ cups)
1 ounce tortilla chips, crushed (¼ cup)
2 tablespoons cumin seeds
4 teaspoons coriander seeds
1 tablespoon paprika
1 tablespoon garlic powder
2 teaspoons dried Mexican oregano
1½ teaspoons black peppercorns
½ teaspoon dried thyme

1 (14.5-ounce) can whole peeled tomatoes
1 tablespoon vegetable oil
1 yellow onion, chopped fine
3 garlic cloves, minced
1–2 teaspoons minced canned chipotle chile in adobo sauce
1 (15-ounce) can pinto beans
2 teaspoons sugar
2 tablespoons cider vinegar

toppings (optional)
Tortilla chips
Lime wedges
Cilantro
Chopped red onion
Chopped tomato
Avocado
Shredded cheese

1. Adjust oven rack to lower-middle position and heat oven to 275 degrees. Combine 2 tablespoons water, salt, and baking soda in medium bowl. Add beef and toss until thoroughly combined. Set aside for 20 minutes.

2. Meanwhile, toast anchos in Dutch oven over medium-high heat, stirring frequently, until fragrant, 2 to 6 minutes; reduce heat if they begin to smoke. Transfer to food processor and let cool for 5 minutes. Add tortilla chips, cumin seeds, coriander seeds, paprika, garlic powder, oregano, peppercorns, and thyme to food processor with anchos and process until finely ground, about 3 minutes; transfer to bowl. Process tomatoes and their juice in now-empty processor until smooth, about 30 seconds.

3. Heat oil in now-empty pot over medium-high heat until shimmering. Add onion and cook until softened, about 5 minutes. Stir in garlic and cook until fragrant, about 30 seconds. Add beef and cook, breaking up meat into ¼-inch pieces with wooden spoon, until browned and fond begins to form on pot bottom, 12 to 14 minutes. Add ancho mixture and chipotle and cook, stirring frequently, until fragrant, 1 to 2 minutes. Stir in processed tomatoes, beans and their liquid, sugar, and remaining 2 cups water, scraping up any browned bits, and bring to simmer. Cover, transfer pot to oven, and cook, stirring occasionally, until beef is tender and chili is slightly thickened, 1½ to 2 hours. Remove pot from oven, stir in vinegar, and season with salt to taste. Portion into containers, let cool, and refrigerate. Package toppings separately.

gift tag

To reheat, bring the chili, covered, to a gentle simmer, stirring often. Adjust the consistency with hot water as desired. Serve with all your favorite toppings.

MURGH MAKHANI

serves: 4 to 6   total time: 1½ hours

66 Rich, creamy, and vibrant, murgh makhani (also known as butter chicken) is one of the most popular Indian dishes in the world, and to me represents an elevated comfort food dinner that is fun to share with friends. It deserves an equally vibrant gift presentation, so why not transform a housewarming gift like glass storage containers or a tiffin by giving them with this superflavorful meal tucked inside? Murgh makhani is usually mildly spiced, but if you know that your recipient likes spicy food, you can reserve, mince, and add the ribs and seeds from the chile."

HOW I GIFT THIS

packaging: It makes for a special presentation to package the components in a tiffin; use a 3-layer tiffin for the rice, chicken, and sauce or a 4-layer tiffin if you're adding naan. You could also package the components in a set of stacking storage containers.

storage: The chicken, sauce, and rice can be refrigerated separately for about 2 days. You could add cilantro to the rice just before giving the gift, or give a cilantro bouquet.

make it a duo: Pair with naan.

make it a basket: In addition to the naan, add a container of raita and a jar of mango chutney.

4 tablespoons unsalted butter, cut into 4 pieces and chilled, divided
1 onion, chopped fine
5 garlic cloves, minced
4 teaspoons grated fresh ginger
1 serrano chile, stemmed, seeded, and minced
1 tablespoon garam masala
1 teaspoon ground coriander
½ teaspoon ground cumin
½ teaspoon pepper
4½ cups water, divided
½ cup tomato paste
1 tablespoon sugar
2½ teaspoons table salt, divided
1 cup heavy cream
2 pounds boneless, skinless chicken thighs, trimmed
½ cup plain Greek yogurt
2 cups long-grain white rice, rinsed
Cilantro (enough for 3 tablespoons chopped)

1. Melt 2 tablespoons butter in large saucepan over medium heat. Add onion, garlic, ginger, and serrano and cook, stirring frequently, until mixture is softened and onion begins to brown, 8 to 10 minutes. Add garam masala, coriander, cumin, and pepper and cook, stirring frequently, until fragrant, about 3 minutes. Add 1½ cups water and tomato paste and whisk until no lumps of tomato paste remain. Add sugar and 1 teaspoon salt and bring to boil. Off heat, stir in cream. Using immersion blender or blender, process until smooth, 30 to 60 seconds. Stir in remaining 2 tablespoons butter until melted. Set aside to cool completely.

2. Adjust oven rack 6 inches from broiler element and heat broiler. Combine chicken, yogurt, and 1 teaspoon salt in bowl and toss well to coat. Using tongs, transfer chicken to wire rack set in aluminum foil–lined rimmed baking sheet. Broil, flipping chicken halfway through, until chicken is evenly charred on both sides and registers 175 degrees, 16 to 20 minutes. Let chicken cool, then cut into ¾-inch pieces.

3. Combine rice, remaining 3 cups water, and remaining ½ teaspoon salt in large saucepan and bring to simmer over high heat. Stir with rubber spatula, dislodging any rice that sticks to bottom of saucepan. Cover, reduce heat to low, and cook for 20 minutes. (Steam should steadily emit from saucepan. If water bubbles out, reduce heat slightly.) Remove from heat and let sit, covered, for 10 minutes. Gently fluff rice with fork. Store chicken, sauce, rice, and cilantro separately; refrigerate.

gift tag

Bring the sauce to a gentle simmer in a medium
saucepan, then stir in the chicken and cook until
warmed through. Stir in 2 tablespoons chopped
cilantro and season with salt to taste. To reheat
the rice, add 3¾ teaspoons water, cover, and
microwave until heated through, stirring once.
Sprinkle the chicken with 1 tablespoon chopped
cilantro and serve with rice.

EASY PULLED PORK

serves: 4 to 6   total time: 3¾ hours, plus 45 minutes cooling

66 Your gift recipient will be guessing that you labored over a grill fire to make this pulled pork. It's up to you whether or not you reveal the truth: This saucy, fall-apart-tender shredded pork came out of your oven. Even though it's an oven rather than a grill recipe, I do like to give it for a gift around Memorial Day, the Fourth of July, or Labor Day. It lends itself so well to picnic-table eating. Combining the cooked and shredded pork with some of the sauce before storing both helps to keep the meat moist and allows the sauce to deepen the flavors of the pork during the storage time. Pork butt roast, a generously marbled cut, is often labeled Boston butt in the supermarket."

HOW I GIFT THIS

packaging: The pork and sauce are best packed in glass storage containers or disposable storage containers (plastic ones may stain). The vinegar can be in a small plastic container and the buns can stay in their plastic bag.

storage: The pork mixture and reserved sauce can be refrigerated separately for about 3 days.

divide it: This is easily divided in half to make two gifts.

make it a basket: Pack an insulated bag or a cooler with storage containers filled with the pork and the sauce. Add soft buns, corn bread, hot sauce, pickles, and plenty of napkins.

1 tablespoon vegetable oil	1½ tablespoons packed brown sugar
1 onion, chopped	1½ tablespoons Worcestershire sauce
3 tablespoons paprika	½ teaspoon table salt
4 garlic cloves, minced	½ teaspoon pepper
1 tablespoon ground cumin	3 pounds boneless pork butt
¼ teaspoon cayenne pepper	roast, trimmed and cut into
1 cup water	2-inch pieces
1 cup ketchup	1 tablespoon cider vinegar
3 tablespoons molasses	4–6 hamburger buns

1. Adjust oven rack to lower-middle position and heat oven to 300 degrees. Heat oil in Dutch oven over medium heat until shimmering. Add onion and cook until softened, about 5 minutes. Stir in paprika, garlic, cumin, and cayenne and cook until fragrant, about 30 seconds. Stir in water, ketchup, molasses, sugar, Worcestershire, salt, and pepper.

2. Nestle pork into sauce and bring to simmer. Cover pot, transfer to oven, and cook pork until tender and fork slips easily in and out of pork, about 3 hours.

3. Remove pot from oven. Using slotted spoon, transfer pork to bowl and let cool slightly. Shred pork into bite-size pieces using potato masher or 2 forks. Let sauce cool completely, about 45 minutes.

4. Skim excess fat from surface of sauce, then transfer 1 cup sauce to storage container. Stir shredded pork into remaining sauce in pot, then transfer to airtight container and refrigerate. Add cider vinegar to small storage container. Package buns separately.

---

gift tag

Combine the pork and cider vinegar in a large pot. Cook over medium-low heat, stirring often, until warmed through, about 10 minutes. Adjust the consistency with hot water as desired and season with salt and pepper to taste. Bring the sauce to a brief simmer in a small saucepan or in the microwave, stirring often. Pile the pork and sauce onto hamburger buns.

CHICKEN ENCHILADAS

serves: 4 to 6   total time: 1¼ hours

66 When I'm invited to a game day
gathering or a Friday game night,
I bring along these hearty enchiladas.
They also make a great gift for a new
homeowner who's too busy to cook but
needs a hearty meal to fuel all that
unpacking. Corn tortillas are traditional,
but flour tortillas are sturdier—this
casserole is delicious made with either
variety. If you prefer, Monterey Jack
cheese can be used instead of cheddar,
or for a mellower flavor and creamier
texture, substitute an equal amount of
queso fresco."

- -

HOW I GIFT THIS

packaging: Use either a disposable
baking dish or a non-disposable dish
that you can make part of your gift.
The shredded cheese for baking and
optional garnishes should go in small
airtight containers.

storage: The enchiladas and the sauce
can be refrigerated separately for
about 3 days. Assemble the toppings
when you're ready to give the gift.

make it a basket: Pack the enchiladas
baking dish in an insulated food carrier
that's part of the gift. Tuck in containers
with the toppings your recipient might
want. Add your recipient's favorite
beer too.

¼ cup vegetable oil, divided
1 onion, chopped fine
3 tablespoons chili powder
3 garlic cloves, minced
2 teaspoons ground coriander
2 teaspoons ground cumin
2 teaspoons sugar
½ teaspoon table salt
1 pound boneless, skinless chicken
    thighs, trimmed and cut into
    ¼-inch-wide strips
2 (8-ounce) cans tomato sauce
⅓ cup water

½ cup minced fresh cilantro
⅓ cup jarred jalapeños, rinsed,
    patted dry, and chopped
10 ounces sharp cheddar cheese,
    shredded (2½ cups), divided
12 (6-inch) corn or flour tortillas

toppings (optional)
Avocado
Salsa
Sour cream
Red onion
Lime wedges

1. Heat 2 tablespoons oil in large saucepan over medium heat until shimmering.
Add onion and cook until softened and lightly browned, 5 to 7 minutes. Stir in chili
powder, garlic, coriander, cumin, sugar, and salt and cook until fragrant, about
30 seconds. Stir in chicken, tomato sauce, and water. Bring to gentle simmer and
cook, stirring occasionally, until chicken is tender and flavors blend, 8 to 10 minutes.

2. Pour mixture through colander into medium bowl, pressing on strained chicken
mixture to extract as much sauce as possible. Transfer sauce to storage container
and set aside to cool completely. Let chicken cool, then combine with cilantro,
jalapeños, and 2 cups cheddar in bowl.

3. Brush both sides of tortillas with remaining 2 tablespoons oil. Stack tortillas, wrap
in damp dish towel, and place on plate; microwave until warm and pliable, about
1 minute. Working with 1 warm tortilla at a time, spread ⅓ cup of chicken mixture
across center of tortilla, roll tortilla tightly around filling, and place seam side down
in greased 13 by 9-inch baking dish, arranging in 2 rows of 6 rolled tortillas. Wrap
dish tightly with plastic wrap. Add remaining ½ cup cheese to separate container.
Refrigerate casserole dish, sauce, and cheese if not giving right away.

gift tag

Spray the top of the enchiladas with vegetable oil spray. Bake the enchiladas uncovered (without the reserved sauce) on the middle rack at 400 degrees until lightly toasted on top, 10 to 15 minutes. Stir the sauce and pour it over the enchiladas, then sprinkle with the shredded cheese. Cover the dish tightly with greased aluminum foil and bake until bubbling around the edges, 20 to 25 minutes. Serve with all your favorite toppings.

STUFFED SHELLS WITH AMATRICIANA SAUCE

serves: 6 to 8   total time: 2 hours

❝ A pasta casserole makes an ideal meal gift since most of the work lies in the assembly. Part of your gift is the time to do that work so your time- or energy-crunched recipient just needs to pop the casserole into the oven. These tender, cheesy jumbo shells with a zesty tomato sauce are gifted as a ready-to-bake refrigerator meal. For pasta meals that can be frozen, see the Hearty Meat Lasagna on page 172 and the Baked Macaroni and Cheese on page 175. When buying pancetta at the deli counter, ask to have it sliced ¼ inch thick. If you can't find pancetta at the deli counter, look for pre-chopped packaged pancetta near where the bacon is sold. You can also substitute 6 ounces of thick-cut, or slab, bacon for the pancetta.❞

HOW I GIFT THIS

packaging: Assemble the shells in the dish your recipient will bake it in, whether that's a disposable aluminum pan or a glass or ceramic baking dish. Basil oxidizes quickly once it's cut, so it's best to gift an entire bunch and let your recipient prep the basil before serving.

storage: The stuffed shells can be refrigerated for about 2 days.

divide it: Instead of baking in a 13 by 9-inch baking dish, you could divide the shells and sauce between two 8-inch baking dishes. The baking time will be the same.

make it a basket: Wrap the casserole in a apron (see page 160 for instructions) and tuck a wedge of Parmesan cheese and a Microplane grater into the pockets. Add a small basket or tote with a bottle of wine, a loaf of bread, and the Garlic Butter (page 160).

1 tablespoon extra-virgin olive oil
6 ounces pancetta, cut into 1 by ¼-inch pieces
1 onion, chopped fine
¾ teaspoon table salt, divided, plus salt for cooking pasta
¼ teaspoon red pepper flakes
2 (28-ounce) cans crushed tomatoes
12 ounces jumbo pasta shells
12 ounces (1½ cups) whole-milk or part-skim ricotta cheese
10 ounces mozzarella cheese, shredded (2½ cups)
3 ounces Parmesan cheese, grated (1½ cups)
2 large eggs, lightly beaten
¼ cup chopped fresh basil
2 garlic cloves, minced
Basil (optional; enough for 2 tablespoons chopped)

1. Heat oil in large saucepan over medium heat until shimmering. Add pancetta and cook until lightly browned and crisp, about 8 minutes. Using slotted spoon, transfer pancetta to paper towel–lined plate.

2. Pour off all but 3 tablespoons fat from saucepan, add onion and ¼ teaspoon salt, and cook until softened, about 5 minutes. Stir in pepper flakes and cook until fragrant, about 30 seconds. Stir in tomatoes, bring to simmer, and cook until slightly thickened, about 10 minutes. Let cool to room temperature, about 45 minutes. Stir in pancetta and season with salt and pepper to taste.

3. Meanwhile, line rimmed baking sheet with clean dish towel. Bring 4 quarts water to boil in large pot. Add pasta and 1 tablespoon salt and cook, stirring occasionally, until just beginning to soften, about 8 minutes. Drain pasta and transfer to prepared baking sheet. Using dinner fork, pry apart any shells that have clung together, discarding any that are badly torn (you should have 30 to 33 good shells).

recipe continues

4. Combine ricotta, 1½ cups mozzarella, 1 cup Parmesan, eggs, basil, garlic, and remaining ½ teaspoon salt in bowl; transfer to zipper-lock bag. Using scissors, cut off 1 corner of bag and pipe 1 tablespoon filling into each shell.

5. Spread 2 cups cooled sauce on bottom of 13 by 9-inch baking dish. Arrange filled shells seam side down in dish. Spread remaining sauce over shells. Sprinkle remaining 1 cup mozzarella and ½ cup Parmesan over sauce. Cover and refrigerate. Package basil for garnish separately, if using.

GARLIC BUTTER

makes: about ¾ cup   **total time:** 10 minutes

  8 tablespoons unsalted butter, softened
  1 head roasted garlic cloves (8–10 cloves)
  1 tablespoon chopped fresh rosemary
  ¼ teaspoon table salt
  ¼ teaspoon pepper

Using fork, mash all ingredients in bowl until combined. (Garlic butter can be refrigerated for 1 week or frozen for 1 month.)

> **gift tag**
>
> Cover the baking dish with greased aluminum foil and bake on a rimmed baking sheet on the middle rack at 400 degrees until the sauce begins to bubble around the edges, 25 to 30 minutes. Remove the foil and bake, uncovered, until the cheese begins to brown, about 10 minutes. Let cool for 10 minutes, then sprinkle with 2 tablespoons chopped basil (optional).

WRAPPING A DISH WITH AN APRON

1. Lay the apron front side down on a flat surface. Fold the top half of the apron toward you just above the front pockets, making sure to smooth out the neck strap as much as possible.

2. Fold the bottom half of the apron away from you, just until you reach the bottom of the front pockets. (You can iron the apron to hold the folds, if desired.)

3. Carefully turn the apron over so that the pockets are facing up and lay the apron horizontally on the casserole dish. Wrap the sides under the pan and bring the strings back over the top.

4. Tie the apron strings to secure the apron in place. Use the pockets to hold additional gifts like a grater and a block of Parmesan cheese.

GET WELL SOON

> In the early stages of cancer treatment, among the most unforgettable moments were when my co-workers here at ATK all stepped in to provide easy meal preps for me and my family members who were visiting in rotation for weeks at a time. This kindness made it possible for my family to give their full attention to me, and I could give all my attention to healing. These meals were truly some of the greatest gifts that really said, 'Get well soon.'"

HOW I GIFT THIS

This is all about giving a friend in need an easy meal, without bells and whistles (or in this case, ribbons and bows). I want to make it as easy as possible for my recipient to get this nourishing, easy-on-the-tummy soup ready to eat. So I package everything up so that it's ready to just open and dump into the broth on the stovetop. I don't want them to have to worry about getting the carrying containers back to me, so I use jars I don't need back and plastic bags (deli containers are also great). I put the Immunitea Herbal Tea Blend in a plastic container and the Ginger Syrup in a tightly capped bottle. I pack everything into an insulated tote bag, a regular tote bag with an ice pack, or a small Styrofoam cooler.

START WITH

Chicken and Ramen Soup (page 164)

Ginger Syrup (page 116)

Immunitea Herbed Tea Blend (page 57)

IF YOU WANT, ADD

Beet chips

Hard-cooked eggs

Seltzer or ginger ale

Soup mug

Cozy scarf or throw

CHICKEN AND RAMEN SOUP

serves: 4 to 6   total time: 30 minutes

66 When I was going through chemotherapy, there were very few meals that were as appetizing as this soothing soup. It has become my go-to recipe when I'm not feeling well, and so it's also one of my go-tos when I want to help a friend or neighbor who's under the weather. It can easily be divided into two gifts, as well. I prefer Shaoxing wine here, but you can substitute dry sherry. The soup calls for small amounts of toasted sesame oil and soy sauce to finish, so consider whether you would like to give your recipient measured amounts in tiny containers or entire bottles of these two items. Hard-cooked eggs and chili crisp also make excellent optional accompaniments, adding even more protein and warm flavors."

HOW I GIFT THIS

packaging: To make this as easy as possible for the recipient, I suggest packing the noodles and sliced cabbage together and the chicken, spinach, and scallion greens together (or you can keep the noodles in their original packaging). The broth, sesame oil, and soy sauce will each need their own containers. Gift all the components in a tote bag with an ice pack or in a small Styrofoam cooler.

storage: All of the prepped and assembled components can be refrigerated for about 2 days.

make it a trio: Team the soup with beautiful ramen bowls and chopsticks and ramen spoons.

make it a basket: This is perfect for the Get Well Soon basket (page 163). Or make a basket with the soup, Chili Crisp (page 67), a bottle of toasted sesame oil, a bottle of soy sauce, and a soup bowl.

1 pound boneless, skinless chicken breasts, trimmed
½ teaspoon table salt
¼ teaspoon pepper
1 tablespoon vegetable oil
5 scallions, white and green parts separated and sliced thin
2 tablespoons grated fresh ginger
2 garlic cloves, minced
8 cups chicken broth
2 cups water
2 tablespoons Shaoxing wine
3 tablespoons soy sauce, divided
2 (3-ounce) packages ramen noodles, seasoning packets discarded
3 cups shredded green cabbage
3 ounces (3 cups) baby spinach
1 tablespoon toasted sesame oil

1. Pat chicken dry with paper towels and sprinkle with salt and pepper. Heat oil in large pot over medium-high heat until just smoking. Brown chicken lightly on both sides, about 5 minutes; transfer to plate.

2. Add scallion whites, ginger, and garlic to fat left in pot and cook over medium heat until fragrant, about 1 minute. Stir in broth, water, Shaoxing wine, and 2 tablespoons soy sauce, scraping up any browned bits, and bring to simmer.

3. Nestle chicken into pot, adding any accumulated juices. Reduce heat to low, cover, and cook until chicken registers 165 degrees, about 15 minutes. Transfer chicken to cutting board, let cool slightly, then shred into bite-size pieces using 2 forks. Let broth cool, then transfer to container. Package noodles and cabbage in container; chicken, spinach, and scallion greens in another container; and sesame oil and remaining 1 tablespoon soy sauce for serving in separate small containers. Refrigerate.

gift tag

Bring the broth to a simmer in a large pot over medium heat. Stir in the noodles and cabbage and cook until the noodles are tender, about 4 minutes. Stir in the chicken, spinach, scallion greens, and toasted sesame oil and cook until warmed through. Season with soy sauce to taste. Hard-cooked eggs and chili crisp also make great accompaniments, if you've got them.

VEGETARIAN CURRIED LENTIL SOUP

serves: 4 to 6   total time: 1¼ hours

66 Full of both nutrition and comfort, lentil soup is a great gift for anyone who's in need of a little physical or emotional nurturing. I love the simple, homey aspect of presenting this soup as a gift to a dear friend. You can give it either freshly made for enjoying within a few days or offer it as a freezer gift in a freezer storage container. Lentilles du Puy, also called French green lentils, are my first choice for this recipe because they won't soften in the fridge or freezer. Brown, black, or regular green lentils will also work (the cooking times will vary depending on the type used)."

HOW I GIFT THIS

packaging: You can give this as either a refrigerator or a freezer gift. Insulated soup mugs are a great way to present the soup and allow you to give multiple gifts, if you like.

storage: The soup can be refrigerated for about 3 days or frozen for about 1 month.

divide it: This is easily split in half to make two gifts.

make it a duo: Pair with the No-Knead Whole-Wheat Rustic Loaf (page 300).

2 tablespoons extra-virgin olive oil
1 large onion, chopped fine
2 carrots, peeled and chopped
3 garlic cloves, minced
1 teaspoon curry powder
1 (14.5-ounce) can diced tomatoes, drained
1 bay leaf
1 teaspoon minced fresh thyme
1 cup lentilles du Puy (French green lentils), picked over and rinsed
¼ teaspoon table salt
½ cup dry white wine
4½ cups vegetable broth
1½ cups water
Parsley (optional; enough for 3 tablespoons chopped)

1. Heat oil in Dutch oven over medium-high heat until shimmering. Stir in onion and carrots and cook until vegetables begin to soften, about 2 minutes. Stir in garlic and curry powder and cook until fragrant, about 30 seconds. Stir in tomatoes, bay leaf, and thyme and cook until fragrant, about 30 seconds. Stir in lentils and ¼ teaspoon salt. Cover, reduce heat to medium-low, and cook, stirring occasionally, until vegetables are softened and lentils have darkened, 8 to 10 minutes.

2. Uncover and increase heat to high. Add wine, scraping up any browned bits, and bring to simmer. Stir in broth and water and bring to boil. Partially cover pot, reduce heat to low, and simmer, stirring occasionally, until lentils are tender but still hold their shape, 30 to 35 minutes.

3. Discard bay leaf. Puree 3 cups soup in blender until smooth, then return to pot. Divide soup among containers and cool to room temperature. Refrigerate or freeze. Package parsley separately, if including.

---

gift tag

If the soup is frozen, thaw in the refrigerator. Bring to a gentle simmer in a covered pot, stirring often. Adjust the consistency with hot water as desired. Stir in 3 tablespoons chopped parsley (optional) and season with salt and pepper to taste.

HEARTY BEEF STEW

serves: 12 to 14   **total time:** 4 hours

66 Beef stew is a perfect make-ahead dish. It's simultaneously homey and fancy, and it freezes and reheats so well that I think it's worth making a big batch, as we do here. This recipe yields enough stew to stock one person's freezer with several meals or to divide into multiple gifts. The stew features chuck-eye roast, which has flavorful, tender meat and a reasonable price tag (especially significant for a big batch of stew). Browning some of the meat develops deep flavor that holds up after freezing, and cooking the assembled stew in a roasting pan in the oven is a great way to cook this large quantity of stew."

- - - - - - - - - - - - - - - - - - - -

HOW I GIFT THIS

packaging: You can give this as either a refrigerator or a freezer gift, in any size storage containers you like.

storage: The stew can be refrigerated for about 3 days or frozen for about 1 month.

divide it: This is easily divided into smaller portions for multiple gifts; plan on about 2 cups per serving.

make it a duo: Pair with the No-Knead Rustic Loaf (page 299).

7 pounds boneless beef chuck-eye roast, pulled apart at seams, trimmed, and cut into 1½-inch pieces

3¼ teaspoons table salt, divided

1⅛ teaspoons pepper

2 tablespoons vegetable oil, plus extra as needed

1¾ pounds carrots, peeled and sliced 1 inch thick

3 bay leaves

1½ tablespoons minced fresh thyme or 1½ teaspoons dried

4 tablespoons unsalted butter

2 pounds onions, chopped

5 garlic cloves, minced

¾ cup all-purpose flour

2 tablespoons tomato paste

1½ cups dry red wine

4 cups chicken broth

2⅔ pounds red potatoes, unpeeled, cut into 1-inch pieces

2 cups frozen peas
Parsley (optional; enough for 6 tablespoons chopped)

1. Adjust oven rack to lower-middle position and heat oven to 325 degrees. Pat beef dry with paper towels and sprinkle with 2¼ teaspoons salt and pepper; transfer half of beef to large roasting pan. Heat oil in Dutch oven over medium-high heat until just smoking. Working in 2 batches, brown remaining beef on all sides, about 8 minutes, adding extra oil if pot looks dry; transfer to roasting pan. Add carrots, bay leaves, and thyme to roasting pan.

2. Melt butter in now-empty pot over medium-low heat. Add onions and remaining 1 teaspoon salt and cook, stirring often, until softened, 7 to 10 minutes. Stir in garlic and cook until fragrant, about 30 seconds. Stir in flour and tomato paste and cook, stirring constantly, until golden, about 1 minute. Slowly whisk in wine, scraping up any browned bits. Gradually whisk in broth until smooth and bring to simmer. Transfer broth mixture to roasting pan with meat mixture. Cover roasting pan tightly with aluminum foil and bake for 1½ hours.

3. Stir in potatoes and continue to cook, covered, until meat is just tender, 2 to 2½ hours.

4. Discard bay leaves, stir in frozen peas, and season with salt and pepper to taste. Divide stew among containers and cool to room temperature. Refrigerate or freeze. Package parsley separately, if including.

┌─ **gift tag** ─────────────────────────

If the stew is frozen, thaw in the refrigerator. Bring
to a gentle simmer in a covered saucepan, stirring
occasionally. Adjust the consistency with hot water as
desired. Remove from the heat, stir in 6 tablespoons
chopped parsley (optional), and season with salt and
pepper to taste.

CHICKEN POT PIE

makes: 2 pies, each serving 4   **total time:** 1¾ hours

66 Chicken pot pies were one of my favorite after-school snacks as a kid. Straight from the freezer to the oven, watching my favorite syndicated shows, it gives me all the nostalgic feels that I love to share with friends. This duo of chicken pot pies was created especially to be made ahead and frozen, making it a natural choice for a food gift (or gifts). All your recipient needs to do is brush the crust with egg wash and bake the pie until it's golden. Two tricks guarantee this pie will taste as good as any freshly baked one: First, using chicken thighs makes for tender, juicy meat (chicken breasts will end up too dry). Second, for a crisp crust, you'll create an aluminum foil barrier between the filling and the crust. This allows the filling to thaw and heat through while the crust thaws and bakes without turning gummy. You will need two 9½-inch disposable aluminum deep-dish pie plates for this recipe."

HOW I GIFT THIS

packaging: This is meant to be given as a freezer gift. Wrap the assembled and covered pies tightly with plastic wrap for freezer storage.

storage: The pot pies can be frozen for about 1 month.

1 tablespoon unsalted butter	½ cup all-purpose flour
2 onions, chopped fine	2½ cups chicken broth
1 pound carrots, peeled and sliced ¼ inch thick	3 pounds boneless, skinless chicken thighs, trimmed
2 celery ribs, sliced ¼ inch thick	½ cup heavy cream
1 teaspoon table salt	2 tablespoons dry sherry
½ teaspoon pepper	1 cup frozen peas
2 teaspoons tomato paste	¼ cup minced fresh parsley
2 teaspoons minced fresh thyme or ½ teaspoon dried	1 package store-bought pie dough

1. Melt butter in Dutch oven over medium heat. Add onions, carrots, celery, salt, and pepper and cook until softened and lightly browned, 8 to 10 minutes. Stir in tomato paste and thyme and cook until browned, about 2 minutes. Stir in flour and cook for 1 minute.

2. Slowly whisk in chicken broth, scraping up any browned bits and smoothing out any lumps. Add chicken and bring to simmer. Reduce heat to medium-low, cover, and simmer, stirring occasionally, until chicken registers 175 degrees and sauce is thickened, 25 to 30 minutes. Off heat, transfer chicken to cutting board, let cool slightly, then shred into bite-size pieces using 2 forks.

3. Stir heavy cream and sherry into sauce, then stir in shredded chicken and any accumulated juices, frozen peas, and parsley. Season with salt and pepper to taste. Divide filling evenly between 2 greased, 9½-inch disposable aluminum deep-dish pie pans and let cool to room temperature, about 30 minutes.

4. Cut out two 12-inch square sheets of aluminum foil and grease both sides lightly. Press sheet of foil flush to surface of each filling, letting excess hang over edges of pans. Unroll each pie dough round, trim to 9-inch round (pie dough should be no wider than pie plate), and cut four 2-inch vents in center. Gently place 1 pie dough round on each pan. Wrap pans tightly with plastic wrap and cover with foil. Freeze.

gift tag

Place the frozen pie on a foil-lined rimmed
baking sheet. Brush the top of the dough with
a lightly beaten egg, cover with greased foil,
and place on the middle rack of a cold oven.
Turn the oven to 400 degrees and bake for
40 minutes. Uncover and continue to bake
until golden, 35 to 40 minutes. Let cool for
15 minutes. Loosen the foil from the pan edges.
Holding the pie crust in place, gently pull the
foil out from underneath crust.

HEARTY MEAT LASAGNA

serves: 8   total time: 1 hour

66 Everybody loves lasagna, but nobody makes it as often as it deserves to be made because it is usually so time-consuming. So assembling and gifting a ready-to-bake lasagna will instantly catapult you to favorite status in the eyes of your recipient. Make-ahead lasagna might have a little bit of a reputation for turning out dry, but that's not a problem with this beauty. The generous amount of liquidy sauce gets absorbed by the thirsty (and convenient) no-boil noodles during baking, and ricotta and Parmesan cheeses blended with an egg keep the layers tender and moist. If you can't find meatloaf mix, use 8 ounces (85 percent lean) ground beef and 8 ounces ground pork."

HOW I GIFT THIS

packaging: This can be given as either a refrigerator or a freezer gift, in a glass or disposable aluminum baking dish. If refrigerating, you can cover it with a baking dish lid. If freezing, wrap the dish tightly in plastic wrap and then aluminum foil.

storage: The lasagna can be refrigerated for about 2 days or frozen for about 1 month.

make it a duo: I like to pair this with a bench scraper. Not only is it a great tool for cleanly slicing the lasagna, it has countless other uses in the kitchen.

sauce

2 tablespoons extra-virgin olive oil
1 onion, chopped fine
1 teaspoon table salt
1 teaspoon pepper
6 garlic cloves, minced
1 pound meatloaf mix
¼ cup heavy cream
1 (28-ounce) can tomato puree
1 (28-ounce) can diced tomatoes, drained
¼ cup chopped fresh basil

lasagna

24 ounces (3 cups) whole-milk or part-skim ricotta cheese
3 ounces Parmesan cheese, grated (1½ cups), divided
¼ cup chopped fresh basil
1 large egg, lightly beaten
½ teaspoon table salt
½ teaspoon pepper
12 no-boil lasagna noodles
1 pound whole-milk mozzarella cheese, shredded (4 cups), divided

1. for the sauce: Heat oil in Dutch oven over medium heat until shimmering. Add onion, salt, and pepper and cook until softened, about 5 minutes. Stir in garlic and cook until fragrant, about 30 seconds. Add meatloaf mix and cook, breaking up meat with wooden spoon, until no longer pink, about 5 minutes. Stir in cream and simmer until liquid evaporates and only fat remains, about 4 minutes. Stir in tomato puree and tomatoes, bring to simmer, and cook until flavors meld, about 5 minutes. Off heat, stir in basil and season with salt and pepper to taste.

2. for the lasagna: Combine ricotta, 1 cup Parmesan, basil, egg, salt, and pepper in bowl. Spread 1 cup sauce (avoiding large chunks of meat) over bottom of 13 by 9-inch baking dish. Lay 3 noodles in dish, spread ⅓ cup ricotta mixture over each noodle, then top with 1 cup mozzarella and 1 cup sauce (in that order). Repeat layering process 2 more times. Top with remaining 3 noodles, remaining sauce, remaining 1 cup mozzarella, and remaining ½ cup Parmesan. Refrigerate or freeze.

> **gift tag**
>
> If the lasagna is frozen, thaw it in the refrigerator. Unwrap the lasagna, then cover the dish tightly with greased aluminum foil, place on a foil-lined rimmed baking sheet, and bake on the middle rack in a 400 degree oven for 15 minutes. Uncover and continue to bake until spotty brown and bubbling around the edges, 25 to 35 minutes. Let cool for 10 minutes.

* HEARTY MEAT LASA
THAW. COVER WITH FOIL (GREA
* PLACE ON RIMMED B
SHEET WITH FOIL. BA
MIDDLE RACK FOR 15 MIN
400 DEGREES. LET COO

BAKED MACARONI AND CHEESE

serves: 6   total time: 1¼ hours

" A classic, homestyle macaroni and cheese appeals to adults and kids alike and will be a most welcome gift to pull out of the freezer (or refrigerator) on any night a cozy, comforting bake-and-serve meal is needed. This one starts with a simple béchamel sauce—butter, flour, and milk, with some chicken broth and spices for savory flavor—and then in goes the duo of shredded cheeses. Panko bread crumbs tossed with melted butter make an indulgent topping that turns crunchy and golden in the oven."

HOW I GIFT THIS

packaging: This can be given as either a refrigerator or a freezer gift, in a glass or disposable aluminum baking dish. If refrigerating, cover the dish with a baking dish lid. If freezing, wrap the covered dish tightly in plastic wrap.

storage: The mac and cheese can be refrigerated for about 2 days or frozen for about 1 month.

divide it: Divide into two 8-inch square dishes. The baking time will remain the same.

make it a duo: Pair with Easy Homemade Hot Sauce (page 68) or Thin and Crispy Chocolate Chip Cookies (page 213).

make it a basket: Tie pot holders onto the dish with a ribbon. Tuck truffle oil, bacon bits, and hot sauce into the opening in the pot holders.

1 cup panko bread crumbs
2 tablespoons unsalted butter, melted, plus 6 tablespoons unsalted butter
1 pound elbow macaroni or small shells
  Table salt for cooking pasta
1 garlic clove, minced
1 teaspoon dry mustard
¼ teaspoon cayenne pepper
6 tablespoons all-purpose flour
3½ cups whole milk
2¼ cups chicken broth
1 pound Colby cheese, shredded (4 cups)
8 ounces extra-sharp cheddar cheese, shredded (2 cups)

1. Adjust oven rack to middle position and heat oven to 350 degrees. Toss panko with melted butter. Spread evenly in aluminum foil–lined rimmed baking sheet and bake, stirring occasionally, until golden brown, about 10 minutes; let cool to room temperature.

2. Bring 4 quarts water to boil in large pot. Add macaroni and 1 tablespoon salt and cook, stirring often, until just starting to soften, about 5 minutes. Drain macaroni and set aside.

3. Dry now-empty pot, add remaining 6 tablespoons butter, and melt over medium heat. Stir in garlic, mustard, and cayenne and cook until fragrant, about 30 seconds. Add flour and cook, stirring constantly, until golden, about 1 minute. Slowly whisk in milk and broth until smooth. Bring to gentle simmer and cook, whisking often, until thickened, about 15 minutes.

4. Off heat, gradually whisk in Colby and cheddar until melted and smooth. Season with salt and pepper to taste. Stir in macaroni, breaking up any clumps. Transfer macaroni mixture to 13 by 9-inch baking dish and sprinkle with panko mixture. Refrigerate or freeze.

┌─ **gift tag**

If the mac and cheese is frozen, thaw in the refrigerator. Unwrap the casserole, then cover the dish tightly with greased aluminum foil, place on a foil-lined rimmed baking sheet, and bake on the middle rack in a 400-degree oven until bubbling around the edges, 25 to 35 minutes. Remove foil and continue to bake until crumbs are crisp, 15 to 20 minutes. Let cool for 20 minutes.

MEATBALLS AND MARINARA

serves: 8 to 12 (makes 30 meatballs and 7 cups sauce)   **total time:** 2 hours

" By making a big pot of meatballs and marinara sauce, you can bring happiness to a whole lot of people. This makes plenty to go around, so you can give one big batch, or easily turn it into multiple smaller gifts. And you can tailor each gift to your recipient's tastes. Package some meatballs and sauce with a favorite dried pasta so a pasta lover can have a hearty pasta night or a leisurely Sunday dinner. Or gift the meatballs and sauce with sub rolls and some provolone cheese for a New Year's Day football-watching gift. Roasting the meatballs in the oven at a high temperature gives them a nice browned crust without the messiness of stovetop frying, and making them medium-size gives them a ratio of crispy crust to tender interior that I find irresistible."

HOW I GIFT THIS

packaging: You can give this as either a refrigerator or a freezer gift, packaging the sauce and meatballs in separate containers. I've also been known to give the sauce in a Dutch oven for a more special housewarming gift! (See page 178 for lid-attaching instructions.) Basil oxidizes quickly, so it's best to gift a whole bunch and let your recipient prep the basil before serving.

storage: The meatballs and sauce can be refrigerated for about 3 days or frozen for about 1 month.

divide it: This is easily divided into multiple gifts.

make it a duo: Gift this with your favorite fancy pasta (you'll need 3½ cups sauce and 15 meatballs for 1 pound of pasta).

make it a trio: Package up sub rolls and sliced provolone cheese for a meatball sub kind of night. For this gift, ⅔ cup sauce and 3 meatballs is just right for a 6- or 7-inch sub roll for one serving.

marinara
- ¼ cup extra-virgin olive oil
- 3 onions, chopped fine
- 8 garlic cloves, minced
- 1 tablespoon dried oregano
- ¾ teaspoon red pepper flakes
- 1 (6-ounce) can tomato paste
- 1 cup dry red wine
- 1 cup water
- 4 (28-ounce) cans crushed tomatoes
- 1 ounce Parmesan cheese, grated (½ cup)

meatballs
- 4 slices hearty white sandwich bread, torn into pieces
- ¾ cup milk
- 8 ounces sweet Italian sausage, casings removed
- 2 ounces Parmesan cheese, grated (1 cup)
- ½ cup chopped fresh parsley
- 2 large eggs
- 2 garlic cloves, minced
- 1½ teaspoons table salt
- 2½ pounds 80 percent lean ground chuck

    Basil (optional; enough for ¼ cup chopped)

1. for the marinara: Heat oil in Dutch oven over medium heat until shimmering. Add onions and cook until softened and lightly browned, 10 to 15 minutes. Stir in garlic, oregano, and pepper flakes and cook until fragrant, about 30 seconds. Transfer half of onion mixture to large bowl and set aside.

recipe continues

2. Add tomato paste to remaining onion mixture in pot and cook over medium-high heat until fragrant, about 1 minute. Stir in wine, scraping up any browned bits, and cook until slightly thickened, about 2 minutes. Stir in water and tomatoes and bring to simmer. Reduce heat to low and simmer until sauce is no longer watery, 45 minutes to 1 hour. Stir in Parmesan and season with salt and pepper to taste.

3. for the meatballs: Meanwhile, adjust oven racks to upper-middle and lower-middle positions and heat oven to 475 degrees. Line 2 rimmed baking sheets with aluminum foil and spray with vegetable oil spray.

4. Mash bread and milk in bowl with reserved onion mixture until smooth. Add sausage, Parmesan, parsley, eggs, garlic, and salt and mash with your hands to combine. Mix in ground beef with your hands until uniform. Pinch off and roll mixture into 2-inch round meatballs (about 30 meatballs total). Arrange meatballs evenly on prepared sheets. Bake until well browned, about 20 minutes, switching and rotating sheets halfway through baking.

5. Divide meatballs and sauce among separate storage containers and let cool. Refrigerate or freeze. Package basil separately, if including.

---

gift tag

If the meatballs and marinara are frozen, thaw in the refrigerator. Bring the sauce and meatballs to a very gentle simmer in a covered saucepan, stirring occasionally, until the meatballs are warmed through. Stir in ¼ cup chopped basil (optional).

SECURING A POT LID

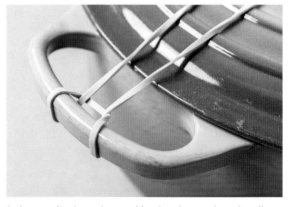

1. Loop or hook one large rubber band around one handle.

2. Stretch it over the pot to hook around the knob on top of the lid. Repeat on the other side with another rubber band.

3. Make sure the bands fit snugly. A 6-inch band will work best on a large pot, while a 4-inch band will be better for a smaller pot.

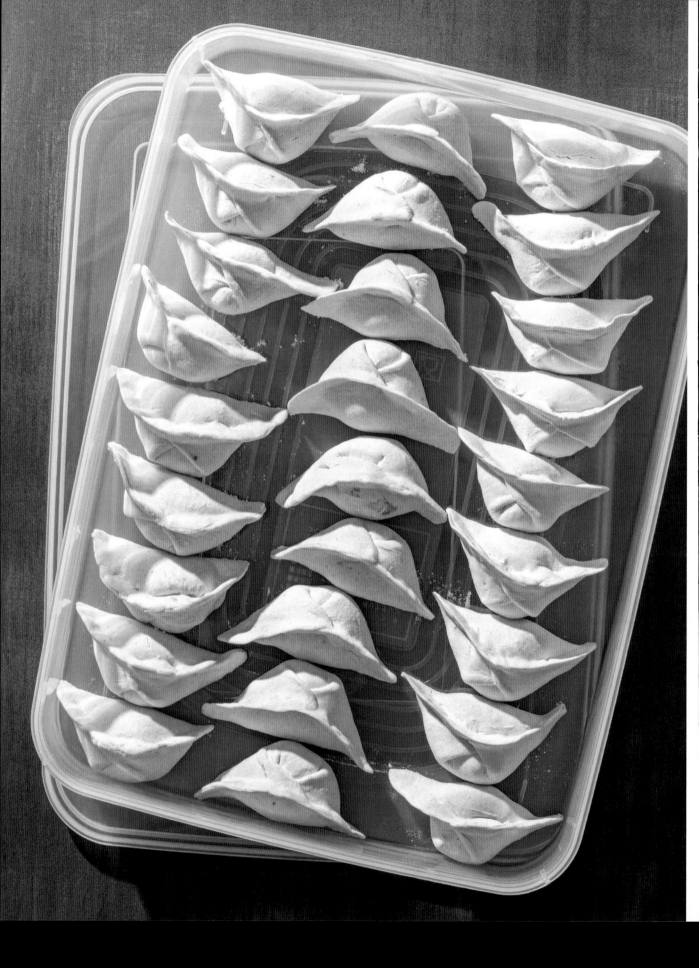

CHINESE PORK DUMPLINGS

serves: 6 to 10 (makes 40 dumplings)   **total time:** 1½ hours

    “ How fun to give the gift of a dumpling party! And with this recipe, you'll have (almost) as much fun making the dumplings as your recipient will have eating them. The simple flour-and-water dough is sturdy, yet easy to stretch and roll out. The flavorful filling is packed with ground pork, cabbage, scallions, sesame oil, soy sauce, ginger, Shaoxing wine, hoisin sauce, and white pepper. Mixing the filling in the food processor is quick and tidy, and the fast-moving blades also help develop myosin, a protein that helps the filling hold together when cooked. There's also a simple sealing method for the filled dumplings. For an accurate measurement of boiling water, bring a full kettle of water to a boil and then measure out the desired amount. To ensure that the dumplings seal completely, use minimal flour when working with the dough so it remains slightly tacky. Keep all the dough covered with a damp towel except when rolling and shaping. A shorter, smaller-diameter rolling pin is ideal here, but a conventional pin will also work.”

HOW I GIFT THIS

packaging: This is meant to be given as a freezer recipe. Once the assembled dumplings are frozen, package them in a zipper-lock freezer bag or plastic freezer container.

storage: The dumplings can be frozen for about 1 month.

make it a trio: Give with a bottle of Chinese black vinegar and a bottle of good-quality Chinese light soy sauce.

make it a basket: Package the frozen dumplings in plastic tubs or in zipper-lock bags tucked into Chinese takeout containers. Use a colorful condiment caddy to present Chili Crisp (page 67 or store-bought), black or rice vinegar, soy sauce, chopsticks, and fortune cookies.

dough
- 2½ cups (12½ ounces) all-purpose flour
- 1 cup boiling water

filling
- 5 cups 1-inch napa cabbage pieces
- ½ teaspoon table salt, plus salt for salting cabbage
- 12 ounces ground pork
- 1½ tablespoons soy sauce
- 1½ tablespoons toasted sesame oil
- 1 tablespoon vegetable oil, plus 2 tablespoons for pan frying
- 1 tablespoon Shaoxing wine or dry sherry
- 1 tablespoon hoisin sauce
- 1 tablespoon grated fresh ginger
- ¼ teaspoon ground white pepper
- 4 scallions, chopped fine

dipping sauces
- Chinese black vinegar or unseasoned rice vinegar
- Soy sauce

1. for the dough: Place flour in food processor. With processor running, add boiling water. Continue to process until dough forms ball and clears sides of bowl, 30 to 45 seconds. Transfer dough to counter and knead with your hands until smooth, 2 to 3 minutes. Wrap dough in plastic wrap and let rest for 30 minutes.

2. for the filling: While dough rests, scrape out any excess dough from now-empty processor bowl and blade. Pulse cabbage in processor until finely chopped, 8 to 10 pulses. Transfer cabbage to medium bowl and stir in ½ teaspoon salt; let sit for 10 minutes. Using your hands, squeeze excess moisture from cabbage. Transfer cabbage to small bowl and set aside.

recipe continues

3. Pulse pork, soy sauce, sesame oil, 1 tablespoon vegetable oil, Shaoxing wine, hoisin, ginger, pepper, and ½ teaspoon salt in now-empty food processor until blended and slightly sticky, about 10 pulses. Scatter cabbage over, add scallions, and pulse until vegetables are evenly distributed, about 8 pulses. Transfer pork mixture to small bowl and, using rubber spatula, smooth surface. Cover with plastic and refrigerate.

4. Line 2 rimmed baking sheets with parchment paper, dust lightly with flour, and set aside. Unwrap dough, roll into 12-inch cylinder, and cut cylinder into 4 equal pieces. Set 3 pieces aside and cover with plastic. Roll remaining piece into 8-inch cylinder. Cut cylinder in half and cut each half into 5 equal pieces. Place dough pieces, cut side down, on lightly floured counter and lightly dust with flour. Using palm of your hand, press each dough piece into 2-inch disk. Cover disks with damp towel.

5. Roll 1 disk into 3½-inch round (wrappers needn't be perfectly round) and re-cover disk with damp towel. Repeat with remaining disks. (Do not overlap disks.) Using rubber spatula, mark filling with cross to divide into 4 equal portions. Transfer 1 portion to small bowl and refrigerate remaining filling. Working with 1 wrapper at a time (keep remaining wrappers covered), place scant 1 tablespoon filling in center of wrapper. Brush away any flour clinging to surface of wrapper. Lift side of wrapper closest to you and side farthest away and pinch together to form 1½-inch-wide seam in center

of dumpling. (When viewed from above, dumpling will have rectangular shape with rounded open ends.) Lift left corner farthest away from you and bring to center of seam. Pinch to seal. Pinch together remaining dough on left side to seal. Repeat pinching on right side. Gently press dumpling into crescent shape and transfer to prepared sheet. Repeat with remaining wrappers and filling in bowl. Repeat dumpling-making process with remaining 3 pieces dough and remaining 3 portions filling. Freeze uncooked dumplings on rimmed baking sheet until solid. Transfer to container. Package vinegar and soy sauce in separate containers.

SHAPING DUMPLINGS

1. Place scant 1 tablespoon filling in center of wrapper. Seal top and bottom edges to form 1½-inch-wide seam.

2. Bring far left corner to center of seam and pinch together. Pinch rest of left side to seal.

3. Repeat process on right side. Gently press dumplings into crescent shape, with seam on top.

SWEETEN SOMEONE'S DAY

PACKING COOKIES AND CANDIES

Cookies are one of the most popular food gifts out there and, in my experience, everyone's biggest question is: How do I pack them so they look good and don't break? Here are some methods I use, along with tips for upping your game when giving homemade candy. If you make any of these sweet treats well ahead of gifting them, I suggest storing them in an airtight container until you're ready to package and present your gift.

HOW TO PACK COOKIES

In a Round Tin

1. Line the bottom and sides of a cookie tin with parchment paper, waxed paper, crinkle-cut paper, or corrugated paper.

2. Cut lengths of corrugated cardboard or paper to fit snugly into the interior of the tin, creating sections for the cookies. Make sure that the cookies fit securely in each section and are not loose. Fold any overhanging parchment over the top before closing the tin.

In a Loaf Pan

For square bars or long cookies such as Scotcheroos (page 241) or Almond Biscotti (page 232), fitting them snugly into a disposable aluminum loaf pan with a lid makes for an easy and attractive gift presentation.

In a Jar

For a cookie jar or other tall vessel, cut pieces of parchment or tissue paper to fit between layers of glazed cookies like Millionaire's Shortbread (page 224).

In a Bag

Round cookies look fantastic stacked tall in a cellophane bag that holds them snugly.

HOW TO PACK CANDIES

Small Candies

Layer small candies like Chocolate Truffles (page 189), Brigadeiros (page 192), and Chocolate-Covered Caramels (page 194) between parchment or waxed paper in a shallow tin or candy box. For added protection, nestle each piece of candy into an individual paper or foil candy cup.

For sticky candies like Salted Caramels (page 195) or a torrone that is cut into individual pieces, wrap individually in squares of waxed paper, then arrange in a tin or box.

Large Candies

Pack larger candy pieces, like Peppermint Bark (page 204) and Chocolate Matzo Toffee (page 207), in a tin or bakery box that holds them snugly, with parchment or waxed paper between layers.

Or arrange large candy shards in a paper take-out box.

You could also slide large candy pieces into a cellophane bag and tie with a ribbon.

Pro Tip
Pack Peppermint Bark separate from other candies and cookies, unless you want everything to taste like peppermint!

CHOCOLATE TRUFFLES

makes: 24 truffles   total time: 30 minutes, plus 1¾ hours chilling

" A chocolate truffle is candy at its most decadent, an elevated confection that carries a luxe price tag in chocolate shops. (But shhh—they are surprisingly easy to make from scratch.) Your recipient will know how highly you think of them when you present a box of these delights for Valentine's Day, an anniversary, or just to say a special thank-you. A rubber spatula is ideal for mixing the ganache, because it doesn't incorporate a lot of air—you want these truffles to be pure, dense, melt-in-your-mouth chocolate."

HOW I GIFT THIS

packaging: Pack them into a candy box or shallow windowed box. Add parchment between layers, or use paper candy cups to cradle each truffle.

storage: The truffles can be refrigerated for about 1 week.

make it a duo: Pair with a bottle of port or another dessert wine.

make it a trio: For a more unexpected combination, gift with stout and a wedge of blue cheese.

¼   cup (¾ ounce) unsweetened cocoa powder
 1   tablespoon confectioners' sugar
 8   ounces bittersweet chocolate, chopped fine
½   cup heavy cream
     Pinch table salt

gift tag

Let the truffles sit at room temperature for 10 minutes before enjoying them.

1. Sift cocoa and sugar through fine-mesh strainer into pie plate; set aside. Microwave chocolate, cream, and salt in bowl at 50 percent power, stirring occasionally with rubber spatula, until melted, about 1 minute. Stir truffle mixture until fully combined; transfer to 8-inch square baking dish and refrigerate until set, about 45 minutes.

2. Using heaping teaspoon measure, scoop truffle mixture into 24 portions, transfer to large plate, and refrigerate until firm, about 30 minutes. Roll each truffle between your hands to form uniform balls (they needn't be perfect).

3. Transfer truffles to reserved cocoa mixture and roll to evenly coat. Lightly shake truffles in your hand over pie plate to remove excess coating and transfer to plate. Refrigerate for 30 minutes.

variations
CHOCOLATE-ALMOND TRUFFLES
Substitute 1 cup whole almonds, toasted and chopped fine, for cocoa mixture coating. Add ½ teaspoon almond extract to chocolate mixture before microwaving in step 1.

CHOCOLATE-SPICE TRUFFLES
Sift ¼ teaspoon ground cinnamon with cocoa powder and sugar for coating. Add 1 teaspoon ground cinnamon and ⅛ teaspoon cayenne pepper to chocolate mixture before microwaving in step 1.

CHOCOLATE-GINGER TRUFFLES
Add 2 teaspoons ground ginger to chocolate mixture before microwaving in step 1.

CHOCOLATE-LEMON TRUFFLES
Add 1 teaspoon grated lemon zest to chocolate mixture before microwaving in step 1.

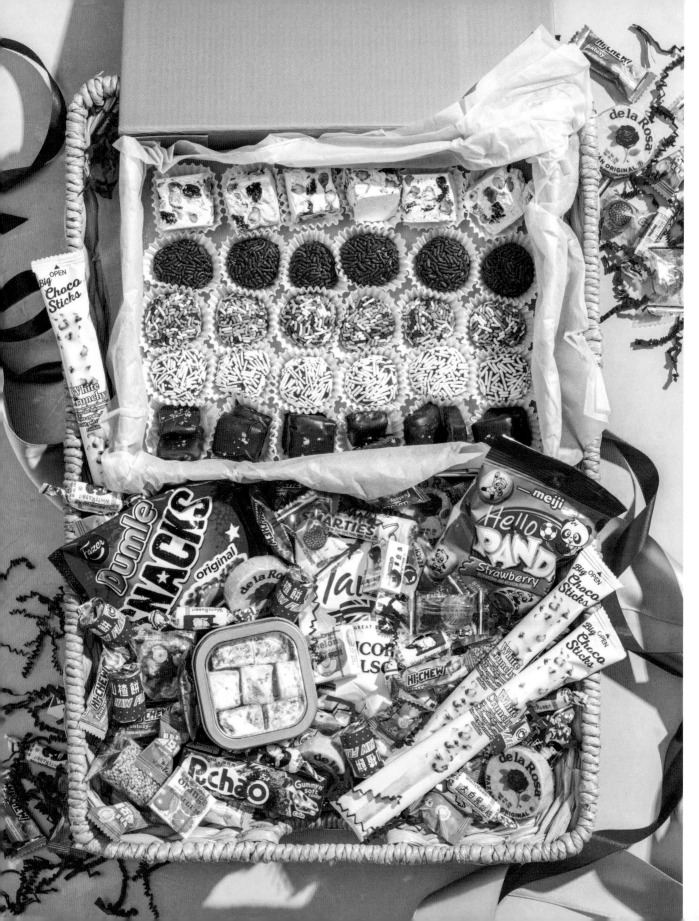

CANDY AROUND THE WORLD

66 Whenever I visit another country, in addition to of course exploring the restaurants, I love to sample as many different kinds of snack food as I can. It's fascinating to learn about the favorite sweet or salty snacks that people of different cultures reach for when they want an everyday treat. And after I return home, I enjoy sharing this type of learning with friends. Thanks to the wonders of online shopping, there's an endless array of international candies readily available to us. So think about your recipient: Where have they traveled to, or where do they want to travel to? What are their favorite cuisines? What is their cultural background? These questions will help you narrow down your journey through the shopping rabbit hole of international candy."

HOW I GIFT THIS

This candy basket starts with homemade Brazilian milk candy, Italian nougat, and French-inspired chocolate-covered caramels with sea salt. I package these homemade candies in a classic shallow candy box with individual paper cup liners for each piece. Or you could wrap pieces individually in cellophane wrappers and jumble them together in a festive candy bag. Then I add plenty of fun store-bought selections: chocolate-cookie candies from Sweden; fruit- and soda-flavored gummies from Japan; soft, chewy licorice from Australia; rosewater Turkish delight from Turkey; and peanut marzipan from Mexico. But let your own imagination run wild here!

START WITH

Brigadeiros (page 192)

Chocolate-Covered Caramels (page 194)

Pistachio-Cherry Torrone (page 197)

IF YOU WANT, ADD

Chocolate Truffles (page 189)

Store-bought international candies

BRIGADEIROS

makes: 30 candies   **total time:** 40 minutes, plus 30 minutes chilling

" These gooey, chocolaty, caramel-y Brazilian candy treats couldn't be easier. Sweetened condensed milk, cocoa powder, and butter are cooked until thick and then poured into a dish and chilled before being rolled into truffle-size nuggets. The last step is simply to coat the brigadeiros in any number of fun toppings. This recipes uses more cocoa powder than is traditional, for a candy that emphasizes the chocolate. Make sure to stir the cocoa mixture frequently or it will burn. You'll know the mixture is done cooking when it becomes so thick that a spatula dragged through it leaves a trail. If the dough sticks to your hands when rolling, spray your hands with a bit of vegetable oil spray."

HOW I GIFT THIS

packaging: Nestle each piece in a paper candy cup, then arrange the cups in a candy box or vintage tin.

storage: The brigadeiros can be refrigerated for about 2 weeks.

big-batch it: This recipe can be doubled and prepped in two 8-inch baking dishes.

make it a duo: For caramel lovers, pair with Salted Caramels (page 195).

- -

 1 (14-ounce) can sweetened condensed milk
 ½ cup (1½ ounces) unsweetened cocoa powder
 2 tablespoons unsalted butter
   Sprinkles, colored sugar, and/or nonpareils

1. Grease 8-inch square baking dish. Cook condensed milk, cocoa, and butter in medium saucepan over low heat, stirring frequently, until mixture is very thick and rubber spatula leaves distinct trail when dragged across bottom of saucepan, 20 to 25 minutes.

2. Pour mixture into prepared dish and refrigerate until firm, at least 30 minutes or up to 24 hours (cover with plastic wrap if chilling overnight).

3. Pinch mixture into approximately 1-tablespoon-size pieces and roll into 1-inch balls. Place desired coatings in small bowls and roll each ball in coating until covered.

CHOCOLATE-COVERED CARAMELS

makes: 64 caramels   **total time:** 1 hour, plus 3 hours cooling, chilling, and firming

66 Gourmet caramel candies dipped in chocolate and sprinkled with sea salt are the ultimate in sweet sophistication. Making them from scratch is a bit of a labor of love, but they make an absolutely spectacular present. My biggest tip for making the caramels is to not turn your back on the sugar syrup while it's cooking, since it can go from golden amber to dark mahogany to burnt beyond recognition faster than you'd think! But as long as you keep that in mind, this recipe cracks the code for chewy, delightfully sticky homemade caramels. When taking the temperature of the caramel in steps 3 and 4, remove the saucepan from the heat and tilt it to one side. This recipe makes enough tempered chocolate to easily dip all the caramels; leftover chocolate can be stored in an airtight container at room temperature for another use."

HOW I GIFT THIS

packaging: Gift chocolate caramels in a vintage tin with layers separated by parchment paper. Pack wrapped Salted Caramels into a cellophane bag.

storage: The caramels can be stored at room temperature for about 2 weeks.

make it a duo: Pair with a container of flake sea salt or smoked salt, Shortbread Cookies (page 220), or salted pretzels.

1 vanilla bean
1 cup heavy cream
5 tablespoons unsalted butter, cut into ¼-inch pieces
1 teaspoon flake sea salt, plus extra for garnish
1⅓ cups (9⅓ ounces) sugar
¼ cup light corn syrup
¼ cup water
1 pound semisweet chocolate (12 ounces chopped, 4 ounces finely grated)

1. Cut vanilla bean in half lengthwise. Using tip of paring knife, scrape out seeds; reserve spent vanilla bean for another use. Bring vanilla bean seeds, cream, butter, and sea salt to simmer in small saucepan over medium heat. Off heat, let steep for 10 minutes.

2. Make parchment sling for 8-inch square baking pan by folding 2 long sheets of parchment paper so each is 8 inches wide. Lay sheets of parchment in pan perpendicular to each other, with extra parchment hanging over edges of pan. Push parchment into corners and up sides of pan, smoothing parchment flush to pan. Grease parchment; set aside.

3. Combine sugar, corn syrup, and water in medium saucepan. Bring to boil over medium-high heat and cook, without stirring, until mixture is golden, 8 to 10 minutes. Reduce heat to low and continue to cook, swirling saucepan occasionally, until amber, 2 to 5 minutes. (Caramel should register 350 degrees.)

4. Off heat, carefully stir in cream mixture (it will bubble and steam). Return saucepan to medium-high heat and cook, stirring frequently, until caramel reaches 248 degrees, about 5 minutes.

5. Carefully transfer caramel to prepared pan. Using greased rubber spatula, smooth surface of caramel. Let cool completely, about 1 hour. Transfer to refrigerator and chill until caramel is completely solid and cold to touch, about 1 hour.

6. Using parchment overhang, lift caramel from pan and transfer to lightly greased cutting board; discard parchment. Using greased chef's knife, cut caramel into 1-inch-wide strips, then cut strips crosswise into 1-inch-wide pieces.

7. Microwave chopped chocolate in bowl at 50 percent power, stirring often, until about two-thirds melted, 2 to 4 minutes. (Melted chocolate should not be much warmer than body temperature; check by holding bowl in palm of your hand.) Add grated chocolate and stir until smooth, returning to microwave for no more than 5 seconds at a time to finish melting if necessary.

8. Line rimmed baking sheet with parchment. Place 1 caramel in chocolate and, using 2 forks, gently flip to coat all sides. Lift caramel out of chocolate with fork. Tap fork against edge of bowl and then wipe underside of fork on edge of bowl to remove excess chocolate from bottom of caramel. Use second fork to slide caramel onto prepared sheet and sprinkle with sea salt. Repeat with remaining caramels, returning chocolate to microwave for no more than 5 seconds at a time if it becomes too firm. Let caramels sit until chocolate is firm, about 1 hour.

variation
SALTED CARAMELS

In step 5, sprinkle caramels with additional ½ teaspoon sea salt. Once caramels are fully chilled, using parchment overhang, remove caramel from pan. Peel off parchment. Cut caramel into ¾-inch-wide strips and then crosswise into ¾-inch pieces. Individually wrap pieces in waxed-paper squares, twisting ends of paper to close. Omit chocolate and steps 6, 7, and 8.

PISTACHIO-CHERRY TORRONE

makes: eight 8-inch logs, sixteen 4-inch logs, or sixty-four 1-inch pieces

total time: 1 hour, plus 2½ hours cooling and chilling

" All my friends know that Italy is my favorite food destination, and whenever I visit, I am undoubtedly inspired by celebratory treats I discover that I immediately want to make and share. This Italian nougat blends the sweetness of caramelized honey, the lightness of meringue, and the crunch of toasted nuts. Torrone is traditionally eaten and gifted around the holiday season and is often served after dinner alongside a digestivo or espresso. Candy making of any kind is not an easy undertaking, but this recipe streamlines the process and makes the torrone very approachable. And nothing will say 'Happy Holidays' to your favorite folks like the care that goes into this stunning confection. I love using Fiori di Sicilia, a mixed-citrus and vanilla extract available from King Arthur Baking, but orange extract is also delicious. Timing is important when working with caramel and meringues. Make sure the caramel is cooled to 280 degrees—but no cooler or it won't pour easily. Be sure that the nuts are still warm when adding them to the nougat for easier incorporation. Edible wafer paper gives torrone its characteristic look and makes it easier to pick up without getting sticky fingers. If your wafer paper has a smooth side and a rough side, the smooth side should be in contact with the torrone."

HOW I GIFT THIS

packaging: Wrap logs tightly in parchment and tie with ribbon on both ends. Place individual pieces in candy cups and then in an airtight gift container.

storage: The torrone can be stored at room temperature for about 2 weeks.

make it a duo: Pair with Baci di Dama (page 227). Or gift with a bottle of amaro, grappa, or Cognac.

make it a trio: Team up with Nutella Rugelach (page 222) and Peppermint Bark (page 204) for a winter holiday trio.

2 (11 by 8-inch) sheets edible wafer paper
3 large egg whites
¼ teaspoon cream of tartar
1¾ cups (12¼ ounces) sugar
¼ cup water
⅛ teaspoon table salt
½ cup honey
¼ cup light corn syrup
1 teaspoon orange extract or Fiori di Sicilia
2 cups (10 ounces) raw pistachios
1 cup dried cherries

1. Adjust oven rack to middle position and heat oven to 350 degrees. Lightly spray bottom and sides of 8-inch square baking pan with vegetable oil spray. Trim edible wafer sheets to match width of bottom of prepared pan (about 7½ inches wide). Press one trimmed wafer sheet, rough side down, into bottom of prepared pan, pressing excess up one side of pan (sheet may extend beyond lip of pan). Set remaining wafer sheet aside.

2. Place egg whites and cream of tartar in bowl of stand mixer fitted with whisk; set aside. Whisk sugar, water, and salt together in bowl. Add honey and corn syrup to large saucepan, then add sugar mixture to center of saucepan, making sure no sugar granules touch sides of saucepan. Cook over medium heat until mixture is bubbling across entire surface, 6 to 8 minutes.

3. Swirl saucepan to even out hot spots, then reduce heat to medium-low and cook, swirling saucepan occasionally, until mixture reaches 320 degrees, 10 to 15 minutes. Remove pan from heat and allow caramel to cool to 280 degrees, about 5 minutes.

recipe continues

4. While syrup cools, whip egg whites and cream of tartar on medium-low speed until foamy, about 1 minute. Increase speed to medium-high and whip until soft peaks form, 2 to 3 minutes.

5. Reduce mixer speed to low. Carefully add 280-degree honey mixture, avoiding whisk and sides of bowl, and mix until incorporated. Increase speed to medium and whip until mixture is pale, stiff, and deflated, about 10 minutes (mixture will almost triple in volume before deflating). Add extract and whip until just combined. While egg white mixture whips, bake nuts on rimmed baking sheet until lightly toasted, about 8 minutes. Transfer sheet to wire rack and set aside.

6. Turn off mixer and remove whisk attachment, scraping nougat from tines of whisk back into bowl. Add warm nuts and cherries to mixer bowl and, using sturdy rubber spatula, fold nuts into nougat. Scrape nougat into center of prepared pan. Press remaining trimmed wafer sheet, rough side facing out, into side of pan opposite wafer overhang. Using greased offset spatula or spoon, spread nougat into even layer. Fold wafer sheet flush across top of nougat, pressing firmly to compress torrone and remove any large air bubbles (sheet may extend beyond lip of pan). Let cool to room temperature, about 30 minutes, then refrigerate until chilled and very firm, about 2 hours.

7. Using excess wafer as handle, pull torrone out of pan and transfer to cutting board. (If torrone sticks to sides of pan, run knife along sides of pan to loosen.) Use kitchen shears to trim excess wafer. Using warm or greased chef's knife, cut torrone into 1-inch-thick slabs, then cut each slab in half crosswise.

variations
ALMOND TORRONE
Substitute 3 cups whole blanched almonds for pistachios and 1 teaspoon vanilla extract for orange extract. Omit dried cherries.

CHOCOLATE-HAZELNUT TORRONE
Substitute 2 cups skinned raw hazelnuts for pistachios and 1 teaspoon vanilla extract for orange extract. In step 6, fold 4 ounces coarsely chopped bittersweet chocolate into nougat with hazelnuts.

USING EDIBLE WAFERS

1. Press one trimmed sheet onto bottom of prepared pan (rough side down if there is a rough side and a smooth side), pressing excess up one side of pan (sheet may extend beyond lip of pan).

2. After adding nougat, press remaining trimmed wafer sheet into side of pan opposite wafer overhang. Spread nougat into even layer using greased offset spatula or spoon.

3. Fold wafer sheet flush across top of nougat, pressing firmly to compress torrone and remove any large air bubbles.

4. Using excess edible wafer paper as handle, pull torrone out of pan and transfer to cutting board. (If torrone sticks to sides of pan, run knife along sides of pan to loosen torrone.)

5. Use kitchen shears to trim excess edible wafer paper.

FLUFFY VANILLA MARSHMALLOWS

makes: 48 marshmallows   **total time:** 50 minutes, plus 4 hours firming

66 If the thought of baking and gifting batches of cookies is a little too much around the holidays, try homemade marshmallows instead. Trust me—they're easier than you think! All you need to do is cook a sugar syrup, stir in gelatin, and whip egg whites in your mixer before streaming in the hot syrup. Then you can sit back and watch the magic: As the mixture whips and cools, it becomes a thick, fluffy cloud. After chilling, it's ready to be cut into squares with a knife or fun shapes with cookie cutters. The egg whites make these lighter and fluffier than store-bought varieties, and a hefty pour of vanilla adds homemade flavor. Or try one of the festive flavor variations (or make them all for a sampler gift). Three ¼-ounce envelopes of gelatin will yield the 2½ tablespoons needed for this recipe. It's important to use an instant-read thermometer. For a cleaner look, you can trim (and snack on) the edges of the marshmallows before cutting them. If you use cookie cutters, remember that your yield will be less than it would be if cutting the 'mallows into 1½-inch squares."

HOW I GIFT THIS

packaging: Regardless of what shape or size you choose, these show off well in a cellophane bag tied with a ribbon and bow or a tin with a clear top.

storage: The marshmallows can be stored at room temperature for about 2 weeks.

make it a trio: Combine with Hot Chocolate Mix (page 52) and either peppermint-stick stirrers or small bottles of rum, brandy, or schnapps.

make it a kit: Create multiple s'mores kits with all the fixings. Get creative with the flavors: I've been known to pack caramelized white chocolate bars with the eggnog marshmallows and lemon curd with the lemon-strawberry marshmallows.

1 cup water, divided
2½ tablespoons unflavored gelatin
2 large egg whites
2 cups (14 ounces) granulated sugar
½ cup light corn syrup
¼ teaspoon table salt
1 tablespoon vanilla extract
⅔ cup (2⅔ ounces) confectioners' sugar
⅓ cup (1⅓ ounces) cornstarch

1. Make foil sling for 13 by 9-inch baking pan by folding 2 long sheets of aluminum foil; first sheet should be 13 inches wide and second sheet should be 9 inches wide. Lay sheets of foil in pan perpendicular to each other, with extra foil hanging over edges of pan. Push foil into corners and up sides of pan, smoothing foil flush to pan. Spray foil with vegetable oil spray.

2. Whisk ½ cup water and gelatin together in bowl and let sit until very firm, about 5 minutes. Add egg whites to bowl of stand mixer fitted with whisk attachment.

3. Combine granulated sugar, corn syrup, salt, and remaining ½ cup water in large saucepan. Bring to boil over medium-high heat and cook, gently swirling saucepan occasionally, until sugar has dissolved completely and mixture registers 240 degrees (soft-ball stage), 6 to 8 minutes. Off heat, immediately whisk in gelatin mixture until gelatin is dissolved.

4. Working quickly, whip whites on high speed until soft peaks form, 1 to 2 minutes. With mixer running, carefully pour hot syrup into whites, avoiding whisk and bowl as much as possible. Whip until mixture is very thick and stiff and bowl is only slightly warm to touch, about 10 minutes. Reduce speed to low and add vanilla. Slowly increase speed to high and mix until incorporated, about 30 seconds, scraping down bowl as needed.

recipe continues

5. Transfer mixture to prepared pan and spread into even layer using greased rubber spatula. Let sit at room temperature until firm, at least 4 hours.

6. Lightly coat chef's knife or cookie cutters with oil spray. Whisk confectioners' sugar and cornstarch together in bowl. Lightly dust top of marshmallows with 2 tablespoons confectioners' sugar mixture. Transfer remaining confectioners' sugar mixture to 1-gallon zipper-lock bag. Place cutting board over pan of marshmallows and carefully invert pan and board. Remove pan and peel off foil.

7. If cutting into squares with knife, cut marshmallows crosswise into 8 strips, then cut each strip into 6 squares (marshmallows will be approximate 1½-inch squares). If using cookie cutters, make shapes as close together as possible to minimize waste.

8. Separate marshmallows and add half to confectioners' sugar mixture in bag. Seal bag and shake to coat marshmallows. Using your hands, remove marshmallows from bag and transfer to colander. Shake colander to remove excess confectioners' sugar mixture. Repeat with remaining marshmallows.

variations

FLUFFY EGGNOG MARSHMALLOWS

Substitute 2 tablespoons dark rum, ⅛ teaspoon ground nutmeg, and pinch ground cinnamon for vanilla.

FLUFFY LEMON-STRAWBERRY MARSHMALLOWS

Grind ½ ounce freeze-dried strawberries to powder in spice grinder. Add ground strawberries with vanilla. Stir in 1 tablespoon grated lemon zest with rubber spatula before transferring marshmallow mixture to prepared pan.

FLUFFY MOCHA MARSHMALLOWS

Add ¼ cup natural unsweetened cocoa powder and 2 tablespoons instant espresso powder with vanilla. Add 2 tablespoons natural unsweetened cocoa powder to confectioners' sugar mixture.

FLUFFY PEPPERMINT SWIRL MARSHMALLOWS

Add ⅛ teaspoon peppermint extract with vanilla. After spreading marshmallow mixture in pan, evenly drop 12 drops red food coloring over marshmallow mixture. Using clean, dry paring knife, swirl food coloring into marshmallow mixture.

MAKING 'MALLOWS

  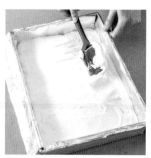 

1. Cook sugar, water, corn syrup, and salt to 240 degrees, or soft-ball stage.

2. With mixer running, pour syrup into egg whites, avoiding sides of bowl and whisk.

3. Transfer marshmallow mixture to greased foil-lined pan and smooth top.

4. Cut marshmallows into 1½-inch squares using greased knife.

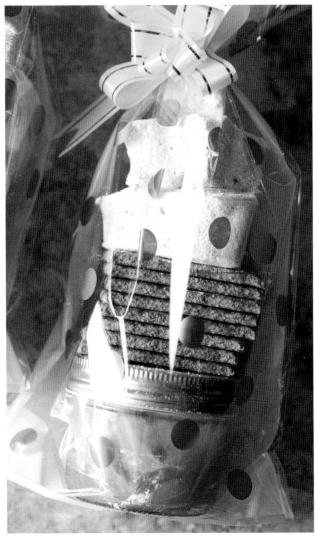

PEPPERMINT BARK

serves: 12   **total time:** 25 minutes, plus 1 hour chilling

" This three-ingredient peppermint bark is more chocolaty, more minty, and way prettier than any $30 store-bought version in a tin. (Hello, holiday price-gouging?) Plus, it's fast, easy, and fun to make. Get rid of holiday stress by crushing those candy canes. Then, revel in a little zen thinking while you swirl the melted white chocolate through the semisweet chocolate in the baking pan and artfully sprinkle the candy over the top. And finally, indulge in a taste-test of your creation before packing it all up into a thrifted or recycled tin, cellophane bags tied with ribbons, or little windowed cardboard boxes. Greetings of the season!"

HOW I GIFT THIS

packaging: The bark looks so festive packaged in a cellophane bag swaddled in beaded tulle and tied up with a ribbon.

storage: The peppermint bark can be refrigerated for about 1 week.

make it a duo: If practical, give with vanilla or chocolate ice cream for a decadent dessert gift.

make it a trio: Combine with Hot Chocolate Mix (page 52) and Fluffy Peppermint Swirl Marshmallows (page 202).

18 mini candy canes or 6 large candy canes or
    20 peppermint candies
 2 cups (12 ounces) semisweet chocolate chips
 2 cups (12 ounces) white chocolate chips

1. Make foil sling for 13 by 9-inch baking pan by folding 2 long sheets of aluminum foil; first sheet should be 13 inches wide and second sheet should be 9 inches wide. Lay sheets of foil in pan perpendicular to each other, with extra foil hanging over edges of pan. Push foil into corners and up sides of pan, smoothing foil flush to pan. Lightly spray foil with vegetable oil spray.

2. Place candy canes in large zipper-lock bag. Seal bag, making sure to press out all air. Use rolling pin to gently pound candy into small pieces (you should have ½ cup pieces); set aside.

3. Microwave semisweet chocolate chips in medium bowl at 50 percent power until mostly melted, 2 to 3 minutes. Remove bowl from microwave and stir with rubber spatula until smooth; set aside. Microwave white chocolate chips in second medium bowl at 50 percent power until mostly melted, 2 to 3 minutes. Remove bowl from microwave and stir with clean rubber spatula until smooth.

4. Use clean rubber spatula to scrape reserved melted semisweet chocolate into prepared pan and smooth top (make sure to get all the way into corners of pan). Pour melted white chocolate over top. Drag tip of clean rubber spatula through chocolate to create swirls. Sprinkle reserved pounded candy canes on top of chocolate. Cover pan with plastic wrap and refrigerate until firm, about 1 hour. Using foil overhang, lift bark out of pan, then break into pieces.

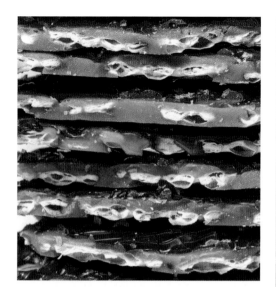

CHOCOLATE MATZO TOFFEE

serves: 8 to 12   **total time:** 45 minutes, plus 30 minutes chilling

66 Matzo toffee is sweet, salty, crunchy, chocolaty, pretty, and stores well, which in my book makes for an ideal giftable treat. This classic Passover offering can be a sweet nibble throughout the week or included as part of a seder dessert spread. It was originally developed by cookbook author and pastry chef Marcy Goldman: Matzo sheets are covered in a layer of bubbling butter and brown sugar, baked, then topped with melted chocolate. In this version, the toffee is made entirely on the stovetop to better control its temperature (be sure to use an instant-read thermometer), creating toffee with a just-right crunch. Breaking up the matzo lets the hot toffee soak in better. Drizzling on tempered chocolate and a sprinkle of flake salt adds to its irresistible flavor and appearance. Feel free to add other toppings like finely chopped nuts, shredded coconut, or sprinkles. If you can only find salted matzo, reduce the table salt to ¼ teaspoon. Grating the chocolate is important for the innovative-yet-easy step of tempering the chocolate in the microwave; the small holes on a box grater work well. To make this kosher for Passover, use kosher for Passover ingredients and follow appropriate food preparation rules. To make this pareve (that is, neutral), use vegan chocolate and 16 tablespoons (8 ounces) unsalted margarine instead of the 20 tablespoons butter. Reduce the heat to medium-low after bringing the sugar mixture to a boil in step 1 to avoid separation between the margarine and sugar."

- -

HOW I GIFT THIS

packaging: Packing the pieces in a pretty tin keeps them nice and crisp.

storage: The matzo toffee can be refrigerated for about 2 weeks.

make it a duo: Pair with Citrus Burst Black Tea Blend (page 57), store-bought macaroons, or a Passover seder plate.

3 sheets plain unsalted matzo

1½ cups packed (10½ ounces) light brown sugar

20 tablespoons (2½ sticks) unsalted butter, cut into 20 pieces

¼ cup water

½ teaspoon table salt

6 ounces bittersweet chocolate (4 ounces finely chopped, 2 ounces grated)

1¼ teaspoons flake sea salt

1. Line rimmed baking sheet with parchment paper. Break matzo into rough 1½-inch square pieces and spread into even layer on prepared sheet (some pieces may overlap; this is OK); place sheet on wire rack and set aside. Combine sugar, butter, water, and table salt in large saucepan. Bring to boil over medium heat, and cook, stirring frequently, until syrup is amber colored and thickened, and registers 300 to 305 degrees, 10 to 20 minutes. (Don't be alarmed if syrup pauses between 230 and 240 degrees.)

2. Working quickly, carefully pour toffee over matzo on prepared sheet, drizzling from side to side and front to back of sheet to distribute evenly. Using offset spatula, spread toffee as evenly as possible over matzo (some edges of matzo may not be fully covered; this is OK). Let toffee cool for 20 minutes.

3. Microwave finely chopped chocolate in bowl at 50 percent power, stirring every 20 to 30 seconds, until about two-thirds melted, 2 to 4 minutes. (Melted chocolate should not be much warmer than body temperature; check by holding bowl in palm of your hand.) Add grated chocolate and stir until smooth. Return chocolate to microwave for no more than 5 seconds at a time to finish melting , if necessary.

4. Drizzle chocolate evenly over cooled toffee, then sprinkle with flake sea salt. Refrigerate until firm, about 30 minutes. Break toffee into large pieces.

STUFFED DATES
(PAGE 210)

STUFFED DATES

Show-stopping stuffed medjool dates are just the thing to give to the person in your life who likes a little glamour. These flavorful little jewels are often given to mark Eid al-Fitr, the holiday celebrating the end of the month-long dawn-to-sunset fasting of Ramadan. But they're also a popular gift to bring to a dinner party at any time of the year. In the Middle East, boxes of stuffed dates line the cases at artisanal candy shops, where they are speckled with vibrant green pistachios, coated in shredded coconut, dipped in chocolate, filled with dried fruit, and more. The flavor possibilities are seemingly endless. It's traditional to give an assortment of flavors, so here are four equally irresistible renditions. Each recipe is scaled to make just 5 dates in order to make it easy for you to mix and match flavors."

HOW I GIFT THIS

packaging: These are traditionally given a grand presentation in an inlaid or wooden box. You could also pack them into rectangular macaron boxes, nestling each one in a paper candy cup, if you like. Presenting a variety of fillings, as is traditional, makes the gift even more visually striking.

storage: The dates can be refrigerated for about 1 month.

big-batch it: Each variation can be easily scaled up to make as many stuffed dates as you want.

make it a trio: Team up with a Turkish coffeepot and a bag of ground Turkish coffee.

WALNUT-POMEGRANATE STUFFED DATES

makes: 5 dates   **total time:** 10 minutes

You can use walnut pieces in place of the walnut halves; you'll need about 1 teaspoon per date.

  5 pitted medjool dates
 10 walnut halves
  1 teaspoon date molasses
  5 teaspoons unsweetened shredded coconut
 ¾ teaspoon freeze-dried pomegranate seeds (optional)

Using paring knife, cut slit down length of each date, without cutting through entirely. Working with 1 date at a time, gently open date at slit and stuff with 2 walnut halves. Place date molasses in small bowl and coconut in second small bowl. Working with one date at a time, dip one end of date in molasses then dip in coconut, pressing to adhere. Sprinkle freeze-dried pomegranates over walnuts, if using.

PISTACHIO-ORANGE STUFFED DATES

makes: 5 dates   total time: 10 minutes

    5 pitted medjool dates
    5 teaspoons pistachios, chopped
    ¼ teaspoon grated orange zest
    ⅛ teaspoon flake sea salt

Using paring knife, cut slit down length of each date, without
cutting through entirely. Combine pistachios, orange zest,
and salt in bowl. Working with 1 date at a time, gently open
date at slit and stuff with 1 teaspoon pistachio mixture.

CHOCOLATE-ALMOND STUFFED DATES

makes: 5 dates   total time: 20 minutes

    5 pitted medjool dates
    5 whole almonds
    2 ounces bittersweet chocolate (1½ ounces chopped
       fine, ½ ounce grated)
    2 tablespoons very finely chopped pistachios

1. Using paring knife, cut slit down length of each date,
without cutting through entirely. Working with 1 date at a
time, gently open date at slit and stuff with one almond;
set aside.

2. Microwave finely chopped chocolate in bowl at 50 percent
power, stirring often, until about two-thirds melted, 2 to
4 minutes. (Melted chocolate should not be much warmer
than body temperature; check by holding bowl in palm of
your hand.) Add grated chocolate and stir until smooth.
Return bowl of chocolate to the microwave for no more than
5 seconds at a time to finish melting (if necessary).

3. Place pistachios in small bowl. Working with one date at
a time, dip each date in chocolate to cover as much of date
as desired, then transfer to bowl with pistachios and toss to
coat. Refrigerate until chocolate is set, about 10 minutes.

SNICKERS STUFFED DATES

makes: 5 dates   total time: 40 minutes

*You won't use the whole jar of coconut butter, so purchase the
smallest size you can find. You'll brown more coconut butter than
you need for this recipe; leftovers can be refrigerated for up to
1 month and are delicious on toast.*

    1 (15-ounce) jar coconut butter
    5 teaspoons chopped unsalted dry-roasted peanuts
    1 teaspoon packed brown sugar
    ¾ teaspoon red miso
    5 pitted medjool dates
    2 ounces bittersweet chocolate (1½ ounces chopped
       fine, ½ ounce grated)

1. Place jar of coconut butter in pot of just-simmering water
until coconut butter is softened. Stir to recombine. Transfer
½ cup coconut butter to small saucepan and cook over
medium-low heat, stirring frequently, until medium brown,
about 5 minutes; transfer to bowl to cool slightly.

2. Combine 1½ tablespoons browned coconut butter,
peanuts, sugar, and miso in now-empty saucepan. Cook
over medium-low heat until sugar dissolves, about 2 minutes.
Transfer peanut mixture to bowl and set aside until cool
enough to handle, about 10 minutes.

3. Using paring knife, cut slit down length of each date,
without cutting through entirely. Working with 1 date at
a time, gently open date at slit and stuff with 1 heaping
teaspoon peanut mixture.

4. Microwave finely chopped chocolate in bowl at 50 percent
power, stirring often, until about two-thirds melted, 2 to
4 minutes. (Melted chocolate should not be much warmer
than body temperature; check by holding bowl in palm of
your hand.) Add grated chocolate and stir until smooth.
Return bowl of chocolate to microwave for no more than
5 seconds at a time to finish melting (if necessary).

5. Working with 1 date at a time, dip each date in chocolate
to cover as much of date as desired, then refrigerate until
chocolate is set, about 10 minutes.

THIN AND CRISPY CHOCOLATE CHIP COOKIES

makes: 16 cookies   **total time:** 50 minutes, plus 20 minutes cooling

> 66 I've got to be honest, most of the time I prefer my chocolate chip cookies chunky and chewy and so fresh from the oven that they're still kind of droopy from the heat. But that's not an easy treat to gift. Instead, when I want chocolate chip cookies that can hold up perfectly to packing for gifting, I turn to this recipe, which creates a thin, crisp cookie that's perfectly flat, almost praline-like in appearance. It also packs a big crunch along with all the flavor you're looking for from semisweet chips, brown sugar, and butter. Incorporating some granulated sugar helps keep them crisp (since it has less moisture than brown sugar), and using egg yolks, rather than whole eggs, helps keep the cookies nice and flat. Note that this recipe calls for cake flour and mini (not full-size) chocolate chips."

HOW I GIFT THIS

packaging: These cookies call for a classic cookie jar–style presentation.

storage: The cookies can be stored at room temperature for about 3 days.

make it a duo: Pair with Hot Chocolate Mix (page 52) or Cold Brew Coffee Concentrate (page 58).

add to a basket: Include in the Summer Supper basket (page 145) or the Snack Care Package (page 84).

1¼ cups (5 ounces) cake flour
¾ teaspoon table salt
¼ teaspoon baking soda
8 tablespoons unsalted butter, melted and cooled
⅓ cup (2⅓ ounces) granulated sugar
⅓ cup packed (2⅓ ounces) dark brown sugar
2 large egg yolks
1½ tablespoons whole milk
2 teaspoons vanilla extract
¾ cup (4½ ounces) mini semisweet chocolate chips

1. Adjust oven rack to middle position and heat oven to 350 degrees. Line 2 rimmed baking sheets with parchment paper. Whisk flour, salt, and baking soda together in bowl.

2. Using stand mixer fitted with paddle, mix melted butter, granulated sugar, and brown sugar on low speed until fully combined. Increase speed to medium-high and beat until mixture is lightened in color, about 1 minute. Reduce speed to low; add egg yolks, milk, and vanilla; and mix until combined. Slowly add flour mixture and mix until just combined, scraping down bowl as needed. Using rubber spatula, stir in chocolate chips.

3. Using greased 1-tablespoon measure, divide dough into 16 heaping-tablespoon portions on prepared sheets, 8 portions per sheet. Divide any remaining dough evenly among portions. Using your moistened fingers, press dough portions to ½-inch thickness. Bake cookies, 1 sheet at a time, until deep golden brown, 16 to 18 minutes, rotating sheet halfway through baking. Transfer sheet to wire rack and let cookies cool completely, about 20 minutes.

SPICY MOCHA SANDWICH COOKIES WITH DULCE DE LECHE

makes: 20 cookies   **total time:** 45 minutes, plus 40 minutes cooling

> " These adorable little sandwich cookies pack a lot of complex flavor in their petite package and would be a total standout at any holiday cookie swap. For a bit of flavor intrigue, the soft chocolate cookies are spiced up with coffee liqueur and cayenne pepper and their exterior is coated with ground almonds. The dulce de leche filling makes for a gooey sweet caramel surprise that complements and enhances the chocolaty cookies. Use either Kahlúa or Tia Maria for the coffee liqueur. "

HOW I GIFT THIS

packaging: These look pretty when jumbled up in a small tin or tucked into empty spaces in a larger cookie basket.

storage: The cookies can be stored at room temperature for about 3 days.

make it a duo: Pair with Baci di Dama (page 227) for the cutest cookie duo ever. Or pair with Coffee Liqueur (page 125) or Dulce de Leche (page 63).

add to a basket: Include in the For the Love of Chocolate basket (page 235).

⅓ cup blanched almonds
1½ cups (7½ ounces) all-purpose flour
¼ cup (¾ ounce) Dutch-processed cocoa powder
½ teaspoon salt
¼ teaspoon cayenne pepper
4 ounces bittersweet chocolate, melted and cooled
12 tablespoons unsalted butter, softened
⅔ cup (4⅔ ounces) sugar
2 large egg yolks
2 tablespoons coffee liqueur
1 teaspoon vanilla extract
¼ cup dulce de leche

1. Adjust oven racks to upper-middle and lower-middle positions and heat oven to 350 degrees. Line 2 baking sheets with parchment paper. Process almonds in food processor until finely ground, about 30 seconds. Combine flour, cocoa, salt, and cayenne in bowl.

2. Microwave chocolate in bowl at 50 percent power, stirring occasionally, until melted, 2 to 4 minutes. Using stand mixer fitted with paddle, beat butter and sugar on medium-high speed until pale and fluffy, about 2 minutes. Add melted chocolate, egg yolks, liqueur, and vanilla and beat until incorporated. Reduce speed to low, add flour mixture in 3 additions, and mix until just combined, scraping down bowl as needed.

3. Working with 2-teaspoon portions at a time, roll into balls and space them 1 inch apart on prepared sheets. Sprinkle ground almonds on top, pressing lightly to adhere. Bake cookies until edges appear dry, 8 to 10 minutes, switching and rotating sheets halfway through baking. Let cookies cool on sheets for 5 minutes, then transfer to wire rack and let cool completely, about 40 minutes.

4. Spread ½ teaspoon dulce de leche over bottom of half of cookies, then top with remaining cookies, pressing gently to adhere.

EASY HOLIDAY SUGAR COOKIES

makes: forty 2½-inch cookies   total time: 1¾ hours plus 4½ hours chilling, cooling, and drying

66 These cookies are my family's go-to recipe for our annual Christmas cookie party, but they can be customized for any holiday. I've been known to use pumpkin cookie cutters and orange-tinted icing for Halloween and daisy cutters and pastel icing for Mother's Day. You can just spread the icing with an icing spatula, or load the icing into a piping bag to make lines, squiggles, dots, or any design your heart desires. Sugar cookies are universally loved and endlessly versatile for any occasion. In step 3, use a combination of rolling and a pushing or smearing motion to form the dough into an oval. The dough scraps can be combined and rerolled once, though the cookies will be slightly less tender. Be sure to use a rimless baking sheet to ensure a perfectly even bake."

HOW I GIFT THIS

packaging: Upcycle your store-bought cookie tins, or look for a secondhand cookie jar or tin to add a personal touch to this gift.

storage: The cookies can be stored at room temperature for about 4 days.

make it DIY: Give the rolled and plastic-wrapped dough, the icing recipe, and fun cookie cutters for an interactive, kid-friendly present.

make it a trio: Give with Hot Chocolate Mix (page 52) and Fluffy Vanilla Marshmallows (page 201).

cookies
- 1 large egg
- 1 teaspoon vanilla extract
- ¾ teaspoon table salt
- ¼ teaspoon almond extract
- 2½ cups (12½ ounces) all-purpose flour
- ¼ teaspoon baking powder
- ¼ teaspoon baking soda
- 1 cup (7 ounces) granulated sugar
- 16 tablespoons unsalted butter, cut into ½-inch pieces and chilled

icing
- 2⅔ cups (10⅔ ounces) confectioners' sugar
- 2 large egg whites
- ½ teaspoon vanilla extract
- ⅛ teaspoon table salt

1. **for the cookies:** Whisk egg, vanilla, salt, and almond extract together in small bowl. Whisk flour, baking powder, and baking soda together in second bowl.

2. Process granulated sugar in food processor until finely ground, about 30 seconds. Add butter and process until uniform mass forms and no large pieces of butter are visible, about 30 seconds, scraping down sides of bowl as needed. Add egg mixture and process until smooth and paste-like, about 10 seconds. Add flour mixture and process until no dry flour remains but mixture remains crumbly, about 30 seconds, scraping down sides of bowl as needed.

3. Turn out dough onto counter and gently knead by hand until smooth, about 10 seconds. Divide dough in half. Place 1 piece of dough in center of large sheet of parchment paper and press into 7 by 9-inch oval. Place second large sheet of parchment over dough and roll dough into 10 by 14-inch oval of even ⅛-inch thickness. Transfer dough with parchment to rimmed baking sheet. Repeat pressing and rolling with second piece of dough, then stack on top of first piece on sheet. Refrigerate until dough is firm, at least 1½ hours (or freeze for 30 minutes). (Rolled dough can be wrapped in plastic wrap and refrigerated for up to 5 days.)

4. Adjust oven rack to lower-middle position and heat oven to 300 degrees. Line rimless cookie sheet with parchment. Working with 1 piece of rolled dough, gently peel off top layer of parchment. Replace parchment, loosely covering dough. (Peeling off parchment and returning it will make cutting and removing cookies easier.) Turn over dough and parchment and gently peel off and discard second piece of parchment. Using cookie cutter, cut dough into shapes. Transfer shapes to prepared cookie sheet, spacing them about ½ inch apart.

Bake until cookies are lightly and evenly browned around edges, 14 to 17 minutes, rotating sheet halfway through baking. Let cookies cool on sheet for 5 minutes, then transfer to wire rack and let cool completely, about 25 minutes. Repeat with remaining dough. (Dough scraps can be patted together, rerolled, and chilled once before cutting and baking.)

5. for the icing: Using stand mixer fitted with whisk attachment, whip all ingredients on medium-low speed until combined, about 1 minute. Increase speed to medium-high and whip until glossy, soft peaks form, 3 to 4 minutes, scraping down bowl as needed. Spread icing onto cooled cookies. Let icing dry completely, about 1½ hours.

CUSTOM COOKIE ASSORTMENT

" For me, cookie gift assortments are synonymous with end-of-year holidays—I know that's when I most often give them, and it's the same for many of my friends. But that doesn't mean they can't also be given for other occasions. Also think about birthdays, graduations, or back-to-school time; a thank-you gift for indispensable folks in your life like the mail carrier, vet, or house cleaner; or a pick-me-up for a friend who's feeling down. You can customize the cookie varieties or the decorations to suit any theme or occasion. I love representing different cultural traditions in my cookie assortments. Iced sugar cookies are a versatile American classic, while biscotti and shortbread reflect European cookie traditions. You can include any cookies you like or that you know are your recipient's favorites."

HOW I GIFT THIS

The photo here shows a go-all-out Christmas-themed "basket," with cookies, candies, and ornaments all tucked into an ornament box. But you could use a decorative tin or box of any size or shape, adding dividers (see page 186) and matching the container to the occasion. Whenever I put together a cookie basket, I make sure to choose at least one or two recipes that can be made reasonably well ahead of gifting time, so that I'm not baking multiple kinds of cookies on the same day.

START WITH

Easy Holiday Sugar Cookies (page 216)

Hazelnut-Rosemary-Orange Biscotti (page 233)

Millionaire's Shortbread (page 224)

IF YOU WANT, ADD

Cinnamon-Walnut Rugelach (page 223)

Spicy Mocha Sandwich Cookies with Dulce de Leche (page 215)

Scotcheroos (page 241)

Assorted store-bought candies or other goodies that match your theme

SHORTBREAD COOKIES

makes: 28 cookies   **total time:** 1¾ hours, plus 1 hour cooling

66 These oaty shortbread cookies, a traditional New Year's cookie in Scotland, are a simple, appealing present for any occasion. I often give them when I need to thank my neighbors for a favor. Rather than shape the dough into wedges, you'll shape it into squared-off logs for slice-and-bake ease. The cookies are certainly delicious enough to be given plain, or you can elevate them by decorating with one of the glaze variations. I like the simplicity of dipping just half of each cookie in the coating, but you'll have enough that you can get creative (try drizzling the coating over the top, or dip one entire side, or try something else that strikes your fancy). Don't substitute quick or instant oats in this recipe. If you don't have a spice grinder, you can pulse the oats in a blender."

HOW I GIFT THIS

packaging: Gift these sweet cookies in a tin (maybe a repurposed shortbread tin) or in a clear bag tied with ribbon to show off the glazes.

storage: The shortbread can be stored at room temperature for about 1 week.

make it a duo: Pair with the Citrus Burst Black Tea Blend (page 57) or Hot Chocolate Mix (page 52). If you're giving unglazed shortbread, you could pair it with a jar of Dulce de Leche (page 63). Or give a holiday shortbread sampler duo by pairing these with the Millionaire's Shortbread (page 224).

½ cup (1½ ounces) old-fashioned rolled oats
1½ cups (7½ ounces) all-purpose flour
⅔ cup (2⅔ ounces) confectioners' sugar
¼ cup (1 ounce) cornstarch
½ teaspoon table salt
14 tablespoons unsalted butter, cut into ⅛-inch-thick slices and chilled

1. Pulse oats in spice grinder until reduced to fine powder, about ten 5-second pulses (you should have ⅓ cup oat flour; discard any extra). Using stand mixer fitted with paddle attachment, mix oat flour, all-purpose flour, sugar, cornstarch, and salt on low speed until combined. Add butter and mix until dough just forms and pulls away from sides of bowl, 5 to 10 minutes.

2. Transfer dough to center of sheet of plastic wrap. Draw edges of plastic over dough and press firmly on sides and top to form rough 8 by 6-inch rectangle. Wrap in plastic wrap and use bench scraper to press sides and top into smooth, compact 7 by 5-inch rectangle, adjusting plastic as needed. Refrigerate dough until firm, at least 30 minutes or up to 3 days.

3. Adjust oven rack to middle position and heat oven to 425 degrees. Line rimmed baking sheet with parchment paper. Using chef's knife, cut dough in half lengthwise (you should have two 7-inch long by 2½-inch wide rectangles). Cut rectangles crosswise into ½-inch-thick slices (you should have 28 slices). Transfer slices, cut side down, to prepared sheet, spacing them about ½ inch apart.

4. If desired, use wooden skewer or fork to poke 8 to 10 holes in center of each slice. Place sheet in oven and immediately reduce oven temperature to 300 degrees. Bake for 40 minutes until pale golden, rotating sheet halfway through baking. Transfer sheet to wire rack and let cool completely, about 1 hour.

CHOCOLATE-DIPPED SHORTBREAD COOKIES

    8 ounces bittersweet chocolate (6 ounces finely
       chopped, 2 ounces grated)
    1 recipe Shortbread Cookies
       Flake sea salt (optional)

Set wire rack in parchment paper–lined rimmed baking sheet. Microwave finely chopped chocolate in bowl at 50 percent power, stirring often, until about two-thirds melted, 2 to 4 minutes. (Melted chocolate should not be much warmer than body temperature; check by holding bowl in palm of your hand.) Add grated chocolate and stir until smooth. Return bowl of chocolate to microwave for no more than 5 seconds at a time to finish melting (if necessary). Working quickly and with 1 shortbread cookie at a time, dip half of cookie into melted chocolate. Lift up from chocolate (do not turn upright) and gently shake side to side to allow excess coating to drip off evenly. Transfer to prepared rack; sprinkle with salt, if using; and let sit until firm, about 1 hour. (If chocolate begins to firm during dipping, microwave chocolate for no more than 5 seconds at a time, stirring after each interval.)

RASPBERRY-DIPPED SHORTBREAD COOKIES

    ½ cup (½ ounce) freeze-dried raspberries
    ½ cup refined coconut oil
    ¾ cup (3⅓ ounces) confectioners' sugar
    1 recipe Shortbread Cookies

Set wire rack in parchment paper–lined rimmed baking sheet. Pulse freeze-dried raspberries in spice grinder until reduced to fine powder, about ten 5-second pulses (you should have ⅓ cup fruit powder). Sift powder through fine-mesh strainer to remove any seeds: discard seeds. Microwave oil in bowl at 50 percent power, stirring occasionally, until melted, 1 to 2 minutes. Stir in fruit powder and sugar until completely smooth. Working quickly, with 1 shortbread cookie at a time, dip half of cookie into oil mixture. Lift up from glaze (do not turn upright) and gently shake side to side to allow excess coating to drip off evenly. Transfer to prepared rack and let sit until firm, about 1 hour. (If glaze begins to firm during dipping, microwave oil until fluid, about 10 seconds. Stir to recombine before continuing.)

NUTELLA RUGELACH

makes: 32 cookies   total time: 1¾ hours, plus 1 hour 20 minutes chilling and cooling

66 Part cookie, part pastry, rugelach are a traditional Jewish bakery snack. They are often given at Hanukkah, and sometimes at Rosh Hashanah, but they make great gifts year-round and always look impressive. I like to enjoy them with a hot cup of coffee or tea on any given Sunday. Their tight curls can contain a variety of bounteous sweet fillings, from nuts and jam to dried fruit to chocolate. The Nutella filling is a modern twist on the more traditional chocolate filling. This recipe uses more flour than most recipes call for, which helps make the dough more workable. A couple of tablespoons of sour cream in addition to the traditional cream cheese makes the cookies even more tender. Be sure to stop processing the dough when the mixture resembles moist crumbs; you do not want the dough to gather into a cohesive mass around the blade of the food processor. If at any point during the cutting and rolling of the crescents the sheet of dough softens and becomes hard to roll, slide it onto a baking sheet and freeze until it is firm enough to handle. When brushing the rugelach with the egg wash, brush only a few cookies at a time and then sprinkle with the demerara sugar. If you brush the egg wash onto all the rugelach at once, it will begin to dry by the time you get to the last rugelach, and the sugar won't stick."

HOW I GIFT THIS

packaging: Pack these into a glass cookie jar, a windowed bakery box, or a cellophane bag tied with a ribbon.

storage: The rugelach can be stored at room temperature for about 3 days.

make it a duo: Pair with one of the Tea Blends (page 57), the Cold Brew Coffee Concentrate (page 58), or the Easy Holiday Sugar Cookies (page 216), cut with Hanukkah-themed cutters.

make it a trio: Add a jar of local honey and a bag of fresh-picked apples for Rosh Hashanah.

1½ cups (7½ ounces) all-purpose flour
¼ cup (1¾ ounces) granulated sugar
¼ teaspoon table salt
6 ounces cream cheese, cut into 3 pieces and chilled
10 tablespoons unsalted butter, cut into ½-inch pieces and chilled
¼ cup sour cream
⅔ cup Nutella, divided
1 large egg, beaten with 1 tablespoon water
1 tablespoon demerara sugar (optional)

1. Process flour, granulated sugar, and salt in food processor until combined, about 3 seconds. Add cream cheese and pulse until large, irregularly sized chunks of cream cheese form with some small pieces interspersed throughout, about 5 pulses. Scatter butter over top and pulse until butter is size of large peas, 5 to 7 pulses.

2. Add sour cream and process until dough forms little clumps that hold together when pinched with your fingers (dough will look crumbly), about 10 seconds.

3. Transfer dough to clean counter and knead briefly until it just comes together, about 3 turns. Divide dough in half (each piece should weigh about 11 ounces) and form each piece into 4-inch disk. Wrap disks individually with plastic wrap and refrigerate for at least 1 hour or up to 2 days.

4. Adjust oven rack to middle position and heat oven to 375 degrees. Line rimmed baking sheet with parchment paper. Roll 1 dough disk into 12-inch circle on lightly floured counter. Using offset spatula, spread ⅓ cup Nutella evenly over entire surface of circle. Using pizza wheel or sharp knife, cut through center of circle to form 16 equal wedges. Starting at wide edge of each wedge, roll dough toward point and transfer to prepared sheet, seam side down.

5. Wipe counter clean, dust counter with additional flour, and repeat with remaining dough disk and remaining ⅓ cup Nutella. Arrange rugelach in 8 rows of four on prepared sheet.

6. Working with few rugelach at a time, brush tops with egg wash, then sprinkle with demerara sugar, if using. Bake until golden brown, 30 to 35 minutes. Let cookies cool completely on sheet tray, about 20 minutes.

variation

CINNAMON-WALNUT RUGELACH

Omit Nutella. Pulse ½ cup walnuts, ½ cup packed (3½ ounces) brown sugar, 1½ teaspoons ground cinnamon, and ¼ teaspoon table salt in food processor until finely ground, about 20 pulses. After rolling 1 dough disk into 12-inch circle in step 4, sprinkle half of walnut mixture over entire surface. Sprinkle remaining walnut mixture over second dough disk in step 5.

MILLIONAIRE'S SHORTBREAD

makes: 40 bars   total time: 1½ hours, plus 2 hours cooling

66 Millionaire's shortbread is by far
one of the most requested cookies
amongst my friends, and what a fitting
name for this impressively rich Scottish
cookie. It has a buttery shortbread base
topped with a caramel-like layer, which
in turn is topped with a layer of shiny
chocolate. It's a beautiful holiday or
host/hostess gift—and the top chocolate layer will maintain its attractive
glossy sheen thanks to the test kitchen's
easy microwave method for tempering
chocolate. The caramel portion of
this cookie is unique, as it's based on
sweetened condensed milk, which
gives it a luxurious creaminess. And
the shortbread itself is just a quick
pat-in-the-pan situation. Make sure
to monitor the caramel's temperature
with an instant-read thermometer."

HOW I GIFT THIS

packaging: For a special mini gift
presentation, tie little stacks of cookies
with parchment and twine. Or layer
the bars in a tin between pieces of
parchment paper.

storage: The shortbread can be stored
at room temperature for about 1 week.

make it a duo: Pair these luxe Scottish
cookies with a bottle of Scotch.

crust
2½ cups (12½ ounces) all-purpose flour
½ cup (3½ ounces) granulated sugar
¾ teaspoon table salt
16 tablespoons unsalted butter, melted

filling
1 (14-ounce) can sweetened condensed milk
1 cup packed (7 ounces) brown sugar
½ cup heavy cream
½ cup corn syrup
8 tablespoons unsalted butter
½ teaspoon table salt

chocolate
8 ounces bittersweet chocolate (6 ounces
chopped fine, 2 ounces grated)

1. for the crust: Adjust oven rack to lower-middle position and heat oven to
350 degrees. Make foil sling for 13 by 9-inch baking pan by folding 2 long sheets
of aluminum foil; first sheet should be 13 inches wide and second sheet should be
9 inches wide. Lay sheets of foil in pan perpendicular to each other, with extra foil
hanging over edges of pan. Push foil into corners and up sides of pan, smoothing
foil flush to pan.

2. Combine flour, granulated sugar, and salt in medium bowl. Add melted butter
and stir with rubber spatula until flour is evenly moistened. Crumble dough evenly
over bottom of prepared pan. Using your fingertips and palm of your hand, press
and smooth dough into even thickness. Using fork, pierce dough at 1-inch intervals.
Bake until light golden brown and firm to touch, 25 to 30 minutes. Transfer pan
to wire rack. Using sturdy metal spatula, press on entire surface of warm crust to
compress (this will make finished bars easier to cut). Let crust cool until it is just
warm, at least 20 minutes.

3. for the filling: Stir all ingredients together in large, heavy-bottomed saucepan.
Cook over medium heat, stirring frequently, until mixture registers between 236 and
239 degrees (temperature will fluctuate), 16 to 20 minutes.

4. Pour filling over crust and spread to even thickness (mixture will be very hot).
Let cool completely, about 1½ hours.

5. for the chocolate: Microwave finely chopped chocolate in bowl at 50 percent power, stirring often, until about two-thirds melted, 1 to 2 minutes. (Melted chocolate should not be much warmer than body temperature; check by holding bowl in palm of your hand.) Add grated chocolate and stir until smooth, returning to microwave for no more than 5 seconds at a time to finish melting if necessary. Spread evenly over filling. Refrigerate shortbread until chocolate is just set, about 10 minutes.

6. Using foil overhang, remove shortbread from pan. Using serrated knife and gentle sawing motion, cut shortbread in half crosswise to create two 6½ by 9-inch rectangles. Cut each rectangle in half to make four 3¼ by 9-inch strips. Cut each strip crosswise into 10 equal pieces.

BACI DI DAMA

makes: 32 cookies   total time: 1¼ hours, plus 1 hour cooling

" These are one of the cutest and most romantic cookies out there. Their name translates from Italian as 'lady's kisses,' because each sandwich cookie is said to resemble a woman's pursed lips. Hailing from the Piedmont region of Italy, these adorable kisses consist of two tiny hazelnut buttons held together by a slim layer of chocolate filling. Letting the melted chocolate cool and thicken for a few minutes before assembling the sandwiches ensures that the chocolate will set and keep the cookies together without dripping out the sides of the sandwiches. Toast the hazelnuts on a rimmed baking sheet in a 325-degree oven until fragrant, 13 to 15 minutes, shaking the sheet halfway through toasting. To skin them, gather the warm hazelnuts in a dish towel and rub to remove some of the skins. A square-cornered metal baking pan works best for shaping the dough. If using a baking dish with rounded corners, be sure to square the corners of the dough before portioning."

HOW I GIFT THIS

packaging: Pile these into a vintage tin lined with parchment or use them as a delicious way to fill spaces in a larger cookie assortment.

storage: The cookies can be stored at room temperature for about 10 days.

make it a duo: Pair with a bag of espresso beans or a bottle of grappa.

¾ cup hazelnuts, toasted and partially skinned
⅔ cup (3⅓ ounces) all-purpose flour
⅓ cup (2⅓ ounces) sugar
⅛ teaspoon table salt
6 tablespoons unsalted butter, cut into ½-inch pieces and chilled
2 ounces bittersweet chocolate, chopped

1. Adjust oven rack to middle position and heat oven to 325 degrees. Line 2 rimmed baking sheets with parchment paper. Line bottom of 8-inch square baking pan with parchment. Process hazelnuts, flour, sugar, and salt in food processor until hazelnuts are very finely ground, 20 to 25 seconds. Add butter and pulse until dough just comes together, 20 to 25 pulses.

2. Transfer dough to counter and knead briefly to form smooth ball. Place in prepared pan and press into even layer that covers bottom of pan. Freeze for 10 minutes. Run knife or bench scraper between dough and edge of pan to loosen. Turn out dough onto counter and discard parchment. Cut dough into 64 squares (8 rows by 8 rows). Roll dough squares into balls and evenly space 32 dough balls on each prepared sheet. Bake, 1 sheet at a time, until cookies look dry and are fragrant (cookies will settle but not spread), about 20 minutes, rotating sheet halfway through baking. Transfer sheet to wire rack and let cookies cool completely, about 30 minutes.

3. Microwave chocolate in small bowl at 50 percent power, stirring every 20 seconds, until melted, 1 to 2 minutes. Let chocolate cool at room temperature until it is slightly thickened and registers 80 degrees, about 10 minutes. Invert half of cookies on each sheet. Using ¼-teaspoon measure, spoon chocolate onto flat surfaces of all inverted cookies. Top with remaining cookies, pressing lightly to adhere. Let chocolate set for at least 15 minutes.

MACARONS WITH RASPBERRY BUTTERCREAM

makes: 30 cookies   total time: 1½ hours, plus 26 hours resting, cooling, and chilling

" I'm not going to sugarcoat it: This recipe isn't for the faint of heart. But oh, how your bravery will be rewarded with these chic confections that look like they just came from a French bakery. In fact, you might have to convince your recipient that you made them from scratch just for them. While most successful baking involves weighing ingredients, the measurements for the flour, sugar, egg whites, and water in the cookies require such precision that they need to be measured in grams (an easy enough switch on your kitchen scale). Lightly beating the egg whites makes it easier to get the exact measurement required. You'll also need a large piping bag with a ½-inch round tip and gel food coloring (liquid food coloring will add too much water to the batter). Whatever shade of gel you choose for the macaron shells to complement the filling flavor, use 3 drops gel for pastel hues and 7 drops for more vibrant color. Each of the butter-cream fillings makes about 1½ cups, which is enough to fill 30 macarons (with a little extra). Make sure to use finely ground almond flour; Blue Diamond or Bob's Red Mill products work well. My final piece of advice: This recipe involves multitasking, so read it carefully and make sure to have your ingredients and equipment in place before you begin. Bonne chance!"

HOW I GIFT THIS

packaging: For maximum visual impact, package the macarons in a windowed bakery box or a tin, or stack them high in a cellophane bag tied with a ribbon.

storage: The macarons can be refrigerated for about 1 week or frozen for about 2 months. Bring to room temperature before serving.

make it a duo: Pair with a bottle of demi-sec Champagne for a fabulously French style.

add to a basket: Add these to the Afternoon Tea basket (page 54).

macaron shells
150 grams blanched, finely ground almond flour
150 grams confectioners' sugar
⅛ teaspoon table salt
113 grams egg whites (measure from lightly beaten whites of 4 large eggs), divided
⅛ teaspoon cream of tartar
150 grams granulated sugar
60 grams water
3–7 drops gel food coloring

raspberry buttercream
10 tablespoons unsalted butter, softened
1¼ cups (5 ounces) confectioners' sugar
Pinch table salt
1 tablespoon heavy cream
½ teaspoon vanilla extract
⅓ cup freeze-dried raspberries

1. for the macaron shells: Using pencil and 1½-inch round biscuit cutter as guide, trace thirty 1½-inch circles on each of 2 pieces of parchment (5 evenly spaced rows of 6 circles on each piece of parchment). Spray 2 rimmed baking sheets with vegetable oil spray. Place templates pencil side down on sheets and smooth to adhere. Sift flour, confectioners' sugar, and salt through fine-mesh strainer into large bowl and set aside.

2. Measure 75 grams of egg whites into bowl of stand mixer fitted with whisk attachment (reserve remaining whites). Add cream of tartar. Start mixer on medium-high speed and whip until soft peaks form, 2 to 3 minutes. Turn mixer to lowest speed and let run while you make sugar syrup.

recipe continues

3. Using heatproof spatula, gently stir granulated sugar and water together in small saucepan. Cook over medium-high heat, without stirring, until sugar dissolves. Continue to cook, checking temperature frequently, until sugar syrup reaches 245 degrees, 4 to 5 minutes.

4. When syrup reaches 245 degrees, quickly remove pan from heat, adjust mixer speed to medium, and carefully pour syrup into whites in thin, steady stream (avoid hitting whisk; aim for side of bowl just above whites). Add food coloring, increase speed to medium-high, and continue to whip until meringue is just shy of stiff peaks (very tip of peak should bend to 2 or 3 o'clock), 3 to 5 minutes.

5. Transfer meringue and reserved 38 grams egg whites to almond flour mixture. Using large rubber spatula, stir to incorporate. Turning bowl, stir and smear batter against sides of bowl, scraping sides and bottom frequently until batter loosens and flows from spatula in slow, wide stream for 8 to 10 seconds and reincorporates into batter within about 30 seconds. (To test consistency, place spoonful of batter on prepared sheet and let sit for 1 minute. If batter spreads into flat, smooth-topped disk, continue with recipe; if it remains domed, continue stirring, taking care not to overmix, and retest.)

6. Transfer batter to pastry bag fitted with ½-inch round tip. Hold bag perpendicular to sheet and about ½ inch above sheet. Using template as guide, pipe batter into 1½-inch-wide disks, keeping bag still as batter flows from tip. To finish each disk, use quick flick of wrist to cut off batter stream. Rap sheets firmly on counter 6 times to release air bubbles. Let rest until shells form skin that can be touched gently with finger without marring surface, about 20 minutes. While shells dry, adjust oven rack to lower-middle position and heat oven to 325 degrees.

7. Bake 1 sheet of shells for 15 minutes. To test for doneness, place your finger gently on top of 1 shell and move it side to side; if center feels loose and jiggly, continue to bake, checking every minute, until firm. Transfer sheet to wire rack and bake remaining shells. Cool shells completely on sheets. While shells cool, make buttercream filling.

8. for the buttercream: Using stand mixer fitted with paddle attachment, beat butter at medium-high speed until smooth, about 20 seconds. Add confectioners' sugar and salt and beat on medium-low speed until most of sugar is moistened, about 45 seconds. Scrape down sides of bowl and beat on medium until mixture is fully combined, about 15 seconds; scrape down bowl. Add cream and vanilla and beat until incorporated, about 10 seconds. Increase speed to medium-high and beat until light and fluffy, about 4 minutes, scraping down bowl once or twice during mixing.

9. Meanwhile, grind raspberries in spice grinder until reduced to fine powder. Sift powder through fine-mesh strainer set over small bowl. Add 1 tablespoon powder to buttercream and beat on medium speed until fully incorporated, about 30 seconds. Add more raspberry powder to taste, as desired. Transfer to pastry bag fitted with ½-inch round or star tip. (Buttercream can be refrigerated for up to 2 days; let stand at room temperature for 30 minutes before using.)

10. Gently peel shells from parchment. (If shells don't release cleanly, place sheets in freezer for 10 minutes.) Holding 1 upturned shell in your hand, pipe about 2 teaspoons filling on top, leaving ⅛-inch border. Place second shell on top of filling, pressing gently until filling spreads to edges. Repeat with remaining shells and filling. Arrange cookies on clean parchment-lined sheet and wrap well. Refrigerate for at least 24 hours before gifting.

variations

COFFEE BUTTERCREAM
Omit freeze-dried raspberries. Before beating butter in step 8, combine 2 tablespoons instant espresso powder with heavy cream and vanilla, stirring to combine. Add heavy cream mixture to fully combined butter, sugar, and salt mixture and continue with recipe.

STRAWBERRY-CARDAMOM BUTTERCREAM
Substitute ½ cup freeze-dried strawberries for freeze-dried raspberries. Add ¼ teaspoon ground cardamom to buttercream along with strawberry powder in step 9.

PISTACHIO BUTTERCREAM
Omit freeze-dried raspberries. Add 3 ounces pistachio paste to light and fluffy butter mixture in step 8, beating on medium speed until fully incorporated, about 30 seconds.

additional fillings
PASSION FRUIT CURD
makes: about 2 cups
total time: 15 minutes, plus 2 hours chilling

- ¾ cup frozen passion fruit puree, thawed
- ½ cup (3½ ounces) sugar
- ¼ cup (1 ounce) cornstarch
- 4 ounces white chocolate, chopped coarse
- 9 tablespoons unsalted butter, cut into 1-tablespoon pieces

Whisk passion fruit puree, sugar, and cornstarch together in medium saucepan. Cook over medium heat, stirring constantly, until thick paste forms, about 4 minutes. Remove from heat and whisk in chocolate until melted, about 1 minute. Let cool slightly, then whisk in butter in three additions until smooth and glossy. Press lightly greased parchment against surface of curd and refrigerate until chilled, about 2 hours.

SEMISWEET CHOCOLATE GANACHE
makes: about 1½ cups
total time: 10 minutes, plus 3 hours cooling

- 9 ounces semisweet chocolate, chopped fine
- ¾ cup heavy cream
- 1 tablespoon light corn syrup

Place chocolate in heatproof bowl. Bring cream and corn syrup to simmer in small saucepan over medium heat (do not let cream boil). Pour cream mixture over chocolate and let stand 2 minutes. Stir until smooth and glossy. Let cool, stirring occasionally, until ganache has consistency of soft frosting, 3 to 4 hours.

MAKING MACARON SHELLS

1. Whip meringues until just shy of stiff peaks (very tip of peak should bend to 2 or 3 o'clock), 3 to 5 minutes.

2. Add meringue and reserved 38 grams egg whites to almond flour mixture.

3. Turning bowl, stir and smear batter against sides of bowl, scraping sides and bottom frequently until batter loosens and flows from spatula in slow, wide stream for 8 to 10 seconds and reincorporates into batter within about 30 seconds.

4. Transfer batter to pastry bag. Hold bag perpendicular to sheet, about ½ inch above sheet. Pipe batter onto template in 1½-inch-wide disks, keeping bag still as batter flows from tip. Use quick flick of wrist to cut off batter stream.

5. Let rest until shells form skin that can be touched gently with finger without marring surface, about 20 minutes.

ALMOND BISCOTTI

makes: 30 cookies   **total time:** 1¾ hours, plus 1 hour cooling

66 The next time you visit with the nonna in your life (whoever she may be), bring these along! Italians typically like their biscotti dry and hard (all the better for dipping into cappuccino, espresso, or vin santo), whereas Americans tend to favor a buttery, tender version that's much closer to being a soft cookie. These biscotti straddle the fence, with plenty of crunch but not so much that you require a dipping liquid to soften them. A judicious amount of butter softens them up, and adding some ground almonds to the dough breaks up the crumb and helps make the cookies more tender. And like traditional biscotti, these keep for a very long time, which makes them ideal for make-ahead gift-giving. The almonds will continue to toast during baking, so toast them just until they're fragrant."

HOW I GIFT THIS

packaging: Pack these sturdy cookies in a cookie jar or tin.

storage: The biscotti can be stored at room temperature for about 1 month.

make it a duo: Pair with a bottle of vin santo, ice wine, or amaretto.

make it a trio: Add a bag of espresso beans and a moka pot.

add to a basket: These are so sturdy and long keeping that they are great in any mailed food gift.

1¼ cups whole almonds, lightly toasted, divided
1¾ cups (8¾ ounces) all-purpose flour
2 teaspoons baking powder
¼ teaspoon table salt
2 large eggs
1 cup (7 ounces) sugar
4 tablespoons unsalted butter, melted and cooled
1½ teaspoons almond extract
½ teaspoon vanilla extract
1 large egg white, beaten with pinch table salt

1. Adjust oven rack to middle position and heat oven to 325 degrees. Using ruler and pencil, draw two 8 by 3-inch rectangles, spaced 4 inches apart, on piece of parchment paper. Grease rimmed baking sheet and place parchment on it, marked side down.

2. Pulse 1 cup almonds in food processor until coarsely chopped, 8 to 10 pulses; transfer to bowl and set aside. Process remaining ¼ cup almonds in now-empty food processor until finely ground, about 45 seconds. Add flour, baking powder, and salt; process to combine, about 15 seconds. Transfer flour mixture to second bowl. Process the 2 eggs in now-empty food processor until lightened in color and almost doubled in volume, about 3 minutes. With processor running, slowly add sugar until thoroughly combined, about 15 seconds. Add melted butter, almond extract, and vanilla and process until combined, about 10 seconds. Transfer egg mixture to medium bowl. Sprinkle half of flour mixture over egg mixture and, using spatula, gently fold until just combined. Add remaining flour mixture and chopped almonds and gently fold until just combined.

3. Divide dough in half. Using your floured hands, form each half into 8 by 3-inch rectangle, using lines on parchment as guide. Spray each loaf lightly with oil spray. Using rubber spatula lightly coated with oil spray, smooth tops and sides of loaves. Gently brush tops of loaves with beaten egg white.

4. Bake until loaves are golden and just beginning to crack on top, 25 to 30 minutes, rotating sheet halfway through baking. Let loaves cool on sheet for 30 minutes, then transfer to cutting board. Using serrated knife, slice each loaf on slight bias into ½-inch-thick pieces. Set wire rack in rimmed baking sheet. Space slices, cut side down, about ¼ inch apart on prepared rack. Bake until crisp and golden brown on both sides, about 35 minutes, flipping slices halfway through baking. Let biscotti cool completely on wire rack, about 30 minutes.

variations
ANISE BISCOTTI
Add 1½ teaspoons anise seeds to flour mixture in step 2. Substitute anise-flavored liqueur for almond extract.

HAZELNUT-ROSEMARY-ORANGE BISCOTTI
Substitute lightly toasted and skinned hazelnuts for almonds. Add 2 tablespoons minced fresh rosemary to flour mixture in step 2. Substitute orange-flavored liqueur for almond extract and add 1 tablespoon grated orange zest to egg mixture with butter in step 2.

PISTACHIO-SPICE BISCOTTI
Substitute shelled pistachios for almonds. Add 1 teaspoon ground cardamom, ½ teaspoon ground cloves, ½ teaspoon pepper, ¼ teaspoon ground cinnamon, and ¼ teaspoon ground ginger to flour mixture in step 2. Substitute 1 teaspoon water for almond extract. Increase vanilla to 1 teaspoon.

FOR THE LOVE OF CHOCOLATE

" It's rare to find someone who doesn't like chocolate. After all, it's a scientific fact that chocolate contains natural chemicals that cause our brains to produce serotonin, a neurotransmitter and hormone that produces feelings of joy. And what's not to like about joy? This blowout basket, however, is for those who truly *love* chocolate. The variety of recipes and the different textures of the treats included in this basket make it a Nobel Prize winner in the food gifts category. Although I like to give this as a special Valentine's gift, it can just as easily be given at the year-end holidays, or for someone's birthday or a wedding anniversary. Any happy occasion is a good occasion for chocolate!"

HOW I GIFT THIS

If you've got a special Valentine that you deem worthy of all this chocolaty goodness, go for it. A heart-shaped box is a must in this situation, but other than that, you don't need to get all lovey-dovey (unless you want to). A silver box filled with pink or light blue crinkle paper and tied with a matching silk ribbon is a really elegant way to present this gift—I think these two colors set off the dark shades of the chocolate goodies particularly well. You could pack everything into one large box for a special someone, or make multiple mini versions with smaller boxes for several Valentines. (I won't spill your secrets.)

START WITH

Chocolate Ganache–Filled Brownies (page 236)

Chocolate-Covered Caramels (page 194)

Spicy Mocha Sandwich Cookies with Dulce de Leche (page 215)

IF YOU WANT, ADD

Dark Chocolate Fudge Sauce (page 62)

Salted pretzels

Stroopwafels

Small store-bought chocolate candies

CHOCOLATE GANACHE–FILLED BROWNIES

makes: 12 brownies   **total time:** 1½ hours, plus 5¼ hours cooling

66 Brownies filled with a rich ganache are the ultimate in chocolate decadence, and individual brownies made in a muffin tin allows every brownie to boast a generous amount of filling with no shortage of crusty edges. Don't want to go all out on the chocolate? Then try one of the equally indulgent variations stuffed with either peanut butter ganache or salted caramel. An optional sprinkle of sea salt on the top seals the deal. The best way to create space for the ganache is to firmly press a greased shot glass into the just-baked brownies. This recipe was developed using Ghirardelli 60% Premium Baking Chips, but you can use semisweet chocolate chips, if you prefer. These brownies are best when made with a high-fat Dutch-processed cocoa powder such as Droste. It's important to indent the centers of the brownies 15 minutes after they come out of the oven, so set your timer!"

HOW I GIFT THIS

packaging: These brownies look beautiful, glossy, and decadent, so I like to show that off. Gift them in their muffin tin for your new neighbors, or arrange them on a beautiful platter or in a bakery box for a party. Take it a step further by using patterned paper or foil liners.

storage: The brownies can be stored at room temperature for about 3 days.

make it a duo: Pair with a jar of flaky sea salt so that your recipient can sprinkle it on top as desired.

make it a trio: For a friend in need of a little self-indulgence, combine with a face mask and a pair of fuzzy socks.

add to a basket: These are a natural for the For the Love of Chocolate basket (page 235).

brownies
- ⅓ cup (2 ounces) bittersweet chocolate chips
- ⅓ cup (1 ounce) Dutch-processed cocoa powder
- ½ cup boiling water
- 2 cups (14 ounces) sugar
- ⅔ cup vegetable oil
- 2 large eggs
- 2 teaspoons vanilla extract
- 1⅓ cups (6⅔ ounces) all-purpose flour
- ¾ teaspoon table salt

ganache filling
- 1⅓ cups (8 ounces) bittersweet chocolate chips
- ½ cup heavy cream
- 1 teaspoon flake sea salt (optional)

1. for the brownies: Adjust oven rack to middle position and heat oven to 350 degrees. Line 12-cup muffin tin with paper or foil liners. Place chocolate chips and cocoa in large bowl. Add boiling water and whisk until chocolate chips are fully melted. Whisk in sugar, oil, eggs, and vanilla until combined. Gently whisk in flour and salt until just incorporated.

2. Using ¼-cup dry measuring cup, portion batter into prepared muffin cups; evenly distribute any remaining batter among cups. Bake until toothpick inserted in center comes out with few moist crumbs attached, 40 to 45 minutes.

3. Let brownies cool in muffin tin on wire rack for 15 minutes. Spray base of 1¼-inch-diameter shot glass (or other object with similar diameter) with vegetable oil spray. Keeping brownies in muffin tin, press base of glass into center of each brownie, about 1 inch deep, respraying glass as needed. Remove brownies from muffin tin and let cool completely on rack, about 1 hour.

4. for the ganache filling: Microwave chocolate chips and cream in bowl at 50 percent power, stirring frequently, until melted, 1 to 3 minutes. Distribute ganache evenly among indentations in brownies (about 1 heaping tablespoon each).

5. Let sit until ganache is set, about 4 hours (or refrigerate brownies until ganache is set, about 1½ hours). Sprinkle ganache evenly with salt, if using.

variations

PEANUT BUTTER GANACHE–FILLED BROWNIES

For ganache filling, substitute milk chocolate chips for bittersweet chocolate chips and creamy peanut butter for heavy cream; add ⅛ teaspoon table salt.

SALTED CARAMEL–FILLED BROWNIES

For ganache filling, substitute 10 ounces soft caramels for chocolate chips, reduce heavy cream to 2 tablespoons, and add ¼ teaspoon table salt. Increase microwaving time to 3 to 5 minutes.

ULTRANUTTY PECAN BARS

makes: 24 bars   total time: 1 hour, plus 1½ hours cooling

" We all know somebody who loves nutty desserts, so here's a pecan bar that puts the focus squarely on the star ingredient. Often pecan bars take the lead from pecan pie and are more about the thick, sugary goo than they are about the nuts. There's nothing wrong with that, but that is not these bars. These ultranutty treats are packed with a full pound of toasted pecans, lightly bound by a dump-and-stir filling that's plenty buttery and caramel-y, but not tooth-achingly sweet. The crust is easy: a pat-in-the-pan dough that doesn't even require parbaking. A final sprinkling of flaky sea salt on the baked bars enhances their flavor and adds a pretty finishing touch (as if they weren't pretty enough already). With so many nuts, these pecan bars have varying textures, with some parts chewy and some crunchy. The contrast will have your recipient reaching back into the tin for another one!"

HOW I GIFT THIS

packaging: Pack these into a cookie tin two ways to show both their layers and their beautiful tops.

storage: The bars can be stored at room temperature for about 5 days.

make it a duo: Embrace the autumnal aspect of this dessert by pairing it with a bag of local apples or a bottle of pumpkin spice–flavored syrup.

crust
- 1¾ cups (8¾ ounces) all-purpose flour
- 6 tablespoons (2⅔ ounces) granulated sugar
- ½ teaspoon table salt
- 8 tablespoons unsalted butter, melted

topping
- ¾ cup packed (5¼ ounces) light brown sugar
- ½ cup light corn syrup
- 7 tablespoons unsalted butter, melted and hot
- 1 teaspoon vanilla extract
- ½ teaspoon table salt
- 4 cups (1 pound) pecans, toasted
- ½ teaspoon flake sea salt (optional)

1. **for the crust:** Adjust oven rack to lowest position and heat oven to 350 degrees. Make foil sling for 13 by 9-inch baking pan by folding 2 long sheets of aluminum foil; first sheet should be 13 inches wide and second sheet should be 9 inches wide. Lay sheets of foil in pan perpendicular to each other, with extra foil hanging over edges of pan. Push foil into corners and up sides of pan, smoothing foil flush to pan. Lightly spray foil with vegetable oil spray.

2. Whisk flour, granulated sugar, and salt together in medium bowl. Add melted butter and stir with wooden spoon until dough begins to form. Using your hands, continue to combine until no dry flour remains and small portion of dough holds together when squeezed in palm of your hand. Evenly scatter tablespoon-size pieces of dough over surface of pan. Using your fingertips and palm of your hand, press and smooth dough into even thickness in bottom of pan.

3. **for the topping:** Whisk brown sugar, corn syrup, hot melted butter, vanilla, and table salt in medium bowl until smooth (mixture will look separated at first but will become homogeneous), about 20 seconds. Fold pecans into sugar mixture until evenly coated.

4. Pour topping over crust. Using spatula, spread topping, pushing to edges and into corners (there will be bare patches). Bake until topping is evenly distributed and rapidly bubbling across entire surface, 23 to 25 minutes.

5. Transfer pan to wire rack and lightly sprinkle with flake sea salt, if using. Let bars cool completely in pan on rack, about 1½ hours. Using foil overhang, lift bars out of pan and transfer to cutting board; discard foil. Cut into 24 bars.

SCOTCHEROOS

makes: 16 bars   total time: 45 minutes, plus 2 hours cooling

" These treats have been a Midwestern favorite with kids and adults alike since they appeared as a recipe on the side of the Kellogg's Rice Krispies box in the 1960s. So here's your chance to surprise a friend with a nostalgic treat—or introduce someone to a new fave. The name traditionally refers to bars made with Rice Krispies, but depending on the ingredients, different names might be used, including Special K bars, Oh Henry! bars, and peanut butter crispy bars. This version gets its crunch from Special K cereal and chunky peanut butter. Butter and corn syrup keep the bars chewy and a little gooey; the corn syrup ensures that they stay soft. The bittersweet chocolate topping balances the sweetness, and a sprinkle of flake salt makes the flavors pop. An equal weight of Rice Krispies cereal can be substituted for the Special K Original cereal."

HOW I GIFT THIS

packaging: Pack in a tin with parchment paper between the bar layers.

storage: The bars can be stored at room temperature for about 3 days.

big-batch it: This recipe can easily be doubled and made in a 13 by 9-inch baking pan.

make it a duo: Pair with Sweet and Salty Kettle Corn Party Mix (page 83) or Thin and Crispy Chocolate Chip Cookies (page 213).

¾ cup (5¼ ounces) sugar
¾ cup light corn syrup
6 tablespoons unsalted butter, cut into 6 pieces
¾ cup chunky or creamy peanut butter
4½ cups (5 ounces) Special K Original cereal
1 cup (6 ounces) bittersweet chocolate chips
½ cup (3 ounces) butterscotch chips
½ teaspoon flake sea salt (optional)

1. Lightly grease 8-inch square baking pan. Make parchment paper sling by folding 2 long sheets of parchment so each is 8 inches wide. Lay sheets of parchment in pan perpendicular to each other, with extra parchment hanging over edges of pan. Push parchment into corners and up sides of pan, smoothing parchment flush to pan. Grease parchment.

2. Bring sugar, corn syrup, and butter to boil in Dutch oven over medium heat, stirring frequently with heat-resistant spatula. Off heat, stir in peanut butter until combined. Gently stir in cereal until fully coated with sugar mixture. Transfer cereal mixture to prepared pan and press firmly into even layer with spatula. Let cool on wire rack for 15 minutes.

3. Microwave chocolate chips and butterscotch chips in bowl at 50 percent power, whisking occasionally, until melted and smooth, 3 to 5 minutes. Let cool for 15 minutes. Using offset spatula, spread chocolate mixture evenly over cereal mixture. Sprinkle with salt, if using. Refrigerate bars until chocolate is firm, about 1 hour.

4. Using parchment overhang, lift bars out of pan and transfer to cutting board. Let bars sit at room temperature for 1 hour. Cut into 16 pieces.

BOX UP THE BAKERY

GIVING LARGER BAKED GOODS

Baked goods beyond cookies and bars can be cozy like muffins, festive like Bundt cakes, or truly showstopping like a whole pie or tart. It's a wide category, and different gifts have different packaging needs depending on their size and decorations. Here are some of my favorite tips and tricks.

HOW TO MAKE A DIY MUFFIN OR CUPCAKE CARRIER

1. Make 4 cuts in a 9- to 10-inch standard paper plate, cutting to the edge of the fluted section.

2. Fold the cut sections inward to form creases, then unfold so the sides stand upright.

3. Use tape to seal the sides closed, forming the shape of an open box.

4. After placing muffins or cupcakes in the carrier, tie twine or ribbon around the outside.

DIY garnish

CANDIED ROSE PETALS

makes: about 2 cups
total time: 30 minutes, plus 1½ hours drying

These make a special garnish for large-format cakes like the Bundt cakes on pages 268–270. Buy food-safe (unsprayed) roses. Use petals from the outer three-quarters of each rose; inner petals are too tightly curled. Excess egg white will cause the sugar to clump, so don't skip dragging the petals along the bowl rim in step 2.

- ½ cup sugar
- 1 large egg white
- 2 teaspoons water
- 2 cups rose petals, divided

1. Place sugar in shallow baking dish or pie plate. Line rimmed baking sheet with parchment paper.

2. Whisk egg white and water together in bowl. Dip 1 petal into mixture and then firmly drag each side against edge of bowl to remove excess. Petal should be coated in thin, even layer of egg wash.

3. Gently lay petal on top of sugar. Using spoon, sprinkle sugar over petal and shake dish to ensure petal is well coated. Carefully slide fork underneath petal and transfer to prepared sheet.

4. Repeat with remaining petals. Let petals stand, uncovered, until dry and crisp, at least 1½ hours or up to 24 hours. (Candied petals can be stored in airtight container at room temperature for up to 2 weeks.)

HOW TO WRAP A QUICK BREAD

If giving loaves on their own (not in a box or cellophane bag), wrapping them in plastic wrap will keep them fresher. Then wrap a rectangle of decorative paper around the waist of the loaf and tie with ribbon.

Parchment Paper Wrapping

1. Place a piece of parchment about four times the width of the loaf on the counter with the long side parallel to the edge. Place the loaf in the center and bring the edges of the paper together over the top.

2. Fold the paper down in several folds until it's loosely flush with the top of the loaf.

3. Fold both of the side ends into points, as though you were wrapping a present.

4. Tuck the folded points under the loaf.

HOW TO KEEP FROSTING AND GLAZES LOOKING GREAT

Frost cupcakes so that the frosting doesn't overhang the edges; this will make them more likely to arrive at their destination looking perfect. Adding sprinkles or decor to the tops can be a proactive way to help hide any messiness from transport.

If you are glazing one of the quick breads, make sure the glaze is fully set before wrapping the bread. Or gift the glaze in a jar that your recipient can pour over the bread before serving.

HOW TO GIVE A WHOLE CAKE, PIE, OR TART

A whole cake can be given in a bakery box or round cake box, on a cake plate or wooden board, or in a cake carrier.

The best way to give a whole pie like the Triple-Berry Slab Pie with Ginger-Lemon Streusel (page 279) is in the pan you bake it in. Give a pan as part of the gift, or bake the pie in a disposable aluminum pan.

Tarts tend to have sturdier crusts than pies so don't need to be given in their pan (unless you want to), but a bakery box goes a long way toward keeping tarts protected.

BRITISH-STYLE CURRANT SCONES

makes: 12 scones   **total time:** 1 hour

❝ There are coffee people, and then there are tea people. These proper scones are a must-gift for all the tea people in your life. I often make multiple gifts from this recipe, pairing a few scones with small jars of jam. Compared to American-style scones, scones from across the pond use less butter and more baking powder, which makes them lighter and fluffier than American scones. British scones are also less sweet—all the better for slathering them with butter or clotted cream and jam for afternoon teatime. I like whole milk in this recipe, but you could use low-fat milk. The dough will be soft and wet, so make sure to dust the counter and your hands liberally with flour.❞

HOW I GIFT THIS

packaging: For a fun visual play on English muffins, I stack these in a cellophane bag or line them up in a rectangular bakery box.

storage: The scones can be stored at room temperature for about 3 days or frozen for about 1 month.

make it a duo: Pair with one of the jams on pages 30–31, one of the Tea Blends (page 57), or a jar of clotted cream.

add to a basket: Add to the Afternoon Tea basket (page 54).

3 cups (15 ounces) all-purpose flour
⅓ cup (2⅓ ounces) sugar
2 tablespoons baking powder
½ teaspoon table salt
8 tablespoons unsalted butter, cut into ½-inch pieces and softened
¾ cup dried currants
1 cup (8 ounces) whole milk
2 large eggs

1. Adjust oven rack to upper-middle position and heat oven to 500 degrees. Line rimmed baking sheet with parchment paper. Pulse flour, sugar, baking powder, and salt in food processor until combined, about 5 pulses. Add butter and pulse until fully incorporated and mixture resembles very fine crumbs with no butter visible, about 20 pulses. Transfer mixture to large bowl and stir in currants. Whisk milk and eggs together in second bowl; set aside 2 tablespoons milk mixture. Stir remaining milk mixture into flour mixture until almost no dry bits of flour remain.

2. Turn out dough onto well-floured counter and gather into ball. Using your floured hands, knead until surface is smooth and free of cracks, 25 to 30 turns. Press gently to form disk then, using floured rolling pin, roll disk into 9-inch round, about 1 inch thick. Using floured 2½-inch round cutter, stamp out 8 scones and arrange on prepared sheet. Gather dough scraps, form into ball, and knead gently until surface is smooth. Roll dough to 1-inch thickness, stamp out 4 scones, and transfer to sheet. Discard remaining dough.

3. Brush tops of scones with reserved milk mixture. Reduce oven temperature to 425 degrees and bake scones until risen and golden brown, 10 to 12 minutes, rotating sheet halfway through baking. Transfer scones to wire rack and let cool for at least 10 minutes.

gift tag

If frozen, reheat the scones in a 300-degree oven for 15 minutes. Serve with butter or clotted cream, plus jam.

BANANA-DATE-WALNUT BREAD

makes: 1 standard loaf, 3 mini loaves, or 12 muffins

66 I don't give plain old banana bread—I surprise my peeps with this sophisticated take that's bold with spices, toffee-like dates, and toasted walnuts. This embellished bread still brings cozy comfort, though. The glaze, made with date molasses (also called date syrup), adds a beautiful sheen reminiscent of sticky date pudding. (You can leave the bread unadorned, if you prefer.) A genius element of this recipe is that you can bake the batter either as a full-size loaf, mini loaves, or muffins, depending on your gifting desires."

HOW I GIFT THIS

packaging: If you're adding the glaze, a bakery box is the way to go. Or give the glaze separately in a small jar for adding later, with a note saying to warm the bread in the oven for a few minutes before pouring on the glaze.

storage: The bread can be stored at room temperature for about 3 days.

add to a basket: Add to the I Brought the Bakery basket (page 288).

1⅔ cups (9⅛ ounces) bread flour
1 tablespoon baking powder
½ teaspoon baking soda
½ teaspoon table salt
½ teaspoon ground cinnamon
⅛ teaspoon ground allspice
⅛ teaspoon ground cardamom
⅛ teaspoon ground cloves
4–5 very ripe large bananas, peeled and coarsely mashed (2 cups)
¾ cup (5¼ ounces) sugar
2 large eggs
⅓ cup vegetable oil
2 teaspoons vanilla extract
⅓ cup chopped dates
⅓ cup chopped toasted walnuts

STANDARD LOAF
total time: 1¼ hours, plus 2 hours cooling

1. Adjust oven rack to middle position and heat oven to 350 degrees. Grease 8½ by 4½-inch loaf pan. Whisk flour, baking powder, baking soda, salt, cinnamon, allspice, cardamom, and cloves together in bowl.

2. Whisk bananas, sugar, eggs, oil, and vanilla in large bowl until fully combined. Add flour mixture and whisk until combined. Stir in dates and walnuts.

3. Pour batter into prepared pan and smooth top. Bake until toothpick inserted in center comes out with few moist crumbs attached, 60 to 70 minutes, rotating loaf halfway through baking. Let loaf cool in pan for 10 minutes. Remove loaf from pan and transfer to wire rack. Let cool completely, about 2 hours.

MINI LOAVES
total time: 1 hour, plus 1 hour cooling

1. Adjust oven rack to middle position and heat oven to 425 degrees. Spray three 5½ by 3-inch mini-loaf pans with vegetable oil spray. Whisk flour, baking powder, baking soda, salt, cinnamon, allspice, cardamom, and cloves together in bowl.

2. Whisk bananas, sugar, eggs, oil, and vanilla in large bowl until combined. Add flour mixture and whisk until combined. Stir in dates and walnuts.

3. Divide batter evenly among prepared pans, leaving about 1-inch headspace, and smooth tops. Bake until toothpick inserted in center comes out with few moist crumbs attached, about 40 minutes. Let loaves cool in pan for 10 minutes. Remove loaves from tins and transfer to wire rack. Let cool completely, about 1 hour.

MUFFINS

total time: 35 minutes, plus 1 hour cooling

1. Adjust oven rack to middle position and heat oven to 425 degrees. Spray 12-cup muffin tin with vegetable oil spray or line with paper liners. Whisk flour, baking powder, baking soda, salt, cinnamon, allspice, cardamom, and cloves together in bowl.

2. Whisk bananas, sugar, eggs, oil, and vanilla in large bowl until combined. Add flour mixture and whisk until combined. Stir in dates and walnuts.

3. Divide batter evenly among prepared muffin cups. Bake until tops are golden brown and toothpick inserted in center comes out clean with few moist crumbs attached, 14 to 18 minutes, rotating pan halfway through baking. Let muffins cool in tin on wire rack for 10 minutes, then transfer to wire rack and let cool completely, about 1 hour.

STICKY DATE GLAZE

total time: 10 minutes

For easy cleanup, glaze the bread or muffins on a wire rack set in a rimmed baking sheet.

¼ cup date molasses
¼ teaspoon ground cinnamon
⅛ teaspoon ground allspice
⅛ teaspoon ground cloves
   Pinch ground cardamom
   Pinch table salt

Microwave all ingredients in bowl at 50 percent power for 30 seconds. After removing bread from pan, brush glaze evenly over top of warm bread or muffins and let cool completely.

BLUEBERRY-LEMON-CARDAMOM BREAD

makes: 1 standard loaf, 3 mini loaves, or 12 muffins

66 I love giving quick breads as gifts because I can make so many at one time and it's all the more fun when I make different variations! This quick bread and its variations start with the same basic batter but have different creative stir-ins, allowing you to customize flavors to the recipient or the occasion—blueberry-lemon-cardamon for a spice-adventurous friend or neighbor; cranberry-orange-pecan for any fall gift; or coffee-chocolate-hazelnut for a favorite coffee break coworker. Each one gets its own optional glaze—stunningly pretty blueberry, zesty orange, or wake-me-up espresso. There's also a streusel topping that could be used on any of the breads instead of a glaze. Or you could go for total simplicity, skip the glaze and streusel, and just sprinkle on a sparkle of coarse sugar before baking. To take the gifting potential of these loaves totally over the top, you can bake any of the batters as 1 full-size loaf, 3 mini loaves, or 12 muffins."

HOW I GIFT THIS

packaging: If you're adding glaze or streusel, a bakery box is a smart way to go for the loaves and muffins. You could also package the glaze separately in a small airtight jar. For a plain bread loaf, you could also wrap it in parchment paper.

storage: The breads (and the glazes if stored separately) can be stored at room temperature for about 3 days.

make it a duo: For a coffee break or teatime treat, pair with Cold Brew Coffee Concentrate (page 58) or Citrus Burst Black Tea Blend (page 57).

make it a basket: Make a breakfast basket by combining a few muffins or mini loaves with Granola (page 60), Cold Brew Coffee Concentrate (page 58), a few British-Style Currant Scones (page 246), store-bought jams, and cultured butter or yogurt.

2 cups (10 ounces) all-purpose flour
1 cup (7 ounces) granulated sugar
1 teaspoon table salt
1 teaspoon baking powder
¼ teaspoon baking soda
1 cup buttermilk
6 tablespoons unsalted butter, melted and cooled
1 large egg
1 cup blueberries (1½ cups if making muffins)
2 teaspoons grated lemon zest
1 teaspoon ground cardamom
3 tablespoons turbinado sugar or 1½ tablespoons granulated sugar, for topping (optional)

STANDARD LOAF

total time: 1½ hours, plus 2 hours cooling

1. Adjust oven rack to middle position and heat oven to 350 degrees. Spray 8½ by 4½-inch loaf pan with vegetable oil spray. Whisk flour, granulated sugar, salt, baking powder, and baking soda together in large bowl. Whisk buttermilk, melted butter, and egg together in bowl then add to bowl with flour mixture and stir until just combined. Sprinkle blueberries, lemon zest, and cardamom over top, then gently fold in; do not overmix.

2. Pour batter into prepared pan and smooth top. Sprinkle with turbinado sugar, if using. Bake until golden brown and toothpick inserted in center comes out with few moist crumbs attached, 1 hour to 1 hour 10 minutes, rotating pan halfway through baking. Let loaf cool in pan on wire rack for 10 minutes, then transfer to wire rack and let cool completely, about 2 hours.

recipe continues

MINI LOAVES
total time: 1 hour, plus 1 hour cooling

1. Adjust oven rack to middle position and heat oven to 350 degrees. Spray three 5½ by 3-inch mini-loaf pans with vegetable oil spray. Whisk flour, granulated sugar, salt, baking powder, and baking soda together in large bowl. Whisk buttermilk, melted butter, and egg together in bowl then add to bowl with flour mixture and stir until just combined. Sprinkle blueberries, lemon zest, and cardamom over top, then gently fold in; do not overmix.

2. Divide batter evenly among prepared pans and smooth tops. Sprinkle with turbinado sugar, if using. Bake until light golden brown and toothpick inserted in center comes out with few moist crumbs attached, 38 to 42 minutes. Let loaves cool in pan on wire rack for 10 minutes, then transfer to wire rack and let cool completely, about 1 hour.

variations
CRANBERRY-ORANGE-PECAN BREAD
Substitute 1½ cups fresh or frozen coarsely chopped cranberries for blueberries and 1 tablespoon grated orange zest for lemon zest. Fold in ½ cup toasted and chopped pecans or walnuts with cranberries in step 1.

MUFFINS
total time: 45 minutes, plus 1 hour cooling

1. Adjust oven rack to middle position and heat oven to 400 degrees. Spray 12-cup muffin tin with vegetable oil spray or line with paper liners. Whisk flour, granulated sugar, salt, baking powder, and baking soda together in large bowl. Whisk buttermilk, melted butter, and egg together in bowl then add to bowl with flour mixture and stir until just combined. Sprinkle blueberries, lemon zest, and cardamom over top, then gently fold in; do not overmix.

2. Divide batter evenly among prepared muffin cups and sprinkle with turbinado sugar, if using. Bake until light golden brown and toothpick inserted in center comes out with few moist crumbs attached, 20 to 22 minutes, rotating pan halfway through baking. Let muffins cool in tin on wire rack for 10 minutes, then transfer to wire rack and let cool completely, about 1 hour.

CHOCOLATE-COFFEE-HAZELNUT BREAD
Substitute ¾ cup mini semisweet chocolate chips for blueberries, 1 tablespoon instant espresso powder for lemon zest, and 1¼ teaspoons ground cinnamon for cardamom. Fold in ½ cup toasted, skinned, and chopped hazelnuts with chocolate chips in step 1.

BLUEBERRY GLAZE

total time: 5 minutes, plus 15 minutes resting

This glaze is a vibrant addition to the Blueberry-Lemon-Cardamom Bread. For easy cleanup, glaze the bread or muffins on a wire rack set in a rimmed baking sheet.

 ½ cup (2½ ounces) blueberries
 1 cup (4 ounces) confectioners' sugar
 2 teaspoons lemon juice

1. Microwave blueberries until they burst and release their juices, 1 to 1½ minutes. Strain berries through fine-mesh strainer into bowl, pressing on solids to extract as much puree as possible. (You should have about 2 tablespoons puree; discard solids.)

2. In second bowl, whisk confectioners' sugar, lemon juice, and 1 tablespoon blueberry puree together until smooth, adding more puree as needed, ½ teaspoon at a time, until glaze is thick but still pourable. Drizzle over cooled bread or muffins and let sit until glaze has hardened, about 15 minutes.

variations

ORANGE GLAZE

total time: 5 minutes, plus 15 minutes resting

This glaze is a perfect topping for the Cranberry-Orange-Pecan Bread. For easy cleanup, glaze the bread or muffins on a wire rack set in a rimmed baking sheet.

Whisk 5 teaspoons orange juice, ¼ teaspoon orange zest, and 1 cup (4 ounces) confectioners' sugar together in bowl, adding more orange juice as needed, ½ teaspoon at a time, until glaze is thick but still pourable. Drizzle over cooled bread or muffins and let sit until glaze has hardened, about 15 minutes.

ESPRESSO GLAZE

total time: 5 minutes, plus 15 minutes resting

This glaze adds a flavorful kick to the Chocolate-Coffee-Hazelnut Bread. For easy cleanup, glaze the bread or muffins on a wire rack set in a rimmed baking sheet.

Whisk 5 teaspoons buttermilk, 1 teaspoon instant espresso powder, and 1 cup (4 ounces) confectioners' sugar together in bowl, adding additional buttermilk as needed, ½ teaspoon at a time, until glaze is thick but still pourable. Drizzle over cooled bread or muffins and let sit until glaze has hardened, about 15 minutes.

BROWN SUGAR STREUSEL

total time: 10 minutes

This streusel is a great topping in lieu of the glazes for any of these quick breads.

 ½ cup packed (3½ ounces) dark brown sugar
 ½ cup (2½ ounces) all-purpose flour
 ½ teaspoon table salt
 4 tablespoons unsalted butter, melted
 ¼ cup hazelnuts, toasted, skinned, and chopped fine (optional)

Combine sugar, flour, and salt in medium bowl. Add melted butter and hazelnuts, if using, and mix until no dry spots remain and mixture forms clumps. After portioning batter, sprinkle evenly over top of bread or muffins and press gently to adhere before baking.

CINNAMON COFFEE CAKE

makes: 1 square cake, 3 mini loaves, or 12 muffins

" One of my favorite 'growing-up' memories is having coffee and coffee cake in the mornings with my granny and aunts as we mapped out meal prep for the holidays. It was and always will be a quick and sweet way to start the day. Topped with a buttery, spice-laced, crumbly streusel, this coffee cake is one that they would definitely approve of. It's always a welcome gift for any occasion or need, whether the recipient is having it with coffee for breakfast or with tea in the afternoon. The ingredient list is pantry-friendly and the cake is easy to prepare. Just like the quick breads on pages 251–252, you can make this recipe as a full-size cake, mini loaves, or muffins. I prefer dark brown sugar here for its richer flavor, but you can use light brown sugar instead."

HOW I GIFT THIS

packaging: Wrap a square cake in a pretty piece of fabric. Wrap loaves in parchment paper and tie with twine. Box up muffins in a bakery box and tie with string, or nestle them into a shallow basket.

storage: The cakes and muffins can be stored at room temperature for about 3 days.

make it a duo: Pair with one of the Tea Blends (page 57) or Cold Brew Coffee Concentrate (page 58).

make it a basket: Make a coffee break basket by adding Chocolate Babka Buns (page 260) and a bag of coffee beans.

streusel
- ¾ cup packed (5¼ ounces) dark brown sugar
- ½ cup (2½ ounces) all-purpose flour
- 1 tablespoon ground cinnamon
- ½ teaspoon table salt
- 4 tablespoons unsalted butter, melted

cake
- 2¼ cups (11¼ ounces) all-purpose flour
- 1¼ cups (8¾ ounces) granulated sugar
- 1¼ teaspoons baking powder
- ½ teaspoon baking soda
- ¾ teaspoon table salt
- 1 cup whole milk
- 12 tablespoons unsalted butter, melted
- 1 large egg plus 1 large yolk, lightly beaten
- 2 teaspoons vanilla extract

SQUARE CAKE
total time: 1¼ hours, plus 2 hours cooling

1. **for the streusel:** Adjust oven rack to middle position and heat oven to 350 degrees. Spray 8-inch square baking pan with vegetable oil spray. Combine brown sugar, flour, cinnamon, and salt in bowl. Stir in melted butter and mix until no dry spots remain and mixture forms clumps; set aside.

2. **for the cake:** Whisk flour, granulated sugar, baking powder, baking soda, and salt together in large bowl. Whisk milk, melted butter, egg and yolk, and vanilla together in separate bowl, then add to flour mixture and stir until just combined.

3. Pour batter into prepared pan and smooth top. Crumble streusel into pea-size crumbs evenly over top, pressing slightly to adhere. Bake until toothpick inserted in center comes out with few moist crumbs attached, 45 to 50 minutes. Let cake cool completely in pan, about 2 hours.

recipe continues

MINI LOAVES

total time: 1¼ hours, plus 1 hour cooling

1. for the streusel: Adjust oven rack to middle position and heat oven to 350 degrees. Spray three 5½ by 3-inch mini-loaf pans with vegetable oil spray. Combine brown sugar, flour, cinnamon, and salt in medium bowl. Stir in melted butter and mix until no dry spots remain and mixture forms clumps; set aside.

2. for the cake: Whisk flour, granulated sugar, baking powder, baking soda, and salt together in large bowl. Whisk milk, melted butter, egg and yolk, and vanilla together in separate bowl, then add to flour mixture and stir until just combined.

3. Divide batter evenly among prepared pans, leaving about ½-inch headspace, and smooth tops. Crumble streusel into pea-size crumbs evenly over tops, pressing slightly to adhere. Bake until toothpick inserted in center comes out with few moist crumbs attached, 45 to 50 minutes. Let loaves cool in pans for 10 minutes, then turn out onto wire rack and let cool completely, about 1 hour.

variations
GINGER-NUTMEG COFFEE CAKE
Add 2 teaspoons ground ginger and ¼ teaspoon ground nutmeg to flour mixture in step 2.

MUFFINS

total time: 1 hour, plus 1 hour cooling

1. for the streusel: Adjust oven rack to middle position and heat oven to 350 degrees. Spray 12-cup muffin tin with vegetable oil spray or line with paper liners. Combine brown sugar, flour, cinnamon, and salt in medium bowl. Stir in melted butter and mix until no dry spots remain and mixture forms clumps; set aside.

2. for the cake: Whisk flour, granulated sugar, baking powder, baking soda, and salt together in large bowl. Whisk milk, melted butter, egg and yolk, and vanilla together in separate bowl, then add to flour mixture and stir until just combined.

3. Divide batter evenly among prepared muffin cups, about ⅓ cup batter per muffin cup. Crumble streusel into pea-size crumbs evenly over tops, pressing slightly to adhere. Bake until toothpick inserted in center comes out with few moist crumbs attached, about 30 minutes, rotating pan halfway through baking. Let muffins cool in tin on rack for 10 minutes, then transfer to wire rack and let cool completely, about 1 hour.

ORANGE-CARDAMOM COFFEE CAKE
Add 1 tablespoon grated orange zest and 1 teaspoon ground cardamom to flour mixture in step 2.

FUROSHIKI-STYLE CLOTH WRAPPING

1. Place gift in middle of fabric square so that corners of fabric draw imaginary line to center of sides of pan.

2. Fold corner of fabric nearest you over pan. Repeat with fabric on opposite side. You can simply fold fabric over or tie loose knot, as you prefer.

3. Gather remaining corners of fabric over top of pan and tie in loose knot.

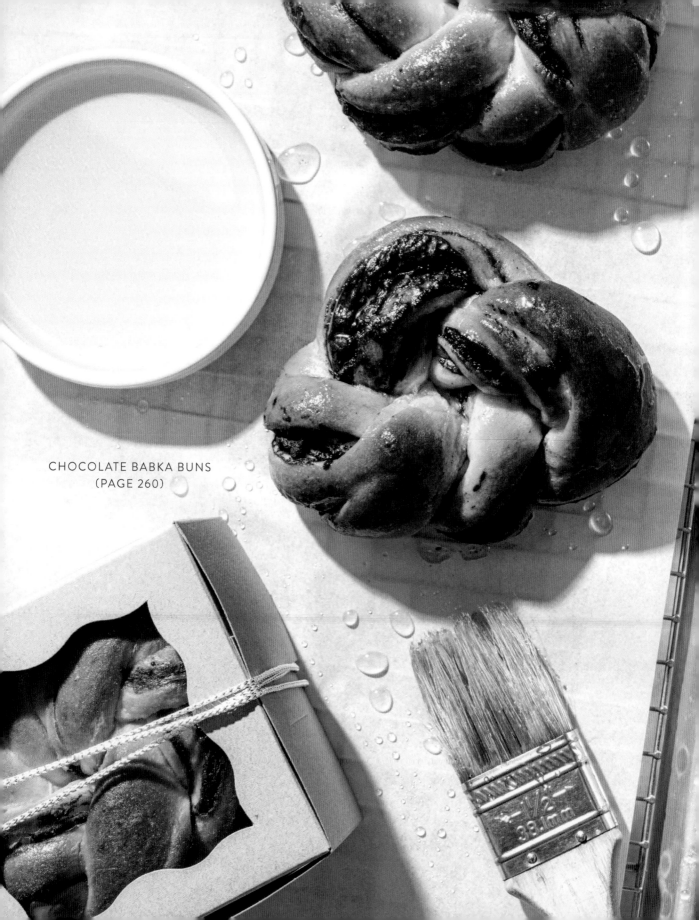

CHOCOLATE BABKA BUNS
(PAGE 260)

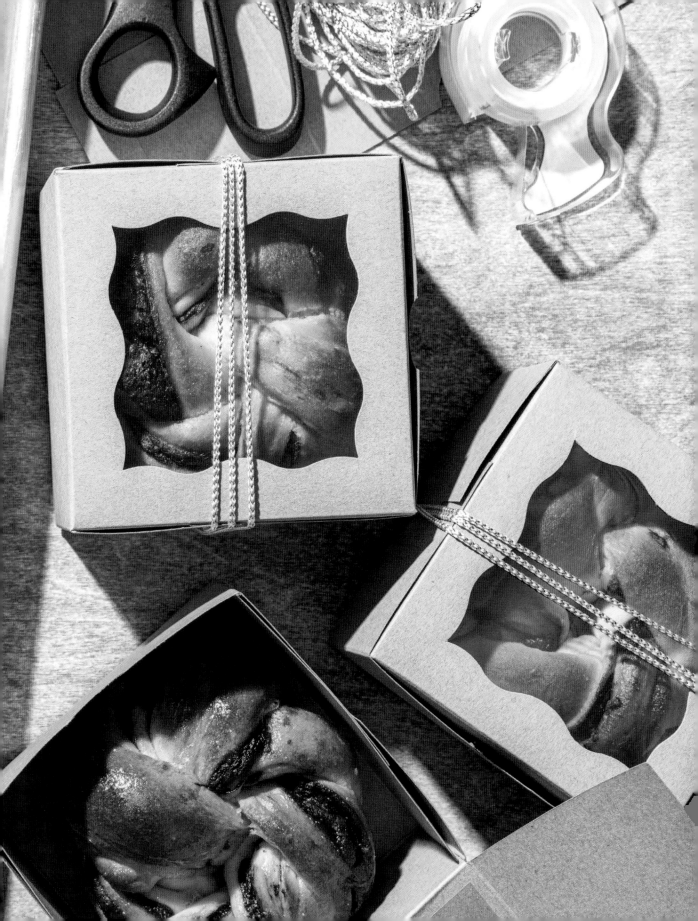

CHOCOLATE BABKA BUNS

makes: 8 buns   **total time:** 2½ hours, plus 4½ hours rising, chilling, and cooling

" Back in my kosher bakery days, I doled out my fair share of babkas. To this day, I still love babka in all its forms and flavors. With these show-stopping braided buns, your lucky recipient gets all the textural contrasts of a whole loaf in an individual package. The origins of babka are found in Poland and Ukraine, and its name, from the Slavic 'babcia' (related to the Yiddish 'bubbe'), translates as 'grandma's cake.' So surprise a grandma in your life the next time you visit her! Jewish versions of this bread evolved in Poland in the early 19th century. In the 1950s, Jewish babka began finding its way into New York City bakeries, and in true NYC style, it began to morph in shape (from round to loaf-shaped) and flavor (the sky is seemingly the limit). I gravitate toward luscious spirals of chocolate in my babka, here with the unexpected but just-right addition of orange zest. A sugar syrup brushed over the warm baked babka makes an extra-special finish."

HOW I GIFT THIS

packaging: A windowed bakery box or boxes will show off these beauties.

storage: The buns can be stored at room temperature for about 2 days.

make it a duo: Give with vanilla ice cream for ice cream sandwiches!

add to a basket: Add to the Let's Fika basket (page 263).

dough
2¼ cups (12⅓ ounces) bread flour
1½ teaspoons instant or rapid-rise yeast
½ cup whole milk
2 large eggs
1 tablespoon grated orange zest
1 teaspoon vanilla extract
¼ cup (1¾ ounces) granulated sugar
½ teaspoon table salt
6 tablespoons unsalted butter, cut into 6 pieces and softened

filling
3 ounces bittersweet chocolate, chopped fine
3 tablespoons unsalted butter, cut into 6 pieces
3 tablespoons confectioners' sugar, sifted
3 tablespoons unsweetened cocoa powder, sifted
¼ teaspoon table salt

syrup
½ cup (3½ ounces) granulated sugar
¼ cup water

1. for the dough: Whisk flour and yeast together in bowl of stand mixer. Add milk, eggs, orange zest, and vanilla. Fit mixer with dough hook and mix on medium-low speed until cohesive dough comes together and no dry flour remains, about 2 minutes. Turn off mixer, cover bowl, and let dough sit for 15 minutes.

2. Add granulated sugar and salt to dough and knead on medium speed until incorporated, about 30 seconds. Increase speed to medium-high and, with mixer running, add butter 1 piece at a time, allowing each piece to incorporate before adding next, about 3 minutes total, scraping down bowl and dough hook as needed. Continue to knead on medium-high speed until dough begins to pull away from sides of bowl, 7 to 10 minutes longer.

3. Transfer dough to greased large bowl. Cover tightly with plastic wrap and let rise at room temperature until slightly puffy, about 1 hour. Refrigerate until firm, at least 2 hours or up to 24 hours.

4. for the filling: Just before removing dough from refrigerator, combine chocolate and butter in medium bowl. Microwave at 50 percent power, stirring often, until chocolate is fully melted and smooth, about 2 minutes. Stir in confectioners' sugar, cocoa, and salt until combined; set aside.

5. Adjust oven rack to upper-middle and lower-middle positions and heat oven to 350 degrees. Line two rimmed baking sheets with parchment paper. Remove dough from refrigerator and turn out onto lightly floured counter. Pat dough into rough rect-angle and divide into 8 equal pieces (about 3 ounces each). Cover loosely with plastic.

6. Working with 1 piece of dough at a time, roll into 10 by 5-inch rectangle on lightly floured counter using floured rolling pin, with short side parallel to counter edge. Spread 1 tablespoon reserved filling evenly over dough, leaving 1-inch border along one long side of rectangle. (If filling becomes too stiff to spread, microwave for no longer than 30 seconds at a time.) Starting on long side opposite 1-inch border, roll dough tightly into cylinder, pinching seam to seal.

7. Place cylinder seam side down. Starting ½ inch from top of cylinder, cut in half lengthwise (leaving top ½ inch intact). Forming tight twist, cross left strand over right strand.

Continue to twist until you reach bottom of cylinder, about 8 twists total; pinch end to seal. Gently form strand into knot, tucking ends underneath. Place buns on prepared sheets and cover loosely with plastic. Let sit for 30 minutes.

8. Bake buns until golden brown, about 25 minutes, switching and rotating sheets halfway through baking.

9. for the syrup: Meanwhile, combine granulated sugar and water in small saucepan and heat over medium heat until sugar dissolves; set aside. Remove babka buns from oven. Brush reserved syrup evenly over entire surface of hot babka (you may not need all of syrup). Let cool for at least 1 hour.

SHAPING BABKA BUNS

1. Roll dough piece into 10 by 5-inch rectangle on lightly floured counter using floured rolling pin, with short side parallel to counter edge.

2. Spread 1 tablespoon filling evenly over dough, leaving 1-inch border along one long side of rectangle.

3. Starting on long side opposite 1-inch border, roll dough tightly into cylinder.

4. Starting ½ inch from top of filled cylinder and leaving top ½ inch intact, cut cylinder in half lengthwise.

5. Cross left strand over right strand and continue to twist tightly until you reach bottom of cylinder, about 8 twists total; pinch each end to seal.

6. Lift both ends of strand together, overlapping ends by about 1 inch to form rough circle.

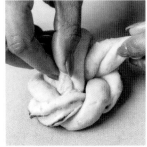

7. Bring end of bottom strand over overlapping point and tuck into center to form knot.

8. Bring end of other strand around bottom of circle and tuck into center. Pinch ends together to seal.

LET'S FIKA

" Like 'gift,' the word 'fika' is both a noun and a verb. So let's have some fun with fika, Swedish for a coffee break. But in Sweden, this long-standing tradition is so much more than just a break for coffee. It's an event, and it can happen at any time of day, when you relax with friends, family, or colleagues to have a coffee (or a tea) with something sweet on the side. It's as much about convivial socializing as it is about the food. My test kitchen colleague Olivia Counter tells such wonderful stories of visiting her family in Sweden and the fika traditions they have, and it's such a treat when she brings back goodies from her travels. In fact, she has inspired the test cooks at ATK to start having a monthly fika break in the kitchen, where anyone is welcome to bring a homemade or store-bought snack to join in the fika festivities."

HOW I GIFT THIS

I like to source a rustic, homey wooden box or crate for this cozy basket. A shallow one can also become the serving tray when it's time to enjoy all the goodies. Flea markets and garage sales are great places to source these types of containers inexpensively. To cushion all the items, coffee beans are a natural choice. You could box up the babka buns in individual bakery boxes or waxed paper bags, or pack a few into a larger bakery box if that works better with the gift container you're using. A tea towel or cloth napkin will cushion coffee glasses or cups, if you're giving those.

START WITH

Chocolate Babka Buns (page 260)

Cold Brew Coffee Concentrate (page 58)

Coffee Liqueur (page 125)

Milk of choice

IF YOU WANT, ADD

Cinnamon Coffee Cake Muffins (page 256)

Biscoff cookies

Coffee beans

Cold brew coffee carafe

Glasses

ULTIMATE CHOCOLATE CUPCAKES WITH GANACHE FILLING

makes: 12 cupcakes   total time: 45 minutes, plus 2 hours chilling and cooling

66 So what makes these cupcakes worthy of the 'ultimate' tag? Well, they succeed at providing intense chocolate flavor combined with a very tender texture. Plus, you can decorate them with sprinkles or other decor for any occasion: a birthday party, Valentine's Day, Halloween, a bachelorette party, or what have you. For an extra-decadent touch, I like to spoon a simple chocolate ganache onto the cupcakes before baking them, which sinks into the middle for a truffle-like center. Though I highly recommend this, you could skip it for a more traditional cupcake."

HOW I GIFT THIS

packaging: A cupcake carrier or covered platter will best protect the frosting and any decorations.

storage: Unfrosted cupcakes can be stored at room temperature for about 2 days. The buttercream can be refrigerated for about 2 days; warm it briefly in the microwave until just slightly softened, 5 to 10 seconds, then stir until creamy. Frosted cupcakes can be stored at room temperature for about 4 hours.

make it a duo: For a kid-friendly celebration, pair with ice cream or Hot Chocolate Mix (page 52). For a grown-up celebration, pair with a bottle of Lambrusco.

filling
- 2 ounces bittersweet chocolate, chopped fine
- ¼ cup heavy cream
- 1 tablespoon confectioners' sugar

cupcakes
- 3 ounces bittersweet chocolate, chopped fine
- ⅓ cup (1 ounce) unsweetened cocoa powder
- ¾ cup brewed coffee, hot
- ¾ cup (4⅛ ounces) bread flour
- ¾ cup (5¼ ounces) granulated sugar
- ½ teaspoon table salt
- ½ teaspoon baking soda
- 6 tablespoons vegetable oil
- 2 large eggs
- 2 teaspoons distilled white vinegar
- 1 teaspoon vanilla extract
- 1 recipe Chocolate Buttercream Sprinkles or other decoration (optional)

1. for the filling: Microwave chocolate, cream, and confectioners' sugar in bowl at 50 percent power until mixture is warm to touch, about 30 seconds. Whisk until smooth, then transfer bowl to refrigerator and let sit until filling is just chilled, no longer than 30 minutes.

2. for the cupcakes: Adjust oven rack to middle position and heat oven to 350 degrees. Line 12-cup muffin tin with paper or foil liners. Place chocolate and cocoa in large heatproof bowl. Pour hot coffee over mixture and let sit, covered, for 5 minutes. Whisk chocolate mixture gently until smooth, then transfer to refrigerator and let cool completely, about 20 minutes.

3. Whisk flour, granulated sugar, salt, and baking soda together in bowl. Whisk oil, eggs, vinegar, and vanilla into cooled chocolate mixture until smooth. Add flour mixture and whisk until smooth.

4. Divide batter evenly among prepared muffin cups. Place 1 slightly rounded teaspoon filling on top of each portion of batter. Bake cupcakes until set and just firm to touch, 17 to 19 minutes, rotating muffin tin halfway through baking. Let cupcakes cool in muffin tin on wire rack for 10 minutes. Remove cupcakes from muffin tin and let cool completely on rack, about 1 hour. Spread or pipe frosting evenly on cupcakes and decorate with sprinkles, if desired.

CHOCOLATE BUTTERCREAM

makes: 2¼ cups (enough for 12 cupcakes)
total time: 20 minutes

The melted chocolate should be cooled to between 85 and 100 degrees before adding to the frosting.

⅓ cup (2⅓ ounces) granulated sugar
2 large egg whites
　 Pinch table salt
12 tablespoons unsalted butter, cut into 12 pieces and softened
6 ounces bittersweet chocolate, melted and cooled
½ teaspoon vanilla extract

1. Combine sugar, egg whites, and salt in bowl of stand mixer. Set bowl over saucepan filled with 1 inch of barely simmering water, making sure that water does not touch bottom of bowl. Cook, whisking gently but constantly, until mixture registers 150 degrees and is slightly thickened and foamy, about 3 minutes.

2. Remove bowl from heat and transfer to stand mixer fitted with whisk attachment. Whip warm egg mixture on medium speed until it has consistency of shaving cream and has cooled slightly, 1 to 2 minutes. Add butter, 1 piece at a time, and whip until smooth and creamy, about 2 minutes. (Frosting may look curdled after half of butter has been added; it will smooth out with additional butter.)

3. Add cooled chocolate and vanilla and mix until combined. Increase speed to medium-high and whip until light and fluffy, about 30 seconds, scraping down bowl as needed. If frosting seems too soft after adding chocolate, chill it briefly in refrigerator, then rewhip until creamy.

PUMPKIN CUPCAKES WITH CREAM CHEESE FROSTING

makes: 12 cupcakes   **total time:** 1 hour, plus 1 hour cooling

" I like to taste *pumpkin* in my pumpkin-flavored treats. 'Pumpkin spice' has morphed into a flavor all its own, separate from pumpkin, and while I'm certainly not going to diss that, it's not what these cupcakes represent. They have undeniable pumpkin flavor thanks to unsweetened pumpkin puree, making them a very appropriate gift for any fall harvest holiday, be it Halloween, Thanksgiving, Sukkot, or a harvest supermoon. The cream cheese frosting, made even tangier with a little sour cream, is an irresistible complement. If the frosting becomes too soft to work with, let it chill in the refrigerator until firm."

HOW I GIFT THIS

packaging: These are sturdy, but I still suggest a cupcake carrier or platter.

storage: Unfrosted cupcakes can be stored at room temperature for about 3 days. The frosting can be refrigerated for about 3 days; let soften at room temperature, about 1 hour, then rewhip on medium speed until smooth, about 2 minutes. Frosted cupcakes can be stored at room temperature for about 4 hours.

make it a basket: Make a fall basket by adding cider doughnuts, apple cider or fresh-picked apples, and an ornamental pumpkin or gourd.

1 cup (5 ounces) all-purpose flour
1 teaspoon ground cinnamon
1 teaspoon baking powder
½ teaspoon baking soda
½ teaspoon table salt
⅛ teaspoon ground allspice
⅛ teaspoon ground ginger
¾ cup canned unsweetened pumpkin puree
7 tablespoons (3 ounces) granulated sugar
½ cup vegetable oil
2 large eggs
1 recipe Cream Cheese Frosting

1. Adjust oven rack to middle position and heat oven to 350 degrees. Line 12-cup muffin tin with paper or foil liners. Whisk flour, cinnamon, baking powder, baking soda, salt, allspice, and ginger together in large bowl. Whisk pumpkin, sugar, oil, and eggs together in second bowl until smooth. Using rubber spatula, stir pumpkin mixture into flour mixture until combined.

2. Divide batter evenly among prepared muffin cups. Bake until toothpick inserted in center comes out with few crumbs attached, 15 to 20 minutes, rotating muffin tin halfway through baking. Let cupcakes cool in muffin tin on wire rack for 10 minutes. Remove cupcakes from muffin tin and let cool completely on rack, about 1 hour. Spread or pipe frosting evenly on cupcakes.

CREAM CHEESE FROSTING
makes: 3 cups (enough for 12 cupcakes)

12 ounces cream cheese, softened
6 tablespoons unsalted butter, cut into 6 pieces and softened
1½ tablespoons sour cream
1 teaspoon vanilla extract
¼ teaspoon salt
1½ cups (6 ounces) confectioners' sugar
Food coloring (optional)

Using stand mixer fitted with paddle, beat cream cheese, butter, sour cream, vanilla, and salt on medium-high speed until smooth, about 2 minutes. Reduce speed to medium-low, slowly add sugar, and beat until incorporated and smooth, about 4 minutes. Add food coloring (if using), increase speed to medium-high, and beat until frosting is light and fluffy, about 4 minutes.

ICED LEMON–POPPY SEED BUNDT CAKE

serves: 12   total time: 1½ hours, plus 3 hours cooling

66 This Bundt is for all the lemon lovers in your life. Lemon zest and juice give the cake and glaze eye-opening lemon flavor, while buttermilk bolsters the overall tanginess of this tender cake. Decorated with Candied Rose Petals (page 244), this makes an elegant Mother's Day gift. (Or if the mother in mind is more on the playful side, put some flowers into the 'hole in this cake!,' like Maria Portokalos did in *My Big Fat Greek Wedding*.) You can also use the batter to make adorable mini Bundt cakes to bring along to a bachelorette weekend. For mini Bundt cakes, make sure to leave at least a ½-inch headspace to prevent the batter from spilling over."

HOW I GIFT THIS

packaging: Bakery boxes work for both the full-size cake and mini Bundts. You can gift the cake glazed, or gift the cake with the glaze in a little jar on the side for the recipient to pour over the top. A domed cake plate, or a round tray or platter that can be covered, would be a dramatic presentation for a glazed cake with rose petals.

storage: The cake and the glaze (together or separately) can be stored at room temperature for about 2 days. Don't refrigerate the glaze or else it will harden, and whisk to combine before using.

make it a duo: Pair with small-batch lemonade, sweet iced tea, sparkling Italian soda, or a jar of lemon curd.

make it a basket: Build an afternoon tea basket around this cake by adding one of the Tea Blends (page 57), Citrus Syrup (page 115), crème fraîche, and a tea infuser or reusable tea bags.

cake

- 3 cups (15 ounces) all-purpose flour
- 3 tablespoons poppy seeds
- 1 teaspoon table salt
- 1 teaspoon baking powder
- ½ teaspoon baking soda
- ¾ cup buttermilk, room temperature
- 3 tablespoons grated lemon zest plus 3 tablespoons juice (3 lemons)
- 1 tablespoon vanilla extract
- 18 tablespoons (2¼ sticks) unsalted butter, cut into 18 pieces and softened
- 2 cups (14 ounces) granulated sugar
- 3 large eggs plus 1 large yolk

glaze

- 2 cups (8 ounces) confectioners' sugar
- 2–3 tablespoons lemon juice
- 1 tablespoon buttermilk

1. for the cake: Adjust oven rack to lower-middle position and heat oven to 350 degrees. Spray 12-cup nonstick Bundt pan with baking spray with flour. Whisk flour, poppy seeds, salt, baking powder, and baking soda together in bowl. Whisk buttermilk, lemon zest and juice, and vanilla together in second bowl.

2. Using stand mixer fitted with paddle, beat softened butter and granulated sugar on medium-high speed until pale and fluffy, about 3 minutes. Add eggs and yolk, one at a time, and beat until combined. Reduce speed to low and add flour mixture in 3 additions, alternating with buttermilk mixture in 2 additions, scraping down bowl as needed. Give batter final stir by hand.

3. Transfer batter to prepared pan and smooth top with rubber spatula. Bake until skewer inserted in center comes out with few crumbs attached, 50 minutes to 1 hour, rotating pan halfway through baking. Let cake cool in pan on wire rack set in rimmed baking sheet for 10 minutes.

4. for the glaze: While cake bakes, whisk confectioners' sugar, 2 tablespoons lemon juice, and buttermilk until smooth, adding more lemon juice as needed, teaspoon by teaspoon, until glaze is thick but still pourable.

5. Invert cake onto rack and remove pan. Whisk glaze to recombine, then pour half of glaze over warm cake and let cool for 1 hour. Whisk remaining glaze to recombine, then drizzle evenly over cake and let cool completely, at least 2 hours, before serving.

variation
MINI LEMON–POPPY SEED BUNDT CAKES
makes: 12 mini Bundt cakes

Thoroughly coat interior of twelve ¾-cup Bundt molds with baking spray with flour. Divide batter evenly among prepared molds and bake for about 50 minutes.

CHOCOLATE-SOUR CREAM BUNDT CAKE

serves: 12   **total time:** 1½ hours, plus 3 hours cooling

66 A simple, perfect chocolate Bundt cake never fails to make people's eyes widen with joy. This one uses bittersweet chocolate and natural cocoa powder, plus brown sugar and sour cream for a moist tanginess. The espresso powder adds a subtlety that will have your recipient asking for the recipe. If you make the 12 adorably giftable mini Bundts, make sure to leave at least a ½-inch headspace to prevent the batter from spilling over."

HOW I GIFT THIS

packaging: Bakery boxes work for both the full-size cake or mini Bundts. A domed cake plate would also look great for the full-size cake. Wrapping mini Bundts furoshiki-style (see page 256) makes for a sweet presentation.

storage: The cake can be stored at room temperature for about 2 days.

make it a duo: Pair with Brandied Cherry and Hazelnut Conserve (page 32) or Coffee Liqueur (page 125).

¾ cup (2¼ ounces) natural unsweetened cocoa powder, plus 1 tablespoon for pan

12 tablespoons unsalted butter, cut into 12 pieces and softened, plus 1 tablespoon, melted, for pan

6 ounces bittersweet chocolate, chopped

1 teaspoon instant espresso powder (optional)

¾ cup boiling water

1 cup sour cream, room temperature

1¾ cups (8¾ ounces) all-purpose flour

1 teaspoon table salt

1 teaspoon baking soda

2 cups packed (14 ounces) light brown sugar

1 tablespoon vanilla extract

5 large eggs, room temperature
   Confectioners' sugar (optional)

1. Adjust oven rack to lower-middle position and heat oven to 350 degrees. Mix 1 tablespoon cocoa and melted butter into paste in bowl. Using pastry brush, thoroughly coat interior of 12-cup nonstick Bundt pan.

2. Combine chocolate; espresso powder, if using; and remaining ¾ cup cocoa in bowl. Pour boiling water over mixture and let sit, covered, for 5 minutes. Whisk mixture gently until smooth. Let cool completely, then whisk in sour cream. Whisk flour, salt, and baking soda together in second bowl.

3. Using stand mixer fitted with paddle, beat softened butter, brown sugar, and vanilla on medium-high speed until pale and fluffy, about 3 minutes. Add eggs, one at a time, and beat until combined. Reduce speed to low and add flour mixture in 3 additions, alternating with chocolate-sour cream mixture in 2 additions, scraping down bowl as needed. Give batter final stir by hand.

4. Transfer batter to prepared pan and smooth top with rubber spatula. Bake until skewer inserted in center comes out with few crumbs attached, 45 to 50 minutes, rotating pan halfway through baking. Let cake cool in pan on wire rack for 10 minutes. Invert cake onto rack, remove pan, and let cool completely, about 3 hours. Dust with confectioners' sugar, if using.

variation
MINI CHOCOLATE-SOUR CREAM BUNDT CAKES
makes: 12 mini Bundt cakes

Increase cocoa powder for pans to 2 tablespoons and melted butter to 2 tablespoons. Thoroughly coat interior of twelve ¾-cup Bundt molds. Divide batter evenly among prepared molds and bake for about 45 minutes.

Chocolate Bundt Cake

Chocolate Bundt Cake

HAPPY BIRTHDAY

66 We all have those people in our lives who are hard to buy for when it comes to birthdays, am I right? Well, I promise you that this consumable gift basket—a portable birthday party, in fact—will be one they remember for a long time. I chose these recipes because I think the flavors appeal to all ages, but there are other options in this chapter if you'd like to design your own flavor ways. Then, depending on the individual who's having the birthday, you can tailor the decorations on the cupcakes and the cake pops accordingly. Including decorated paper plates and napkins is another fun way to customize this memorable birthday basket."

HOW I GIFT THIS

I pack all the goodies into a colorful plastic tub with a tight-fitting lid, arranging the elements attractively so that the recipient is ready to party as soon as they open it up! Wrapping the cake pops individually in cellophane (like lollipops) and then gathering them together with tissue paper and a ribbon to make a bouquet is a festive touch—and also serves to visually divide the cupcakes from the cream pies. Depending on how large the birthday celebration is, you may need more than one tub—or conversely, you may have some leftover treats to keep for yourself or give to neighbors or co-workers. If you're giving plates, napkins, and utensils, wrap those separately or slip them into a paper gift bag.

START WITH

Party Cake Pops (page 274)

Ultimate Chocolate Cupcakes with Ganache Filling (page 264)

Banana-Caramel Pie in a Jar (page 294)

IF YOU WANT, ADD

Dulce de Leche (page 63)

Extra whipped cream (you can never have enough!)

Ice cream

Party plates, napkins, and utensils

Candles for the cupcakes

PARTY CAKE POPS

makes: about 36 cake pops   **total time:** 1 hour, plus 3½ hours cooling, freezing, and resting

66 Everybody loves food on a stick; my top choice is corn dogs, but the first runner up is cake pops! These pops are all-ages friendly because they aren't tooth-achingly sweet like pops that call for cake mix and store-bought frosting. The homemade yellow cake provides enough crumbs for about three dozen pops. Milk and confectioners' sugar bind them together, and freezing the cake balls briefly firms them up before coating them with chocolate. A 2-cup liquid measuring cup is great for this, because its tall, narrow sides allow for easier dipping. You'll need a floral foam block (available at craft stores and online) to stand the cake pops upright as the coating sets. Or stand the dipped pops upside-down on a parchment paper–lined baking sheet (note that this will give the tops a flat appearance). To make different colors for the coating, add food coloring to the melted white chocolate chips."

HOW I GIFT THIS

packaging: Tie a few cake pops with twine and wrap them with tissue or parchment paper, like a bouquet. Or decorate the foam block and gift the pops in the block. Or wrap pops individually, like lollipops.

storage: The cake pops can be refrigerated for about 3 days.

make it a duo: Pair with the Cookies and Cream Cake Pops (page 276).

1½ cups (7½ ounces) all-purpose flour
1 cup (7 ounces) granulated sugar
1½ teaspoons baking powder
½ teaspoon table salt
8 tablespoons unsalted butter, softened
½ cup sour cream
1 large egg plus 2 large yolks, room temperature
1½ teaspoons vanilla extract
¼ cup milk
2 tablespoons confectioners' sugar
2½ cups (15 ounces) white chocolate chips or semisweet chocolate chips
Lollipop sticks
Multicolored nonpareil sprinkles

1. Adjust oven rack to middle position and heat oven to 350 degrees. Grease 8-inch square baking pan, line with parchment paper, grease parchment, and flour parchment.

2. Whisk flour, granulated sugar, baking powder, and salt together in bowl of stand mixer. Fit stand mixer with paddle and add butter, sour cream, egg and yolks, and vanilla. Beat on medium speed until smooth and satiny, about 30 seconds. Scrape down bowl with rubber spatula and stir by hand until smooth and no flour pockets remain.

3. Scrape batter into prepared pan and smooth top with rubber spatula. Gently tap pan on counter to release air bubbles. Bake until light golden and toothpick inserted in center comes out clean, 25 to 30 minutes, rotating pan halfway through baking. Let cake cool in pan on wire rack for 10 minutes. Remove cake from pan, discarding parchment, and let cool completely on rack, about 2 hours. (Cake can be wrapped in plastic wrap and stored at room temperature for up to 24 hours.)

4. In clean, dry bowl of stand mixer fitted with paddle, break cake into rough 1-inch pieces. Add milk and confectioners' sugar and beat on medium-low speed until broken into fine, evenly moistened crumbs and cohesive dough begins to form, about 1 minute, scraping down bowl as needed.

5. Line rimmed baking sheet with parchment. Working with 1 packed tablespoon cake mixture at a time, roll into balls and place in single layer on prepared sheet. Cover with plastic wrap and freeze until firm but still pliable, 45 minutes to 1 hour.

6. Microwave 2 cups chocolate chips in 2-cup liquid measuring cup at 50 percent power, stirring occasionally, until melted, 1 to 2 minutes. Working with 1 cake ball at a time, insert lollipop stick into cake ball, stopping at center. Dip entire cake ball into melted chocolate and turn until completely coated (tipping measuring cup to the side as needed). Lift up from chocolate (do not turn upright) and gently shake side to side to allow excess coating to drip off evenly. Turn cake pop upright, gently twist back and forth

to even out coating, and insert stick into foam block. Sprinkle with nonpareils. Stir and rewarm chocolate in microwave as needed to stay fluid; add remaining ½ cup chocolate chips and melt when chocolate level becomes too low to dip easily. (If cake balls become too soft, refreeze until firm.)

7. Let cake pops sit at room temperature until coating is set, about 30 minutes.

COOKIES AND CREAM CAKE POPS

makes: about 36 cake pops   total time: 1½ hours, plus 3½ hours cooling, freezing, and resting

" Flavor variations for cake pops are so wide-ranging that it's hard to choose my favorites for gifting. Cookies and cream is a whimsical, universally popular favorite among kids and kids-at-heart. These pops use a fudgy cake base, and the cake balls are dipped into melted white chocolate chips (the 'cream' element of the pops) then rolled in crushed Oreo cookies for a crunchy exterior. A 2-cup liquid measuring cup is great for melting the chocolate chips, because its tall, narrow sides allow for easier dipping. You'll need a floral foam block (available at craft stores and online) to stand the cake pops upright as the coating sets. Or stand the dipped cake pops upside-down on a parchment paper–lined baking sheet (note that this will give the tops a flat appearance). Don't substitute natural cocoa powder for the Dutch-processed. To make different colors for the coating, add food coloring to the melted white chocolate chips."

HOW I GIFT THIS

packaging: Cut the foam block to fit inside a flowerpot and give an edible potted plant! Or decorate the foam block and gift the pops standing in the foam block.

storage: The cake pops can be refrigerated for about 3 days.

make it a duo: Pair with Party Cake Pops (page 274).

¾ cup (5¼ ounces) sugar
10 tablespoons (3⅛ ounces) all-purpose flour
¼ teaspoon baking soda
¼ teaspoon table salt
½ cup plus 2 tablespoons whole milk
4 ounces bittersweet chocolate, chopped fine
6 tablespoons (1⅛ ounces) Dutch-processed cocoa powder
⅓ cup vegetable oil
2 large eggs
½ teaspoon vanilla extract
6 Oreo cookies
2½ cups (15 ounces) white chocolate chips
Lollipop sticks

1. Adjust oven rack to middle position and heat oven to 325 degrees. Grease 8-inch square baking pan, line with parchment paper, grease parchment, and flour parchment.

2. Whisk sugar, flour, baking soda, and salt together in medium bowl; set aside. Combine ½ cup milk, bittersweet chocolate, and cocoa in medium saucepan. Place saucepan over low heat and cook, whisking frequently, until chocolate is melted and mixture is smooth. Remove from heat and let cool slightly, about 5 minutes. Whisk oil, eggs, and vanilla into chocolate mixture (it may initially look curdled) until smooth and homogeneous. Add sugar mixture and whisk until combined, making sure to scrape corners of saucepan.

3. Scrape batter into prepared pan and smooth top with rubber spatula. Gently tap pan on counter to release air bubbles. Bake until toothpick inserted in center comes out clean, 30 to 35 minutes, rotating pan halfway through baking. Let cake cool in pan on wire rack for 10 minutes. Remove cake from pan, discarding parchment, and let cool completely on wire rack, about 2 hours. (Cake can be wrapped in plastic wrap and stored at room temperature for up to 24 hours.)

4. In bowl of stand mixer fitted with paddle, break cake into rough 1-inch pieces. Add remaining 2 tablespoons milk and beat on medium-low speed until broken into fine, evenly moistened crumbs and cohesive dough begins to form, about 1 minute, scraping down bowl as needed.

5. Line rimmed baking sheet with parchment. Working with 1 packed tablespoon cake mixture at a time, roll into balls and place in single layer on prepared sheet. Cover with plastic wrap and freeze until firm but still pliable, 45 minutes to 1 hour.

6. Place cookies in zipper-lock bag and crush with rolling pin until broken into small pieces; transfer to small bowl. Microwave 2 cups chocolate chips in 2-cup liquid measuring cup at 50 percent power, stirring occasionally, until melted, 1 to 2 minutes. Working with 1 cake ball at a time, insert lollipop stick into cake ball, stopping at center. Dip entire cake ball into melted chocolate and turn until completely coated. Lift up from chocolate (do not turn upright) and gently shake side to side to allow excess coating to drip off evenly. Turn cake pop upright and gently twist back and forth to even out coating. Dip into crushed cookies, pressing gently to adhere. Turn cake pop upright and insert stick into foam block. Stir and rewarm chocolate in microwave as needed to stay fluid; add remaining ½ cup chocolate chips and melt when chocolate level becomes too low to dip easily. (If cake balls become too soft, refreeze until firm.)

7. Let cake pops stand at room temperature until coating is set, about 30 minutes.

TRIPLE-BERRY SLAB PIE WITH GINGER-LEMON STREUSEL

makes: two 11 by 8-inch pies (each serves 9 to 12)   total time: 2 hours, plus 4 hours chilling and cooling

66 Nothing says summer to me quite like a homemade pie bursting with fresh berries, and this is one of my favorite recipes to make and share with my special people after I've gone berry picking. It uses blueberries, blackberries, and raspberries, so you can make it all through the summer, as each of these berries comes into U-pick season. It makes two quarter sheet pan–size pies that will disappear fast at a backyard BBQ, Fourth of July bonfire, or neighborhood block party. The streusel top is just right, too: more summery and somehow more casual than a double-crust pie. Make sure to weigh the flour for this recipe. In the mixing stage, the dough will be moister than most pie doughs, but as it chills it will absorb much of the excess moisture. Be sure to roll the dough on a well-floured counter. You'll need two small rimmed baking sheets with a cooking surface measuring at least 11 by 8 inches for this recipe."

HOW I GIFT THIS

packaging: Using a small rimmed baking sheet lid makes gifting this pie a breeze. The cover snaps right on and keeps the pie protected and intact.

storage: The pie can be refrigerated for about 3 days.

make it a duo: I think all this really needs for a perfect pairing is to add a pie server or a small metal pancake turner.

dough

- 24 tablespoons (3 sticks) unsalted butter, divided
- 2¾ cups (13¾ ounces) all-purpose flour, divided
- 2 tablespoons granulated sugar
- 1 teaspoon table salt
- ½ cup ice water, divided

streusel

- 1½ cups (7½ ounces) all-purpose flour
- ½ cup packed (3½ ounces) light brown sugar
- ½ cup crystallized ginger, chopped fine
- ¼ cup (1¾ ounces) granulated sugar
- 1 tablespoon ground ginger
- 1 teaspoon grated lemon zest
- ¼ teaspoon table salt
- 10 tablespoons unsalted butter, melted and cooled

filling

- 1 cup (7 ounces) granulated sugar
- 6 tablespoons instant tapioca, ground
- 1 teaspoon grated lemon zest
- ¼ teaspoon table salt
- 1¼ pounds (4 cups) blackberries
- 1¼ pounds (4 cups) blueberries
- 1¼ pounds (4 cups) raspberries

1. for the dough: Grate 5 tablespoons butter on large holes of box grater and place in freezer. Cut remaining 19 tablespoons butter into ½-inch cubes.

2. Pulse 1¾ cups flour, granulated sugar, and salt in food processor until combined, about 2 pulses. Add cubed butter and process until homogeneous paste forms, 40 to 50 seconds. Using your hands, carefully break paste into 2-inch chunks and redistribute evenly around processor blade.

recipe continues

Add remaining 1 cup flour and pulse until mixture is broken into pieces no larger than 1 inch (most pieces will be much smaller), 4 to 5 pulses. Transfer mixture to bowl. Add frozen grated butter and toss until butter pieces are separated and coated with flour.

3. Sprinkle ¼ cup ice water over mixture. Toss with rubber spatula until mixture is evenly moistened. Sprinkle remaining ¼ cup ice water over mixture and toss to combine. Press dough with spatula until dough sticks together. Using spatula, divide dough into 2 equal portions. Transfer each portion to sheet of plastic wrap. Working with 1 portion at a time, draw edges of plastic over dough and press firmly on sides and top to form compact, fissure-free mass. Wrap in plastic and form into 5 by 6-inch rectangle. Refrigerate dough for at least 2 hours or up to 2 days. (Wrapped dough can be frozen for up to 1 month. If frozen, let dough thaw completely on counter before rolling.)

4. Let chilled dough sit on counter to soften slightly, about 10 minutes, before rolling. Line 1 small rimmed baking sheet with parchment paper. Roll each dough square into 15 by 12-inch rectangle on floured counter; stack dough on prepared sheet, separated by second sheet of parchment. Cover loosely with plastic wrap and refrigerate until dough is firm but still pliable, about 10 minutes.

5. Spray 1 small rimmed baking sheet with vegetable oil spray. Using parchment as sling, transfer one chilled dough rectangle to counter and return sheet with second dough rectangle to refrigerator. Starting at short side of dough rectangle on counter, loosely roll around rolling pin, then gently unroll over one short side of greased sheet, leaving about 2 inches of dough overhanging each edge.

6. Ease dough into sheet by gently lifting edges of dough with your hand while pressing into sheet bottom with your other hand. Trim overhang to ½ inch beyond edge of sheet. Tuck overhang under itself; folded edge should be flush with edge of sheet. Crimp dough evenly around edge of sheet with tines of fork. Cover loosely with plastic and refrigerate until firm, about 30 minutes. Repeat process with second dough rectangle, removing it from baking sheet and greasing baking sheet with vegetable oil spray before fitting with dough.

7. for the streusel: Meanwhile, adjust oven racks to lower-middle and lowest positions and heat oven to 375 degrees. Combine flour, brown sugar, crystallized ginger, granulated sugar, ground ginger, lemon zest, and salt in bowl. Stir in melted butter until mixture is completely moistened; let sit for 10 minutes.

8. for the filling: Whisk granulated sugar, tapioca, lemon zest, and salt together in large bowl. Add blackberries, blueberries, and raspberries and gently toss to combine. Spread half of berry mixture evenly over one chilled dough-lined sheet. Sprinkle half of streusel evenly over fruit, breaking apart any large chunks. Repeat with second chilled dough-lined sheet, remaining filling, and remaining streusel. Place large sheet of aluminum foil directly on lower rack (to catch any bubbling juices). Place pies on upper rack (short sides facing you) and bake until crusts and streusels are deep golden brown and juices are bubbling, 45 to 50 minutes, rotating sheets halfway through baking. Let pies cool on wire rack until filling has set, about 1½ hours.

GRAPEFRUIT TART WITH PUMPERNICKEL-CARAWAY CRUST

serves: 8 to 10   **total time:** 1½ hours, plus 5 hours cooling and chilling

" This showstopping tart is definitely 'outside the box' and an impressive gift for someone who enjoys unexpected flavors. It hits the right notes for a Mother's Day or intimate engagement party gift. Toasted caraway seeds in the crust are a warm, peppery nod to pumpernickel bread. The striking contrast of the pink-orange filling against the dark crust makes it look as good as it tastes. Garnishing the tart with whipped cream mellows the zesty flavors—and this stable whipped cream can be added to the tart either before or after gifting. You can substitute rye flour for pumpernickel, if you prefer. This recipe calls for a rectangular tart pan; or you can use four 4-inch tart pans with removable bottoms or one 9-inch round tart pan with removable bottom (you may have leftover filling). The baking times will be the same."

HOW I GIFT THIS

packaging: A windowed bakery box protects the tart and makes it look professional.

storage: The tart can be refrigerated, covered, for about 3 days. If any moisture collects on top, gently dab with a paper towel before gifting.

make it a duo: Pair with sparkling Moscato, a nonalcoholic sparkler, or a liqueur like Grand Marnier.

dough
- ¾ teaspoon caraway seeds
- ¾ cup (4⅛ ounces) pumpernickel flour
- ¼ cup (1¼ ounces) all-purpose flour
- ¼ cup (2¼ ounces) packed dark brown sugar
- ¼ teaspoon table salt
- 8 tablespoons unsalted butter
- 1½ tablespoons water

filling
- ¾ cup (5¼ ounces) granulated sugar
- 3 large eggs plus 4 large yolks
- 1 tablespoon cornstarch
- ½ teaspoon table salt
- 1 tablespoon grated grapefruit zest plus 1 cup juice
- 3 tablespoons lemon juice
- 5 tablespoons unsalted butter, cut into 10 pieces and chilled
- 6 drops red liquid food coloring

whipped cream
- 1 cup heavy cream
- 1 teaspoon granulated sugar

1. for the dough: Adjust oven rack to middle position and heat oven to 350 degrees. Toast caraway seeds in small skillet over medium-low heat until fragrant, 3 to 5 minutes; let cool. Grind seeds fine in spice grinder. Whisk pumpernickel flour, all-purpose flour, brown sugar, caraway, and salt in bowl. Melt butter in small saucepan over medium-high heat, swirling pan occasionally, until butter melts, about 3 minutes. Reduce heat to medium-low and cook, stirring and scraping bottom of pan with spatula, until milk solids are dark golden brown and butter has nutty aroma, 3 to 5 minutes. Remove pan from heat and add water (it will bubble vigorously). When bubbling subsides, add butter to flour mixture and stir until combined.

2. Using your hands, crumble three-quarters of dough over bottom of 14¼ by 4¾-inch rectangular tart pan with removable bottom. Press dough to even thickness in bottom of pan. Crumble remaining dough and scatter evenly around edge of pan, then press dough into sides of pan to even thickness. Place pan on rimmed baking sheet and bake until edges of tart shell darken slightly, 25 to 30 minutes, rotating sheet halfway through baking. Transfer sheet with tart shell to wire rack.

3. for the filling: Whisk granulated sugar, eggs and yolks, cornstarch, and salt in medium bowl until smooth. Bring grapefruit juice and lemon juice to simmer in medium saucepan over medium-high heat. Whisking constantly, slowly pour hot juice mixture into egg mixture and whisk until smooth; transfer egg mixture to now-empty saucepan.

4. Cook egg mixture over medium heat, stirring constantly, until mixture clings to spoon and registers 165 to 170 degrees in multiple places, 3 to 5 minutes. Off heat, stir in chilled butter and food coloring. Once butter is melted and fully incorporated, strain curd through fine-mesh strainer into small bowl. Whisk in grapefruit zest.

5. Pour filling into tart shell (shell doesn't need to be fully cooled). Bake until edges of filling are just set but center jiggles when pan is gently shaken, 15 to 20 minutes. Transfer sheet to wire rack and let tart cool completely, about 1 hour. Refrigerate, uncovered, until filling is well chilled, about

4 hours. Remove outer metal band of pan. Slide thin metal spatula between tart and pan bottom, then carefully slide tart onto plate.

6. for the whipped cream: Process cream and granulated sugar in food processor for 45 seconds. Pulse in 5-second intervals for 15 to 20 seconds, until cream is thickened and has consistency of buttercream frosting. Either transfer whipped cream to storage container or add to pastry bag fitted with pastry tip and pipe onto tart as desired. (Whipped cream can be refrigerated for up to 2 weeks.)

LEMON TARTLETS

makes: 6 tartlets   total time: 1 hour 20 minutes, plus 2 hours cooling

66 Whole tarts are obviously impressive to make and give, but individual tartlets are coveted darlings of pastry cases everywhere. Giving someone the experience of enjoying a sleek fluted tart that's all their own will turn you into a star pastry chef in their eyes. Give these for bridal or baby showers or for Teacher Appreciation Day. This is an easy tartlet too, with a pat-in-the-pan crust that you blind bake first so that it stays crisp after pouring in the bright, tart lemon filling for the final bake. Once the lemon curd ingredients are combined, cook them immediately; otherwise, the curd will be grainy. Add the filling to the tart shells while they are still warm; if the shells have cooled, rewarm them in the oven for 5 minutes first. You'll need six 4-inch tart pans with removable bottoms for these tartlets."

HOW I GIFT THIS

packaging: Give the tartlets individually in cellophane bags or small bakery boxes. Or present them all on a tray. If you like, dust the tartlets with confectioners' sugar just before gifting. Or put some confectioners' sugar in a small shaker to include with the gift.

storage: The tarts can be refrigerated for about 3 days.

make it a trio: Combine with a bottle of limoncello and a lemon thyme plant. Or team with a bottle of Sauternes and fresh berries.

crust
- 2 cups (10 ounces) all-purpose flour
- ½ cup (3½ ounces) sugar
- ¾ teaspoon table salt
- 14 tablespoons unsalted butter, melted

filling
- 3 large eggs plus 9 large yolks
- 1 cup (7 ounces) sugar
- 3 tablespoons grated lemon zest plus ¾ cup juice (4 lemons)
- ¼ teaspoon table salt
- 6 tablespoons unsalted butter, cut into 6 pieces
- 3 tablespoons heavy cream, chilled

1. **for the crust:** Adjust oven racks to middle and lowest positions and heat oven to 350 degrees. Spray six 4-inch tart pans with removable bottoms with vegetable oil spray. Whisk flour, sugar, and salt together in bowl. Add melted butter and stir until dough forms.

2. Divide dough into 6 equal pieces. Working with 1 piece of dough at a time, press two-thirds of dough into bottom of 1 prepared pan using your fingers. Press remaining dough into sides of pan. Press and smooth dough with your fingers to even thickness.

3. Line tart pans with double layer of aluminum foil, covering edges to prevent burning, and fill with pie weights. Place pans on wire rack set in rimmed baking sheet and bake on lower rack until edges are beginning to turn golden, about 25 minutes. Carefully remove foil and weights, rotate sheet, and continue to bake until tart shells are golden brown and firm to touch, 10 to 15 minutes; set aside (tart shells must still be warm when filling is added).

4. **for the filling:** Whisk eggs and yolks together in medium saucepan. Whisk in sugar until combined, then whisk in lemon zest and juice and salt. Add butter and cook over medium-low heat, stirring constantly, until mixture thickens slightly and registers 170 degrees, about 5 minutes. Immediately pour mixture through fine-mesh strainer into bowl. Stir in cream.

5. With tarts still on wire rack, divide warm lemon filling evenly among warm tart shells. Bake on upper rack until filling is shiny and opaque and centers jiggle slightly when shaken, about 10 minutes, rotating sheet halfway through baking. Let tartlets cool completely on wire rack in sheet, about 2 hours. To remove tarts from pans, remove outer ring of tart pans, then slide thin metal spatula between tartlets and pan bottoms.

EGG TARTS

makes: 12 tarts   **total time:** 1¾ hours, plus 1¾ hours chilling and cooling

" I love visiting bakeries in Boston's vibrant Chinatown, and Cantonese egg tarts are among my favorite treats to bring home. For special gifting and for Chinese New Year, I make these iconic specialties from scratch. The cheerful, sunflower-yellow tartlets will transport your recipient to a teahouse or dim sum parlor. The flaky pastry crust filled with sweet, milky egg custard is perfect for any time of day, from breakfast through late-night snacking. This recipe was developed using twelve individual 3-inch tart pans, which are available online or in kitchen supply stores. You can substitute a 12-cup muffin tin; you'll need to pleat the dough disks around the edge to create a uniform fit. If dough becomes too soft while shaping at any point, refrigerate it until firm to touch, about 10 minutes, before continuing."

HOW I GIFT THIS

packaging: Wrap the tartlets individually in cellophane bags or gift them in a bakery-style box.

storage: The tarts can be refrigerated for about 2 days.

make it a duo: Include some loose-leaf or bagged Chinese black tea.

make it a basket: Build a dim sum basket with Chinese Pork Dumplings (page 181), Chili Crisp (page 67), and Chinese black or jasmine tea.

crust
- 1½ cups (7½ ounces) all-purpose flour
- 1 tablespoon sugar
- ½ teaspoon table salt
- 10 tablespoons unsalted butter, cut into ½-inch pieces and chilled
- 6 tablespoons ice water

custard
- 1 cup warm water (110 degrees)
- ½ cup (3½ ounces) sugar
- 2 large eggs plus 2 large yolks
- ½ cup evaporated milk
- 1 teaspoon vanilla extract
- ⅛ teaspoon table salt

1. for the crust: Process flour, sugar, and salt in food processor until combined, about 5 seconds. Scatter butter over top and pulse until butter pieces are size of small peas, about 10 pulses. Continue to pulse, slowly streaming ice water in until dough begins to form small curds that hold together when pinched with fingers, about 10 pulses.

2. Transfer mixture to lightly floured counter and gather into rectangular-shaped pile. Starting at farthest end, use heel of hand to smear small amount of dough against counter. Continue to smear dough until all crumbs have been worked. Gather smeared crumbs together in another rectangular-shaped pile and repeat process. Form dough into 5-inch square, wrap tightly in plastic wrap, and refrigerate for at least 1 hour or up to 2 days.

3. Evenly space twelve 3-inch metal tart pans on parchment paper–lined rimmed baking sheet and spray with vegetable oil spray; set aside. Divide dough in half. Working with one half of dough at a time, roll into 8 by 12-inch rectangle on lightly floured counter. Using 4-inch round dough cutter, cut out 6 dough rounds. Working with 1 round at a time, center over prepared tart pan and use fingers to press dough evenly into bottom and up sides of pan. Trim any overhang ¼ inch beyond lip of pan. Repeat with remaining 5 dough rounds and then repeat rolling and shaping 6 more rounds with remaining dough half. Lightly prick shells all over with fork, cover loosely with plastic, and refrigerate until dough is firm, about 15 minutes.

4. for the custard: Adjust oven rack to lowest position and heat oven to 400 degrees. Whisk water and sugar in bowl until sugar has dissolved. Let cool to room temperature, about 10 minutes. Whisk eggs, yolks, evaporated milk, vanilla, and salt together in separate large bowl. Whisk sugar-water mixture into egg mixture until combined. Strain egg mixture through fine-mesh strainer set over 4-cup liquid measuring cup or bowl.

5. Divide custard evenly among pastry shells, leaving ¼-inch space below rim of tart pan. (You may have extra filling.) Using fork or toothpick, pop any large bubbles on surface of custard. Carefully transfer sheet to oven and bake until shells are golden brown and crisp and edges of custard are just set and center of custard jiggles slightly when gently shaken, 20 to 25 minutes. Let tarts cool in pans on wire rack for 10 minutes. Gently unmold tarts and let cool on wire rack.

I BROUGHT THE BAKERY

66 I love browsing through mail-order catalogs from famous bakeries. Their gift ideas are so creative and mouthwatering—and usually very expensive. It's much more personal and special to give someone a from-scratch basket of home-baked goods. And with the choices here, there's no skimping on creativity. This is my 'anytime' basket, but you can lean into an autumn theme by subbing Cranberry-Orange-Pecan Bread (page 252) for the blueberry bread, or a chocolate theme by subbing Chocolate-Coffee-Hazelnut Bread (page 252) for the blueberry bread and Mini Chocolate–Sour Cream Bundt Cakes (page 270) for the pies. Let your creativity rise!"

HOW I GIFT THIS

I line a wooden crate with parchment paper and fill it to the brim for a really generous-looking gift. I'm always on the lookout at flea markets, vintage markets, and antique warehouses for food-themed crates like the oh-so appropriate baking powder crate here. Or I pack everything into a large, sturdy bakery box tied with twine, as though I've just come from a fancy bakery. For quicker prep, you could bake the blueberry bread as muffins instead of a full-size loaf. Though you can make the pie dough ahead and freeze it, I've been known to save time on the pies by using store-bought dough. (I've also been known to keep a few extra pies or muffins for myself, freezing the latter.) I usually either leave off any optional glazes or give them separately, to be drizzled on just before serving time.

START WITH

Banana-Date-Walnut Muffins (page 249)

Pear-Rosemary Muffin Tin Pies (page 291)

Blueberry-Lemon-Cardamom Bread (page 251)

IF YOU WANT, ADD

Sticky Date Glaze (page 249) in a small airtight jar

Blueberry Glaze (page 253) in a small airtight jar

One of the Tea Blends (page 57)

Cold Brew Coffee Concentrate (page 58)

Crème fraîche or cream cheese for the muffins and bread

PEAR-ROSEMARY MUFFIN TIN PIES

makes: 10 pies   total time: 1 hour 40 minutes, plus 3 hours 10 minutes cooling and chilling

66 Here's how I shrink a full-size pie. These little gems are no less satisfying for their petiteness, and they're always a huge hit when I bring a batch to Friendsgiving, a Sunday football gathering, or even a post–leaf peeping picnic. A plentiful amount of juicy fruit filling fits in each pie shell, nestled under a crumbly streusel topping. They are cleverly baked in a muffin tin for individual portions that you can divide up however suits you for gift giving. The tapioca that helps thicken the filling may be sold as 'minute' tapioca. Measure it before grinding to a powder (use a spice grinder or mini food processor). Be sure to spray both the muffin tin cups and the surface between cups with vegetable oil spray to prevent sticking. You can use our recipe for pie dough or use store-bought; you'll need 4 store-bought dough rounds in order to make 10 pies."

HOW I GIFT THIS

packaging: These pies are pretty sturdy, so they can be gifted in individual cellophane bags or a bakery-style box. Or you could give them in the muffin tin you bake them in.

storage: The pies can be stored at room temperature for about 2 days.

make it a duo: Pair with Citrus Burst Black Tea Blend (page 57).

make it a trio: Pair with apple cider (or pear cider if you can find it) and a package of mulling spices.

1 recipe Classic Double-Crust Pie Dough (page 292)

filling
2½ pounds ripe but firm Bosc pears, peeled, halved, cored, and cut into ½-inch pieces
3 tablespoons packed brown sugar, divided
¼ teaspoon table salt
1 tablespoon instant tapioca, ground
¾ teaspoon minced fresh rosemary

streusel
⅔ cup (3⅓ ounces) all-purpose flour
½ cup walnuts, chopped fine
6 tablespoons packed (2⅔ ounces) brown sugar
½ teaspoon table salt
6 tablespoons unsalted butter

1. Line rimmed baking sheet with parchment paper. Roll each dough piece into 16 by 11-inch rectangle on floured counter; stack on prepared sheet, separated by second sheet of parchment. Cover loosely with plastic wrap and refrigerate until dough is firm but still pliable, about 10 minutes.

2. Spray the outer cups of 12-cup muffin tin (so the 2 center cups will be left empty) as well as surface in between cups with vegetable oil spray. Using parchment as sling, transfer chilled dough rectangles to counter. Using 5-inch round biscuit or cookie cutter, cut 5 rounds from each dough rectangle. Reserve dough scraps for another use. Return rounds to sheet, still on parchment, and cover loosely with plastic. Refrigerate until firm but still pliable, about 10 minutes.

recipe continues

3. Center 1 dough round over an outer muffin tin cup. Using your fingers, press center of dough into bottom of cup, then press dough into corners and against sides, smoothing out any overlapping creases. (You should have about ½ inch dough overhanging rim of cup.) Fold overhang over itself; fold edge over rim of cup to rest on surface of muffin tin. Repeat with remaining 9 dough rounds and outer muffin tin cups. (If dough rounds become too soft to work with, refrigerate tin and rounds until firm.) Cover and refrigerate muffin tin until dough is firm, about 30 minutes.

4. **for the filling:** Toss pears, 1 tablespoon sugar, and salt together in bowl. Microwave until pears soften slightly and release their juices, 6 to 8 minutes, stirring once halfway through microwaving. Drain pears thoroughly in colander set over bowl; discard juices and return pears to now-empty bowl. Let pears cool completely, about 30 minutes, while you make the streusel.

5. **for the streusel:** Meanwhile, adjust oven rack to lower-middle position and heat oven to 375 degrees. Whisk flour, walnuts, sugar, and salt together in medium bowl. Melt butter in 10-inch skillet over medium-high heat and cook, swirling skillet constantly, until butter is browned and has nutty aroma, 3 to 5 minutes. Stir butter into flour mixture until completely moistened.

6. To finish the filling, whisk remaining 2 tablespoons sugar, tapioca, and rosemary together in small bowl. Add to pears and toss to combine. Divide pear mixture evenly among dough-lined cups. Sprinkle streusel evenly over fruit, breaking apart any large clumps. Bake until crusts are deep golden brown and juices are bubbling, 35 to 45 minutes, rotating muffin tin halfway through baking. Transfer muffin tin to wire rack and let pies cool for 10 minutes. Run paring knife around edges of pies, transfer to wire rack, and let cool until filling has set, about 2 hours.

CLASSIC DOUBLE-CRUST PIE DOUGH

makes: one 9-inch double crust
total time: 20 minutes, plus 1 hour chilling

- 2½ cups (12½ ounces) all-purpose flour
- 2 tablespoons sugar
- 1 teaspoon table salt
- 8 tablespoons vegetable shortening, cut into ½-inch pieces and chilled
- 12 tablespoons unsalted butter, cut into ¼-inch pieces and chilled
- 6 tablespoons ice water, plus extra as needed

1. Process flour, sugar, and salt in food processor until combined, about 5 seconds. Scatter shortening over top and process until mixture resembles coarse cornmeal, about 10 seconds. Scatter butter over top and pulse until mixture resembles coarse crumbs, about 10 pulses.

2. Transfer mixture to large bowl. Sprinkle ice water over mixture. Stir and press dough with spatula until dough sticks together. If dough does not come together, stir in up to 2 tablespoons ice water, 1 tablespoon at a time, until it does.

3. Using spatula, divide dough into 2 equal portions. Transfer each portion to sheet of plastic wrap and form each into 4-inch disk. Wrap each piece tightly in plastic and refrigerate for at least 1 hour or up to 2 days. Let chilled dough sit on counter to soften slightly, about 10 minutes, before rolling. (Wrapped dough can be frozen for up to 1 month. If frozen, let dough thaw completely on counter before rolling.)

MAKING PEAR-ROSEMARY MUFFIN TIN PIES

1. Center 1 dough round over an outer muffin tin cup. Using your fingers, press center of dough into bottom of cup.

2. Press dough into corners and against sides, smoothing out any overlapping creases. (You should have about ½ inch of dough overhanging rim of cup.)

3. Fold overhang over itself, then fold edge over rim of cup to rest on surface of muffin tin.

BANANA-CARAMEL PIE IN A JAR

makes: 10 jars   total time: 1 hour, plus 1¾ hours resting and chilling

66 No-bake pies are among my favorite summertime food gifts—and here they get a gifty mini-pie treatment. Bring a batch of these multilayered treats for Mother's Day, Father's Day, or a Fourth of July barbecue. Everything gets layered into a clear glass container for maximum show-off potential: a fresh banana pastry cream, gooey caramel sauce, whipped cream, and sliced bananas. Crumbled graham crackers make the 'crust,' but in this case they're really the topping, which keeps them crisp. If you know your recipient won't be eating these right away, consider giving a separate bag with the crushed crackers for sprinkling on before serving. You'll need ten 6-ounce wide-mouthed jars or other clear containers with lids for these pies."

HOW I GIFT THIS

packaging: Any cute 6-ounce wide-mouthed jar will look good; they don't all have to match. If you give the crushed graham crackers on the side, include a note letting the receiver know to top the whipped cream with the crackers.

storage: The assembled jars can be refrigerated for about 1 day.

make it a duo: Pair with the Chocolate Cream Pie in a Jar (page 297). Or pair with a bottle of bourbon.

add to a basket: Add to the Easy Pulled Pork meal basket (page 154) for a Southern-style dinner.

banana cream filling
- 4 tablespoons unsalted butter, cut into 4 pieces, divided
- 2 ripe bananas, peeled and sliced ½ inch thick
- 2½ cups heavy cream
- ⅛ teaspoon ground cinnamon
- ½ cup plus 2 tablespoons (4⅓ ounces) sugar
- 6 large egg yolks
- ¼ teaspoon table salt
- 3 tablespoons cornstarch
- 1 teaspoon vanilla extract

caramel sauce
- ¾ cup plus 2 tablespoons (6⅛ ounces) sugar
- ¼ cup water
- 2 tablespoons light corn syrup
- ½ cup heavy cream
- ½ teaspoon vanilla extract
- ⅛ teaspoon table salt

whipped cream
- 2 cups heavy cream
- 2 teaspoons sugar
- ½ teaspoon vanilla extract

- 3 ripe bananas
- 2 teaspoons lemon juice
- 6 whole graham crackers, crushed into coarse crumbs, divided

1. for the banana cream filling: Melt 1 tablespoon butter in medium saucepan over medium-high heat. Add sliced bananas and cook until they begin to soften, about 2 minutes. Add heavy cream and cinnamon, bring to boil, and cook for 30 seconds. Remove from heat, cover, and let sit for 40 minutes.

2. Whisk sugar, egg yolks, and salt together in large bowl until smooth. Whisk in cornstarch. Strain cooled banana-cream mixture through fine-mesh strainer into yolk mixture (do not press on bananas) and whisk until incorporated; discard cooked bananas. Clean saucepan.

3. Transfer egg mixture to clean, dry saucepan. Cook over medium heat, whisking constantly, until mixture is thickened and registers 180 degrees, 4 to 6 minutes (mixture should have consistency of thick pudding). Off heat, whisk in vanilla and remaining 3 tablespoons butter until smooth. Strain mixture through fine-mesh strainer into clean bowl. Spray piece of parchment paper with vegetable oil spray and press directly against surface of filling. Refrigerate until chilled, at least 1 hour or up to 24 hours. Clean saucepan and set aside.

4. for the caramel sauce: Bring sugar, water, and corn syrup to boil in clean, dry saucepan over medium-high heat. Cook, without stirring, until mixture is straw-colored, 6 to 8 minutes. Reduce heat to low and continue to cook, swirling saucepan occasionally, until mixture is amber-colored and registers between 360 and 370 degrees, 2 to 5 minutes longer.

5. Off heat, quickly but carefully stir in cream, vanilla, and salt (mixture will bubble and steam). Continue to stir until sauce is smooth. Transfer to 1 cup liquid measuring cup and set aside. (Sauce can be refrigerated for up to 2 weeks. Reheat in microwave, stirring frequently, until warm and smooth before using.)

6. for the whipped cream: Process cream, sugar, and vanilla in food processor for 45 seconds. Pulse in 5-second intervals for another 15 to 20 seconds, until cream has reached consistency of buttercream frosting. (Whipped cream can be refrigerated for up to 2 weeks.)

7. Peel bananas, then slice ¼ inch thick on bias and toss with lemon juice in bowl. Divide banana cream filling evenly among ten 6-ounce wide-mouthed containers (about ¼ cup per container). Top each container with about 1½ tablespoons caramel sauce, followed by about 3 tablespoons whipped cream, and banana slices. Just before gifting, sprinkle each container with ¼ cup graham cracker crumbs.

CHOCOLATE CREAM PIE IN A JAR

makes: 12 jars   total time: 30 minutes, plus 1 hour chilling

66 The next time your book club or movie-night gang is looking for someone to bring the snacks, step up with these fast, fun, and very chocolaty little pies. They also make a kid-friendly Valentine's treat. Dolloping the pudding into individual jars and topping with stabilized whipped cream makes mini desserts that taste as irresistible as they look. An upside-down hack is to layer a crumbled Oreo cookie 'crust' on top of the pies to keep the crumbs crisp. Go slow when whisking the half-and-half mixture into the egg mixture or the yolks will scramble. Chilling the pudding in a shallow bowl cools it faster. If you know your recipient won't be eating these right away, consider giving a separate bag with the crumbled cookies for sprinkling on before serving. You'll need twelve 6-ounce wide-mouthed jars or other clear containers with lids for these pies."

HOW I GIFT THIS

packaging: Any cute 6-ounce wide-mouthed jar will look good; they don't all have to match. If you give the crushed Oreos on the side, include a note letting the receiver know to top the whipped cream with the Oreos.

storage: The assembled jars can be refrigerated for about 1 day.

make it a duo: Pair with fresh berries, Italian maraschino cherries, or a jar of flake sea salt or smoked salt.

chocolate cream filling
- 2½ cups half-and-half
- ⅓ cup (2⅓ ounces) sugar, divided
- Pinch table salt
- 6 large egg yolks
- 2 tablespoons cornstarch
- 6 tablespoons unsalted butter, cut into 6 pieces
- 6 ounces semisweet chocolate, chopped fine
- 1 ounce unsweetened chocolate, chopped fine
- 1 teaspoon vanilla extract

whipped cream
- 2 cups heavy cream
- 2 teaspoons granulated sugar
- ½ teaspoon vanilla extract

- 20 Oreo cookies, broken into coarse crumbs

1. for the chocolate cream filling: Bring half-and-half, 3 tablespoons sugar, and salt to simmer in medium saucepan over medium heat, stirring occasionally. Whisk egg yolks, cornstarch, and remaining sugar in medium bowl until smooth. Slowly whisk 1 cup warm half-and-half mixture into yolk mixture to temper, then slowly whisk tempered yolk mixture into remaining half-and-half mixture in saucepan.

2. Cook half-and-half mixture over medium heat, whisking constantly, until mixture is thickened and registers 180 degrees, about 2 minutes (mixture should have consistency of thick pudding). Off heat, whisk in butter, semisweet chocolate, unsweetened chocolate, and vanilla until smooth. Strain mixture through fine-mesh strainer into clean bowl. Spray piece of parchment paper with vegetable oil spray and press directly against surface of filling. Refrigerate until chilled, at least 1 hour or up to 24 hours.

3. for the whipped cream: Process cream, sugar, and vanilla in food processor for 45 seconds. Pulse in 5-second intervals for another 15 to 20 seconds, until cream has reached consistency of buttercream frosting. (Whipped cream can be refrigerated for up to 2 weeks.)

4. Divide chocolate cream filling evenly among twelve 6-ounce wide-mouthed containers (about ½ cup per container), then top each with about 2½ tablespoons whipped cream. Just before gifting, sprinkle each container with cookie crumbs.

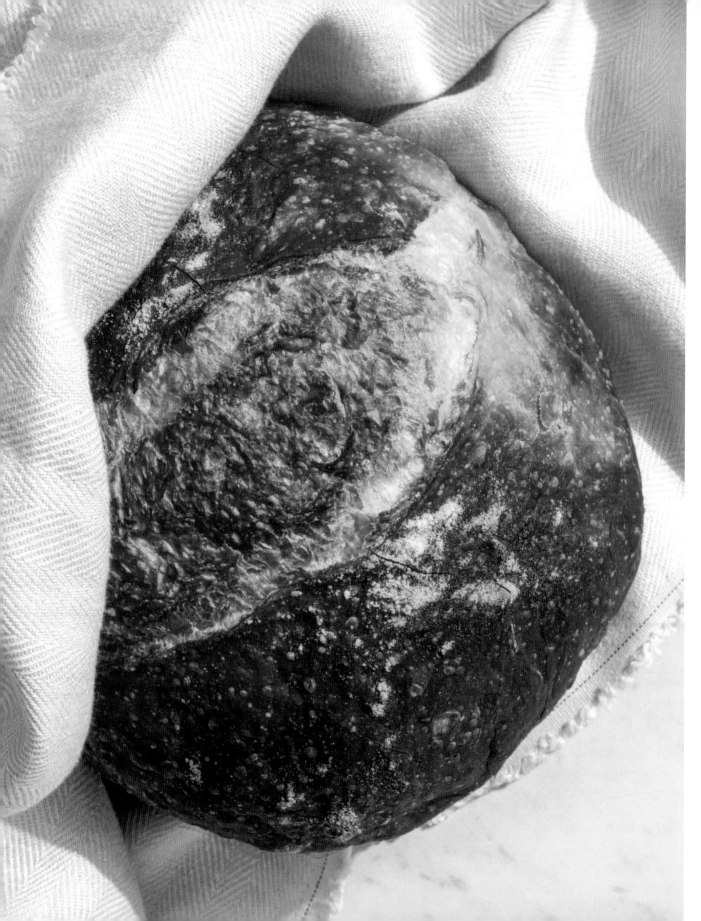

NO-KNEAD RUSTIC LOAF

makes: 1 loaf   total time: 1¾ hours, plus 12 hours rising and cooling time

66 A gorgeous bronzed loaf that looks and tastes like it came from the bakery is such an elemental yet elevated food gift. Even if you've never baked yeasted bread before, you'll find this rustic round loaf easy and approachable. Instead of kneading, this exemplary loaf relies on a very wet dough, a long rest, and some easy folding techniques to build structure and develop a strong gluten network. Baking the bread in the humid environment of a preheated Dutch oven results in an open crumb and gloriously chewy texture. Use a mild American lager, such as Budweiser; strongly flavored beers will make the bread taste bitter. The beer adds great flavor, but you can substitute an equal amount of water. You'll need a bowl that is at least 9 inches wide and 4 inches deep to cover the dough in step 6."

HOW I GIFT THIS

packaging: Wrap this loaf in a tea towel or parchment paper and tie with ribbon or twine.

storage: The bread can be stored at room temperature for about 3 days.

make it a duo: Pair with any of the following: Chocolate-Hazelnut Spread (page 28), Classic Strawberry Jam (page 30), Basil Pesto (page 41), Marinated Green and Black Olives (page 75), Vegetarian Curried Lentil Soup (page 167), or Hearty Beef Stew (page 168).

make it a trio: Pair the bread with a serrated bread knife and wooden cutting board. Or for a traditional housewarming gift, give the bread with a bottle of wine and a container of salt.

make it a basket: I like to give the rye variation bundled with smoked salmon, cream cheese, capers, and a bouquet of dill. The spelt variation is a great breakfast bread that I like to combine with cultured butter and an assortment of marmalades and jams.

2¾ cups (15⅛ ounces) bread flour
1½ teaspoons table salt
¼ teaspoon instant or rapid-rise yeast
¾ cup plus 2 tablespoons (7 ounces) water, room temperature
½ cup (4 ounces) mild lager, room temperature
1 tablespoon distilled white vinegar

1. Whisk flour, salt, and yeast together in large bowl. Using rubber spatula, fold water, beer, and vinegar into flour mixture, scraping up dry flour from bottom of bowl and pressing dough until cohesive and shaggy and all flour is incorporated.

2. Cover bowl tightly with plastic wrap and let sit at room temperature for at least 8 hours or up to 18 hours.

3. Using greased bowl scraper or your wet fingertips, fold dough over itself by lifting and folding edge of dough toward middle and pressing to seal. Turn bowl 90 degrees and fold dough again; repeat turning bowl and folding dough 6 more times (for a total of 8 folds). Flip dough seam side down in bowl, cover with plastic, and let rest for 15 minutes.

4. Lay 18 by 12-inch sheet of parchment paper on counter and spray lightly with vegetable oil spray. Transfer dough seam side up onto lightly floured counter and pat into rough 9-inch circle using your lightly floured hands. Using bowl scraper or your floured fingertips, lift and fold edge of dough toward center, pressing to seal. Repeat 5 more times (for a total of 6 folds), evenly spacing folds around circumference of dough. Press down on dough to seal, then use bench scraper to gently flip dough seam side down.

recipe continues

5. Using both hands, cup side of dough farthest away from you and pull dough toward you, keeping pinky fingers and side of palm in contact with counter and applying slight pressure to dough as it drags to create tension. (If dough slides across surface of counter without rolling, remove excess flour. If dough sticks to counter or hands, lightly sprinkle counter or hands with flour.) Rotate dough ball 90 degrees, reposition dough ball at top of counter, and repeat pulling dough until taut round ball forms, at least 4 more times. Using your floured hands or bench scraper, transfer dough seam side down to center of prepared parchment.

6. Cover dough with inverted large bowl. Let rise until dough has doubled in size and springs back minimally when poked gently with your finger, 1 to 2 hours.

7. Thirty minutes before baking, adjust oven rack to middle position, place Dutch oven with its lid on rack, and heat oven to 475 degrees. Using sharp knife or single-edge razor blade, make one 6-inch-long, ½-inch-deep slash with swift, fluid motion along top of loaf. Carefully remove hot pot from oven and, using parchment as sling, gently transfer dough and parchment to hot pot. Working quickly and reinforcing score in top of loaf if needed, cover pot and return to oven.

8. Reduce oven temperature to 425 degrees and bake loaf in covered pot for 30 minutes. Remove lid and continue to bake until loaf is deep golden brown and registers at least 205 degrees, 10 to 15 minutes. Using parchment sling, carefully remove loaf from hot pot and transfer to wire rack; discard parchment. Let cool completely, about 3 hours, before slicing.

variations
WHOLE-WHEAT RUSTIC LOAF
Reduce bread flour to 2 cups (11 ounces) and add 1 cup (5½ ounces) whole-wheat flour. Increase water to 1 cup (8 ounces).

SPELT RUSTIC LOAF
Reduce bread flour to 2 cups (11 ounces) and add 1 cup (5½ ounces) spelt flour. Increase water to 1 cup (8 ounces).

RYE RUSTIC LOAF
Reduce bread flour to 2 cups (11 ounces) and add 1 cup (5½ ounces) medium rye flour. Increase water to 1¼ cups plus 2 tablespoons (11 ounces) and omit lager.

SHAPING THE DOUGH

1. Fold dough toward middle of bowl; turn bowl 90 degrees and fold again; repeat for a total of 8 turns and folds. Turn dough seam side down, cover with plastic, and let rest for 15 minutes.

2. Transfer dough seam side up to lightly floured counter. Pat dough into 9-inch circle.

3. Lift and fold edge of dough toward center, pressing to seal. Repeat folds 5 more times, evenly spacing folds around circumference of dough.

4. Cup dough with both hands and pull toward you, applying slight pressure to dough. Rotate 90 degrees and repeat until taut round ball forms.

CANNING AND PICKLING PRIMER

Some of the recipes in this book, including the jams, pickles, and tomato sauce in Chapter 1, can be canned and processed for either short-term or long-term storage. Short-term canning, for which you simmer the empty jars in water to sterilize them and then fill them with food, keeps the food fresh for a couple of months. Long-term canning takes the process a step further by simmering the jars again after they are filled with food, which hermetically seals the jars. This method is called boiling-water processing and allows the (unopened) food to be safely stored for long periods of time at room temperature. Both methods are a great way to make food gifts well ahead of time—and long-term canning also allows your recipient more flexibility in deciding when to use their food gift. Here are some basics that you need to know if you plan to do any canning.

LOW-TEMPERATURE PROCESSING

For delicate vegetables, such as zucchini, we find it best to process the jars in hot water rather than boiling water. This process is called "low-temperature pasteurization treatment" by the USDA and is used to help keep pickles crisp. Although it requires a thermometer and a watchful eye to maintain the water in the canning pot between 180 and 185 degrees during the processing time, we love the snappy texture this technique produces in the Sweet Zucchini Pickle Chips (page 34). While perfectly suited for vegetables such as cucumber and zucchini, this method is not recommended for other types of vegetables.

---

a note about altitude and canning

The boiling point of water decreases as altitude increases, which means that when canning at higher elevations you must process food longer in a boiling-water canner. At sea level, the temperature of boiling water is 212 degrees Fahrenheit. The boiling point of water drops 2 degrees for every 1,000-foot increase in elevation. The altitude of America's Test Kitchen is 50 feet, or basically sea level. Google the altitude of where you live to determine your elevation.

THE ATK DIY CANNING KIT

You don't need to buy anything too fancy or expensive; you really only need to invest in a good canning pot and a handful of other key pieces, all of which you can find at a good kitchen supply store or online.

1. A large (18- to 21-quart) canning pot is handy for heating empty jars and key for processing filled jars. A pot that has silicone-coated handles allows for easy gripping, and a clear lid lets you monitor what is going on inside.

2. A canning rack with handles that fits inside the pot keeps the jars off the bottom of the pot and makes pulling the hot jars out of boiling water easy. Canning pots are often sold with a rack.

3. Glass canning jars (aka Mason jars) are sold with flat metal lids and threaded metal screw rings that hold the lids in place during processing for long-term canning. The USDA discourages use of latch-style jars in boiling-water canning because they don't form a consistent seal. Beautiful-looking jars in this style are fine for recipes that will be refrigerated for short-term storage, but they shouldn't be used in boiling-water processing for long-term storage.

4. A canning-specific jar lifter works better than tongs when putting hot filled jars in and taking them out of boiling water because it allows you to grasp the heavy jars firmly.

5. A wide-mouthed stainless-steel canning funnel makes pouring liquids and channeling pieces of fruit and vegetables into jars easier and tidier.

6. A ladle makes transferring cooked foods and pouring hot cooking liquid or brine into jars much simpler and neater.

7. Wooden skewers help to release the air bubbles around the inside of each jar once the jars are filled.

KEY INGREDIENTS

Bottled Lemon Juice and Lime Juice

Achieving the proper acidity (pH) level is key for preservation. Without the right pH, boiling-water canning is not considered safe. Likewise, without enough acid, unprocessed foods will have a short lifespan, even in the fridge. Acidity also plays a key role in the gelling abilities of pectin; without a consistent pH it can be difficult to predict how a jam or jelly will set. Fresh lemon juice varies too much from lemon to lemon to consistently predict how much it will increase the acidity of a given preserve; bottled lemon juice has a tightly controlled pH that is always consistent.

Vinegar

When making pickles, vinegar provides not only flavor but also acidity, which helps preserve the pickles and ensure they're safe to eat. Getting pickles to the proper pH is particularly important when boiling-water canning, which is only safe for high-acid foods. The two most common vinegars used are cider vinegar and distilled white vinegar; both are available at a 5 percent acetic acid level, meaning they have a consistent pH. Always use the variety of vinegar called for in the recipe.

Water

Pickles are made using water, vinegar, and salt, so the quality of the water matters. Fluoride and other elements may interfere with the pickling process, and water may contain enough chlorine to delay fermentation. If the water is highly chlorinated, that smell can carry through to the food. The minerals in hard water can interfere with the formation of acid and might also discolor the pickles. Soft tap water or filtered tap water are preferable for pickling. If you have any concerns about your water, use bottled.

Ball Pickle Crisp

To help pickled vegetables retain their fresh, crisp texture, we find it beneficial to add Ball Pickle Crisp, which is simply a granulated form of calcium chloride. It reinforces the naturally occurring pectin in vegetables and helps to keep pickles crunchy after being processed and stored for months in brine. It's easy to use; you add a measured amount to each jar before filling.

A NOTE ABOUT BOTULISM

Food-borne botulism is a rare but serious illness, and most cases are due to improperly home-canned foods. Luckily, avoiding botulism is very easy if you follow our recipes exactly. The processing times given in our recipes are derived from the *USDA Complete Guide to Home Canning*; these times are long enough to neutralize any dangerous toxins inside the jars.

We measured the pH of every canning recipe in the book and have been careful to stay well below the minimum level (pH of 4.6) for food safety and botulism in canned goods. The pH for your batches at home will be the same as long as you use bottled lemon or lime juice and don't substitute other types of vinegar. Be sure to work cleanly. Thoroughly wash the food, jars, rings and lids, counter, sink, and your hands before starting a home-canning project to reduce the possibility of contamination. Last, when in doubt, throw it out. Always discard food from jars that have lost their seal during storage, as it is a sign that bacteria, mold, or other toxins might be growing inside the jar. Also, if a jar is still sealed but the food inside looks or smells off when you open it, you should discard it.

CANNING STEP-BY-STEP

1. heat the jars

The empty jars need to be heated before being filled with hot food or the glass may shatter. The easiest way to do this is in the canning pot. The lids do not need to be heated before using.

2. fill the jars

As soon as the food has finished cooking, it needs to be portioned into the hot jars. Given that both the food and the jars are hot, it's best to use a wide-mouthed canning funnel. The large opening makes filling the jars go quickly (which helps to keep the food hot), and the funnel nestles securely into the jar so it's less likely to tip over when full of hot liquid.

3. measure the headspace

It's important to leave headspace between the top of the food and the rim of the jar, which allows for the food to expand as it heats up during processing. If canning larger pieces of fruit or vegetables in liquid, make sure the solids are fully covered by the liquid and then measure the distance between the liquid and the rim of the jar. Each recipe spells out how much headspace is required. If you have too much or too little headspace, it can prevent the lid from sealing properly during processing.

4. release the air bubbles

After filling the jars and measuring the headspace, use a wooden skewer to remove any trapped air bubbles. For thick jams, draw the skewer upward to release the bubbles. For larger pieces of fruit or vegetables in liquid, press the skewer against the food to press the air bubbles out. If left unchecked, the air bubbles will collect at the top of the jar during processing and alter the headspace, which can prevent the jar from sealing properly. Once the air bubbles have been removed, add extra jam or liquid as needed so that the headspace measurement is correct.

5. add the lids and rings

Wipe the rim of the jar clean of any drips. Once clean, place the lids on top and screw on the rings until fingertip-tight. Don't overtighten the rings, or you will prevent air from escaping the jars during processing, which is a key part of the canning process. Although lids cannot be reused, rings can be used several times as long as they are in good shape. The screw-on variety of lids and rings are the only type recommended by the USDA for boiling-water processing. Lids that use the combination glass top and rubber gasket can yield an inconsistent seal and result in unsafe canning.

6. process the jars

Lower the hot, filled jars into the rack inside the pot of boiling water. Make sure the jars are covered by at least 1 inch of water. Bring the water back to a boil and then process the jars for the amount of time specified. Be sure to start the timer only after the water has returned to a boil. Processing times will vary based on the size of the jars, your altitude, and the type of food. We follow USDA guidelines in all of our recipes. If you choose to stray from the jar sizes we recommend in our recipes, note that your processing times will vary.

7. let the jars seal themselves

After the processing time is up, turn off the heat and let the jars sit in the hot water for 5 minutes. This allows the boiling-hot food to settle down and starts the lid-sealing process. After 5 minutes, remove the jars from the pot and allow them to cool at room temperature for 24 hours. As the food cools, it contracts, which creates a small vacuum inside the jar. The pull of this vacuum pops the flexible metal lid inward, an indication that the jar has been hermetically sealed and oxygen can no longer pass through. To test the seal, press on the lid with your finger; a sealed lid will feel firm, while an unsealed lid will flex under the pressure and make a small popping sound.

8. store the jars

The combination of the sterilized food and the hermetically sealed lid is the reason the jar can be stored for at least 1 year in a dark, cool place. Storing the jars without their rings lets you quickly tell if the seal has been broken before using. If the seal pops at any time during storage, you must discard the food; it could contain harmful bacteria or toxins.

NUTRITIONAL INFORMATION FOR OUR RECIPES

To calculate the nutritional values of our recipes per serving, we used The Food Processor SQL by ESHA research. When using this program, we entered all the ingredients, using weights wherever possible. We also used our preferred brands in these analyses. Any ingredient listed as "optional" was excluded from the analyses. If there is a range in the serving size, we used the highest number of servings to calculate nutritional values. We did not include additional salt or pepper for food that's seasoned to taste.

	CALORIES	TOTAL FAT (G)	SAT FAT (G)	CHOL (MG)	SODIUM (MG)	TOTAL CARB (G)	DIETARY FIBER (G)	TOTAL SUGARS (G)	PROTEIN (G)
PRESENT A PANTRY									
Chocolate-Hazelnut Spread (2 tbsp)	100	8	0.5	0	910	7	1	5	2
Classic Strawberry Jam (1 tbsp)	60	0	0	0	0	15	1	14	0
Classic Raspberry Jam	60	0	0	0	0	15	1	14	0
Classic Peach Jam	50	0	0	0	0	13	0	12	0
Brandied Cherry and Hazelnut Conserve (1 tbsp)	40	1	0	0	20	7	1	6	0
Apple-Shallot Chutney (1 tbsp)	25	0	0	0	40	5	1	4	0
Sweet Zucchini Pickle Chips	60	0	0	0	450	15	0	14	1
Sweet and Spicy Zucchini Pickle Chips	60	0	0	0	450	15	0	14	1
Summer Tomato Sauce	30	0	0	0	250	6	2	4	1
Basil Pesto (¼ cup)	310	32	4.5	5	340	2	1	0	4
Dukkah	30	2.5	0	0	150	2	1	0	1
Hazelnut-Nigella Dukkah	40	3.5	0	0	120	2	1	0	1
Herbes de Provence	10	0	0	0	0	2	1	0	0
Advieh	10	0	0	0	150	2	1	0	0
Shichimi Togarashi	15	1	0	0	0	2	1	0	1
Taco Seasoning	25	1	0	0	760	5	2	0	1
Thai Panang Curry Paste	30	0	0	0	20	7	0	4	1
Vanilla Extract	10	0	0	0	0	0	0	0	0
Pancake Mix	440	0	0	0	1930	96	0	22	11
Hot Chocolate Mix	170	8	4.5	0	85	28	2	18	4
Malted Hot Chocolate Mix	150	8	4.5	0	85	24	2	14	3
Mexican Hot Chocolate Mix	170	8	4.5	0	90	28	2	18	4
Mint Hot Chocolate Mix	170	8	4.5	0	85	28	2	18	4
Mocha Hot Chocolate Mix	170	8	4.5	0	85	29	2	18	4

	CALORIES	TOTAL FAT (G)	SAT FAT (G)	CHOL (MG)	SODIUM (MG)	TOTAL CARB (G)	DIETARY FIBER (G)	TOTAL SUGARS (G)	PROTEIN (G)
PRESENT A PANTRY (CONT.)									
Immunitea Herbal Tea Blend	10	0	0	0	55	2	1	0	0
Cozy and Calm Herbal Tea Blend	20	0	0	0	5	4	2	1	1
Citrus Burst Black Tea Blend	5	0	0	0	0	1	1	0	0
Cold Brew Coffee Concentrate	150	6	1	0	35	23	7	0	6
Pumpkin-Spiced Cold Brew Coffee Concentrate	150	6	1	0	35	23	7	0	6
Star Anise–Orange Cold Brew Coffee Concentrate	150	6	1	0	35	23	7	0	6
Granola (¾ cup)	140	6	4	0	25	20	2	4	3
Cocoa-Coconut Granola	210	10	7	0	35	27	4	8	4
Peanut Butter–Banana Granola	220	11	6	0	30	25	3	7	5
Green Granola	210	11	5	0	70	22	3	5	8
Dark Chocolate Fudge Sauce (2 tbsp)	240	12	7	15	80	37	2	32	3
Dark Chocolate–Orange Fudge Sauce	240	12	7	15	80	37	2	32	3
Dark Chocolate–Peanut Butter Fudge Sauce	290	16	8	15	190	39	2	33	4
Dulce de Leche (2 tbsp)	100	2.5	1.5	10	85	17	0	17	2
Chili Crisp (1 tbsp)	120	12	2	0	160	4	2	1	1
Easy Homemade Hot Sauce	25	2	0	0	105	3	0	2	0
GIVE A SNACK OR SIP									
Marinated Green and Black Olives (¼ cup)	190	20	2.5	0	410	3	1	0	0
Marinated Olives with Pearl Mozzarella	270	26	7	30	280	2	0	0	6
Marinated Green Olives with Feta	230	23	6	20	520	3	0	1	3
Cinnamon-Ginger Spiced Nuts (¼ cup)	260	19	1.5	0	200	19	5	12	8
Saffron–Orange Blossom Spiced Nuts	310	22	2	0	340	21	5	12	10
Sichuan Spiced Nuts	280	22	2	0	450	17	5	8	10
Cheesy Garlic Popcorn Seasoning	5	0	0	0	130	1	0	0	0
Spiced Chocolate Popcorn Seasoning	5	0	0	0	40	1	0	1	0
Dill Pickle Popcorn Seasoning	5	0	0	0	125	1	0	0	0
Firecracker Party Mix (1 cup)	210	13	4	10	380	19	0	2	5
Fisherman's Friend Party Mix	120	5	2.5	10	300	17	0	1	2
BBQ Party Mix	130	8	2.5	10	170	13	1	2	2
Sweet and Salty Kettle Corn Party Mix	100	4	2.5	10	210	15	0	3	1
Southern Cheese Straws	50	3.5	2	10	70	3	0	0	2
Bacon Jam (2 tbsp)	230	18	6	30	310	10	0	8	6
Caponata (½ cup)	130	9	1	0	190	12	2	8	2

	CALORIES	TOTAL FAT (G)	SAT FAT (G)	CHOL (MG)	SODIUM (MG)	TOTAL CARB (G)	DIETARY FIBER (G)	TOTAL SUGARS (G)	PROTEIN (G)
GIVE A SNACK OR SIP (CONT.)									
Smoked Trout Pâté (⅓ cup)	80	6	2.5	25	170	1	0	1	6
Ultracreamy Hummus (¼ cup)	100	7	1	0	310	7	2	0	3
Spiced Walnut Topping (1 tbsp)	190	19	2.5	0	170	3	1	1	1
Whipped Feta Dip (¼ cup)	120	11	5	25	260	2	0	1	4
Whipped Feta and Roasted Red Pepper Dip	120	11	5	25	280	2	0	2	4
Whipped Feta Dip with Dill and Parsley	120	11	5	25	260	2	0	1	4
Beet Muhammara (¼ cup)	160	13	1.5	0	320	9	2	5	3
Blue Cheese Log with Pistachio Dukkah and Honey	140	12	7	30	230	5	0	4	4
Goat Cheese Log with Hazelnut-Nigella Dukkah	170	15	8	35	170	2	0	1	6
Feta Cheese Log with Advieh and Olive Oil	160	16	7	35	210	2	0	1	3
Roasted Tomato–Lime Salsa (2 tbsp)	20	0	0	0	410	5	1	3	1
Gruyère, Mustard, and Caraway Cheese Coins	35	2	1	5	50	2	0	0	1
Blue Cheese and Celery Seed Cheese Coins	30	2	1.5	5	45	2	0	0	1
Pimento Cheese Coins	30	2	1	5	35	2	0	0	1
Seeded Pumpkin Crackers	40	1.5	0	5	35	5	1	2	1
Tonic Syrup (1 oz)	50	0	0	0	10	14	0	13	0
Simple Syrup (½ oz)	35	0	0	0	0	9	0	9	0
Herb Syrup	35	0	0	0	0	10	0	9	0
Citrus Syrup	35	0	0	0	0	9	0	9	0
Spiced Syrup	35	0	0	0	0	9	0	9	0
Ginger Syrup (½ oz)	50	0	0	0	0	12	0	10	0
Coquito (6 oz)	210	8	8	5	45	20	0	20	2
Bloody Mary Mix (8 oz)	100	1	0	0	850	21	6	14	4
Fruits of the Forest Liqueur (1 oz)	80	0	0	0	0	7	1	6	0
Strawberry–Black Pepper Rim Sugar	15	0	0	0	0	4	0	3	0
Coffee Liqueur (1 oz)	90	0.5	0	0	0	8	1	6	1
Sweet Vermouth (1 oz)	50	0	0	0	0	7	0	6	0
BOARD THE MEAL TRAIN									
Turkish Bride Soup in a Jar	280	10	1.5	0	40	40	7	5	11
Mushroom Risotto in a Jar	340	17	8	30	400	43	3	1	7
Earl Grey Baked Oatmeal in a Jar	310	14	4.5	20	230	40	4	17	9
Sichuan Chili–Ginger Chicken Salad	320	17	2.5	110	480	6	2	2	36

	CALORIES	TOTAL FAT (G)	SAT FAT (G)	CHOL (MG)	SODIUM (MG)	TOTAL CARB (G)	DIETARY FIBER (G)	TOTAL SUGARS (G)	PROTEIN (G)
BOARD THE MEAL TRAIN (CONT.)									
Turkey Picnic Sandwich with Sun-Dried Tomato Spread	740	42	10	50	1970	66	3	11	28
Capicola Picnic Sandwich with Artichoke Spread	820	44	15	70	2750	72	4	10	37
Ham Picnic Sandwich with Olive Spread	640	35	8	50	1890	60	2	10	25
Overnight Kale Salad with Roasted Sweet Potatoes and Pomegranate Vinaigrette	550	34	5	5	690	55	11	23	11
Italian Pasta Salad	640	34	11	70	990	59	3	2	25
Best Ground Beef Chili									
Murgh Makhani	440	29	16	190	1000	12	2	8	35
Easy Pulled Pork	580	34	12	140	1200	30	2	23	38
Chicken Enchiladas	520	30	12	120	1280	35	3	5	31
Stuffed Shells with Amatriciana Sauce	520	26	13	115	1350	43	2	8	31
Garlic Butter (1 tsp)	25	2.5	1.5	5	15	0	0	0	0
Chicken and Ramen Soup	270	8	1	55	1830	26	2	3	23
Vegetarian Curried Lentil Soup	190	5	0.5	0	890	24	5	6	8
Hearty Beef Stew	510	15	6	155	1100	36	6	9	55
Chicken Pot Pie	560	26	11	165	960	43	3	6	40
Hearty Meat Lasagna	780	44	23	165	1510	51	3	11	45
Baked Macaroni and Cheese	1010	57	35	165	1020	81	3	9	44
Meatballs and Marinara	500	29	10	110	1390	28	4	14	31
Chinese Pork Dumplings	260	11	3	25	320	28	1	1	10
SWEETEN SOMEONE'S DAY									
Chocolate Truffles (2 pieces)	70	6	3.5	5	10	6	1	0	1
Chocolate-Almond Truffles	100	8	3.5	5	5	6	1	0	2
Chocolate-Spice Truffles	70	6	3.5	5	5	6	1	0	1
Chocolate-Ginger Truffles	70	6	3.5	5	10	6	1	0	1
Chocolate-Lemon Truffles	70	6	3.5	5	10	6	1	0	1
Brigadeiros (2 pieces)	70	2.5	1	5	15	11	0	9	1
Chocolate-Covered Caramels	80	4	2.5	5	30	10	0	9	1
Salted Caramels	40	2	1.5	5	45	5	0	5	0
Pistachio-Cherry Torrone (one 4-inch log)	300	14	1	0	35	40	3	36	6
Almond Torrone	250	7	1	0	35	45	2	41	4
Chocolate-Hazelnut Torrone	280	14	2.5	0	30	42	2	36	4

	CALORIES	TOTAL FAT (G)	SAT FAT (G)	CHOL (MG)	SODIUM (MG)	TOTAL CARB (G)	DIETARY FIBER (G)	TOTAL SUGARS (G)	PROTEIN (G)
SWEETEN SOMEONE'S DAY (CONT.)									
Fluffy Vanilla Marshmallows	50	0	0	0	20	13	0	11	0
Fluffy Eggnog Marshmallows	50	0	0	0	20	13	0	11	0
Fluffy Lemon-Strawberry Marshmallows	50	0	0	0	20	13	0	11	0
Fluffy Mocha Marshmallows	60	0	0	0	20	14	0	11	1
Fluffy Peppermint Swirl Marshmallows	50	0	0	0	20	13	0	11	0
Peppermint Bark	320	18	11	5	30	42	2	37	3
Chocolate Matzo Toffee	350	22	14	50	300	38	0	32	2
Walnut-Pomegranate Stuffed Dates	110	3.5	1.5	0	0	20	2	18	1
Pistachio-Orange Stuffed Dates	80	1	0	0	70	19	2	16	1
Chocolate-Almond Stuffed Dates	140	5	2	0	10	26	2	21	2
Snickers Stuffed Dates	180	9	5	0	40	28	3	22	3
Thin and Crispy Chocolate Chip Cookies	160	9	5	40	130	20	1	13	1
Spicy Mocha Sandwich Cookies with Dulce de Leche	300	11	6	40	65	46	0	12	6
Easy Holiday Sugar Cookies	120	4.5	3	15	65	19	0	12	1
Shortbread Cookies	170	10	6	25	75	18	0	5	2
Chocolate-Dipped Shortbread Cookies	240	14	9	25	75	27	0	13	3
Raspberry-Dipped Shortbread Cookies	250	17	13	25	75	24	0	11	2
Nutella Rugelach	120	8	5	15	40	11	1	5	1
Cinnamon-Walnut Rugelach	110	7	3.5	20	60	10	0	5	2
Millionaire's Shortbread	200	10	6	25	90	26	0	16	2
Baci di Dama (Italian Hazelnut Cookies)	60	4.5	2	5	10	6	0	2	1
Macarons with Raspberry Buttercream	130	6	2.5	10	25	17	1	15	2
Macarons with Coffee Buttercream	120	6	2.5	10	25	16	1	15	1
Macarons with Strawberry-Cardamom Buttercream	130	6	2.5	10	25	17	1	15	2
Macarons with Pistachio Buttercream	140	7	2.5	10	25	18	1	15	2
Macarons with Passion Fruit Curd	190	11	6	20	30	24	1	21	2
Macarons with Semisweet Chocolate Ganache	190	11	6	15	25	22	1	20	2
Almond Biscotti	110	5	1.5	15	55	14	1	7	3
Anise Biscotti	110	5	1.5	15	55	14	1	7	3
Hazelnut-Rosemary-Orange Biscotti	100	4.5	1.5	15	55	14	1	7	2
Pistachio-Spice Biscotti	100	4	1.5	15	55	14	1	7	2
Chocolate Ganache–Filled Brownies	470	27	10	45	360	59	2	43	5
Peanut Butter Ganache–Filled Brownies	500	27	8	35	240	62	2	46	7
Salted Caramel–Filled Brownies	630	19	5	35	270	108	2	51	10
Ultranutty Pecan Bars	280	20	6	20	105	24	2	12	3
Scotcheroos	310	16	7	10	135	39	1	20	6

	CALORIES	TOTAL FAT (G)	SAT FAT (G)	CHOL (MG)	SODIUM (MG)	TOTAL CARB (G)	DIETARY FIBER (G)	TOTAL SUGARS (G)	PROTEIN (G)
BOX UP THE BAKERY									
British-Style Currant Scones	260	9	5	55	340	39	1	13	6
Banana-Date-Walnut Bread (12 servings)	300	9	1.5	30	300	51	3	29	5
Sticky Date Glaze	20	0	0	0	15	4	0	4	0
Blueberry-Lemon-Cardamom Bread (12 servings)	250	10	4	30	290	38	2	18	4
Cranberry-Orange-Pecan Bread	220	7	4	30	290	38	1	19	4
Chocolate-Coffee-Hazelnut Bread	290	12	6	30	290	43	2	23	5
Blueberry Glaze	40	0	0	0	0	10	0	9	0
Orange Glaze	40	0	0	0	0	10	0	10	0
Espresso Glaze	40	0	0	0	0	10	0	9	0
Brown Sugar Streusel	90	4	2.5	10	100	12	0	8	1
Cinnamon Coffee Cake (12 servings)	400	16	10	75	350	58	0	33	5
Ginger-Nutmeg Coffee Cake	400	16	10	75	350	58	0	33	5
Orange-Cardamom Coffee Cake	400	16	10	75	350	58	0	33	5
Chocolate Babka Buns	450	19	11	80	240	61	2	22	9
Ultimate Chocolate Cupcakes with Ganache Filling; Chocolate Buttercream	430	28	13	65	180	43	1	30	5
Pumpkin Cupcakes with Cream Cheese Frosting	380	26	10	75	340	33	1	23	4
Iced Lemon–Poppy Seed Bundt Cake (12 servings)	490	18	11	110	340	77	0	54	5
Mini Lemon–Poppy Seed Bundt Cakes	490	18	11	110	340	77	0	54	5
Chocolate–Sour Cream Bundt Cake (12 servings)	440	21	12	120	340	60	0	43	6
Mini Chocolate–Sour Cream Bundt Cakes	440	21	12	120	340	60	0	43	6
Party Cake Pops	140	7	4.5	25	70	18	0	13	2
Cookies and Cream Cake Pops	140	8	3.5	15	50	17	0	13	2
Triple-Berry Slab Pie with Ginger-Lemon Streusel	350	16	10	45	150	48	3	21	3
Grapefruit Tart with Pumpernickel-Caraway Crust	500	33	20	245	260	47	3	28	7
Lemon Tartlets	840	49	28	480	440	88	0	51	12
Egg Tarts	220	12	7	90	150	23	0	10	4
Pear-Rosemary Muffin Tin Pies	590	34	16	55	410	66	4	25	6
Classic Double-Crust Pie Dough	340	23	11	35	230	28	0	3	4
Banana-Caramel Pie in a Jar	580	33	15	55	410	66	4	25	6
Chocolate Cream Pie in a Jar	470	37	21	170	150	35	1	25	6
No-Knead Rustic Loaf	200	0	0	0	440	40	2	0	7
Whole-Wheat Rustic Loaf	220	0	0	0	440	43	3	0	8
Spelt Rustic Loaf	220	0.5	0	0	440	43	4	0	8
Rye Rustic Loaf	220	0	0	0	440	44	4	0	7

CONVERSIONS AND EQUIVALENTS

Some say cooking is a science and an art. We would say that geography has a hand in it, too. Flours and sugars manufactured in the United Kingdom and elsewhere will feel and taste different from those manufactured in the United States. So we cannot promise that the loaf of bread you bake in Canada or England will taste the same as a loaf baked in the States, but we can offer guidelines for converting weights and measures. We also recommend that you rely on your instincts when making our recipes. Refer to the visual cues provided. If the dough hasn't "come together in a ball" as described, you may need to add more flour— even if the recipe doesn't tell you to. You be the judge.

The recipes in this book were developed using standard U.S. measures following U.S. government guidelines. The charts below offer equivalents for U.S. and metric measures. All conversions are approximate and have been rounded up or down to the nearest whole number.

Example:

1 teaspoon = 4.9292 milliliters, rounded up to 5 milliliters
1 ounce = 28.3495 grams, rounded down to 28 grams

VOLUME CONVERSIONS

U.S.	Metric
1 teaspoon	5 milliliters
2 teaspoons	10 milliliters
1 tablespoon	15 milliliters
2 tablespoons	30 milliliters
¼ cup	59 milliliters
⅓ cup	79 milliliters
½ cup	118 milliliters
¾ cup	177 milliliters
1 cup	237 milliliters
1¼ cups	296 milliliters
1½ cups	355 milliliters
2 cups (1 pint)	473 milliliters
2½ cups	591 milliliters
3 cups	710 milliliters
4 cups (1 quart)	0.946 liter
1.06 quarts	1 liter
4 quarts (1 gallon)	3.8 liters

WEIGHT CONVERSIONS

Ounces	Grams
½	14
¾	21
1	28
1½	43
2	57
2½	71
3	85
3½	99
4	113
4½	128
5	142
6	170
7	198
8	227
9	255
10	283
12	340
16 (1 pound)	454

CONVERSIONS FOR COMMON BAKING INGREDIENTS

Baking is an exacting science. Because measuring by weight is far more accurate than measuring by volume, and thus more likely to produce reliable results, in our recipes we provide ounce measures in addition to cup measures for many ingredients. Refer to the chart below to convert these measures into grams.

Ingredient	Ounces	Grams
Flour		
1 cup all-purpose flour*	5	142
1 cup cake flour	4	113
1 cup whole-wheat flour	5½	156
Sugar		
1 cup granulated (white) sugar	7	198
1 cup packed brown sugar (light or dark)	7	198
1 cup confectioners' sugar	4	113
Cocoa Powder		
1 cup cocoa powder	3	85
Butter†		
4 tablespoons (½ stick or ¼ cup)	2	57
8 tablespoons (1 stick or ½ cup)	4	113
16 tablespoons (2 sticks or 1 cup)	8	227

* U.S. all-purpose flour, the most frequently used flour in this book, does not contain leaveners, as some European flours do. These leavened flours are called self-rising or self-raising. If you are using self-rising flour, take this into consideration before adding leaveners to a recipe.

† In the United States, butter is sold both salted and unsalted. We generally recommend unsalted butter. If you are using salted butter, take this into consideration before adding salt to a recipe.

OVEN TEMPERATURES

Fahrenheit	Celsius	Gas Mark
225	105	¼
250	120	½
275	135	1
300	150	2
325	165	3
350	180	4
375	190	5
400	200	6
425	220	7
450	230	8
475	245	9

CONVERTING TEMPERATURES FROM AN INSTANT-READ THERMOMETER

We include doneness temperatures in many of the recipes in this book. We recommend an instant-read thermometer for the job. Refer to the table above to convert Fahrenheit degrees to Celsius. Or, for temperatures not represented in the chart, use this simple formula:

Subtract 32 degrees from the Fahrenheit reading, then divide the result by 1.8 to find the Celsius reading.

Example:
"Roast chicken until thighs register 175 degrees."

To convert:
175°F − 32 = 143°
143° ÷ 1.8 = 79.44°C, rounded down to 79°C

INDEX

Note: Page references in *italics* indicate photographs.